a handbook of
COMPUTER
BASED
TRAINING

a handbook of
COMPUTER BASED TRAINING

**Christopher Dean
and Quentin Whitlock**

Kogan Page, London
Nichols Publishing Company, New York

First published in Great Britain in 1983 by
Kogan Page Ltd, 120 Pentonville Road, London N1 9JN

British Library Cataloguing in Publication Data

Dean, Christopher
    A handbook of computer-based training.
    1. Computer-assisted instruction
    I. Title   II. Whitlock, Quentin
    371.3'9445   LB1028.46

    ISBN 0-85038-557-1

First published in the United States of America in 1983 by
Nichols Publishing Company, PO Box 96, New York, NY 10024

Library of Congress Cataloging in Publication Data

Dean, Chris.
    A handbook of computer-based training.
    1. Computer managed instruction – Handbooks,
    manuals, etc. I. Whitlock, Quentin A. II. Title.
    LB1028.46.D4 1982   371.3'9445   82-3546
    ISBN 0-89397-132-4   AACR2

Printed in Great Britain by Nene Litho,
And bound by Woolnough Bookbinding Ltd.,
both of Wellingborough, Northants.

Contents

Introduction

Many, if not all readers of this book, will have had some experience of 'conversing' with computers. They may own their own microcomputer; they may use a terminal from the main company computer at work, or they may own a television set with a viewdata facility. Those who do not have this experience may well have observed the staff at an airline check-in or a building society branch office sitting at their desks, pressing keys on a typewriter-like keyboard and reading information presented on a television-type screen, like the one illustrated on page 8. In such a situation the check-in clerk or the branch cashier is using the computer to obtain information (eg to find out if a seat is booked) or to amend information (eg to change a customer's name and address).

How do these operations come to be learned by the staff concerned? There are various possibilities. A colleague or supervisor can show them and then leave them to their own devices until they run into problems. They may go to a group training session where an instructor explains basic procedures, possibly with some practice on terminals, or they may be given a printed manual explaining the procedures and containing exercises. Combinations of these strategies are also possible.

One approach which has grown increasingly popular over the past few years is to arrange a situation in which 'lessons', explaining the procedures to be learned and giving examples and practice in those procedures, appear on the screen which is used for the performance of the task. These lessons include explanatory information and diagrams and set and mark exercises just like the group instructor. They will almost always require supplementary printed materials. How these lessons come to be developed is the subject of this book.

As we will show, such lessons need not be restricted only to those procedures for which computer terminals are already used. The introduction of the computer may enhance the teaching of many aspects of science, business or the arts. It is not our contention that computer-based training is invariably superior to the more traditional methods. Clearly there will be a strong case for this approach in tasks which involve the use of terminals. But even here the use is not always self-evident. In some circumstances a simple, printed performance aid may be cheaper and more effective. In others there may be good reasons for retaining a human instructor.

This book attempts to bring together relevant aspects of two specialist areas – educational technology and computing, so that the reader, who may

be an expert in neither, one, or both these fields, can easily select the areas that are important to study in depth. Part 1 discusses the design of learning sequences with particular reference to computer-based training and is particularly important for computer experts. Experienced trainers may wish to skim through parts of this section. Part 2, on the other hand, is designed for trainers who know little about computers and it aims to give an introduction to the subject and the sorts of devices that can be supported. Part 3 covers the subject of computer-based training from deciding on equipment and authoring systems through the composition of a design team, to deciding how to structure the training material on the screen and thus validating the course.

As its title implies, this book is designed to be a handbook for the newcomer to this exciting area of training as well as a useful reference work for practitioners. It is hoped that it will be of use to trainers and educators with an interest in, or requirement to learn about, computer-based training. It should also be useful to management and computer personnel.

In places, we have found it convenient to use the masculine gender. Readers should interpret this as meaning a person of either sex. We hope that no one will be offended.

Part 1
The design of
learning sequences

INTRODUCTION

Training is very fashion-conscious. A bewildering (and expensive) variety of techniques and apparatus has appeared over the past 25 years to baffle or entice trainers and their bosses. This part of the book deals with a procedure for course design which is not new – although it may be to some – but which seems to work.

The underlying standpoint of this procedure is that effective occupational training is performance-oriented. In the words of one writer:

> It is not what is presented to the student but what the student is led to do that results in learning.
>
> Whether you choose to file this under the 'active response principle' of old-time programmed instruction or under the effects of questioning on student retention in the more recent mathemagenic research tradition, or under the new interest in levels of processing in the most recent cognitive research, the principle is axiomatic. One way transmission to passive audiences is passé in all media.[1]

The design procedures outlined in Part 1 lead to the development of inter-active learning sequences for students working individually to improve their performance. These procedures may appear unnecessarily detailed to some. However, they have been written for the trainer with little or no previous experience of authorship of self-instructional courseware. The experienced classroom instructor, however able he may be, will find that the development of individualized materials is not simply an extension of what he does already. His absence from the scene when the student confronts his course means that the quick-wittedness and flexibility he customarily employs to deal with misunderstandings and wrong sequencing in group instruction count for nothing. He must plan carefully the content and sequence of the lesson relating these features to the learners' existing capabilities and steering towards a clearly-defined goal.

We hope that the procedures we describe will assist authors to these ends. They do not constitute an inviolable rubric; features may be adapted or pruned to suit personal styles and circumstances. We do suggest, however, that the major steps comprise a planning routine which it would be risky to ignore.

[1]*Teaching Conceptual Networks* Susan M Markle, NSPI Journal, February 1978

1. Analysing performance and setting objectives

INTRODUCTION

Computer-based training (CBT), like other forms of individualized learning, is a manifestation of training technology. Technology is an overworked expression and open to several interpretations. For many people, understandably, it suggests machines and apparatus, and certainly the work of the educational and training technologist often requires the use of mechanical devices. Yet the educational technologist's own definition of his technology is unlikely to refer specifically to machines. It is more likely that he will concur with Professor J K Galbraith in that:

> Technology means the systematic application of scientific or other organized knowledge to practical tasks.
>
> Its most important consequence, at least for the purposes of economics, is in forcing the division and subdivision of any such task into its component parts.
>
> Thus, and only thus, can organized knowledge be brought to bear on performance.[1]

In educational and training technology this process of dividing and subdividing problems and subject matter is known as task analysis. The planning stages of training design – of which task analysis is one – are well known to experienced trainers from textbooks, pamphlets from training boards and other bodies. Figure 1.1 is a general summary of the course design process.[2] Implicit in this figure is a point fundamental to the whole training process. A training scheme is developed to solve a problem. Training problems are usually caused by inadequate or deficient performance. Courses are designed to enable their participants to acquire the capability or the knowledge necessary to enhance the performance of their duties and thus make good the deficiency.

To restate this point one might say that without training, the participants could not perform the task demonstrated in the training course even if their life depended on it. This rather melodramatic phraseology is chosen to stress the point that training, computer-based or any other, should be considered a last resort.

[1] *The New Industrial State* J K Galbraith, Penguin Special, 1974
[2] Adapted from *The Sheffield System* E Hudson, PAVIC (revised edition in print)

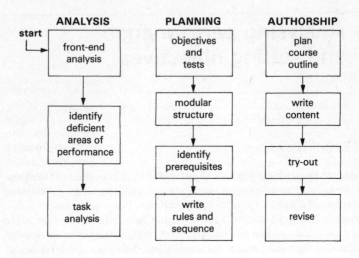

Figure 1.1 The steps of training design

IDENTIFYING TRAINING NEEDS

Front-end analysis

Reactive

As we have stated, training serves to make good deficient performance. This is the focus of the first step in our flowchart. A detailed description of the techniques involved in this stage of training development is beyond the scope of this book.[1] However it will suffice to say that the main function of front-end analysis (otherwise known as pre-analysis, diagnosis or training needs analysis) is to identify deficient performance, establish its cause and to propose an appropriate solution. That solution will often be something other than training. Occasionally people fail to perform adequately because their work is unpleasant or unrewarding or because their working environment is unsatisfactory. In other cases they may never be told how their work fails to meet standards or which jobs have priority. In these sort of circumstances the problem may be rectified by one or more of a variety of solutions, any of which is probably less costly than training. These solutions may range from redesigning the job, apparatus or documentation, to providing a regular system of feedback on achievement. The only grounds for contemplating training would be where inadequate performance is caused by a genuine lack

[1] *cf Training Needs Analysis* T Boydell, BACIE; *An Ounce of Analysis is worth a Pound of Objectives* J H Harless, Stipes Publishing; *Analysing Performance Problems* R F Mager, P Pipe, Fearon

of knowledge or skills. Even here suitable alternatives may suggest them-selves. (One such alternative might be to recruit staff whose experience includes the understanding and capability currently lacking.)

Proactive
The procedure employed to analyse problems of inadequate current per-formance on existing tasks may be called reactive analysis. A slightly differ-ent circumstance occurs when one is faced with an impending performance problem as a result of the introduction of new systems or procedures. The analysis employed to explore this kind of problem we may call proactive needs analysis. In these circumstances it may well be that few, if any, of the existing staff possess any relevant knowledge or skill. It would be rash, how-ever, to conclude that the firm would therefore need to provide equal train-ing for all its staff.

Consider for example the change to decimalization in the UK in 1971. This innovation impinged upon a wide variety of skills such as change-giving, writing invoices, calculating and verbal skills. Conventional, group-based training was quite inadequate to cope with the situation. The student num-bers were too vast and the subject experts non-existent. As a consequence, many companies commissioned self-instructional packages or instructor-support kits to send out, comprising all the necessary lesson plans, exercises and aids for local supervisors to conduct their own training.

A common characteristic of such prestructured materials was their modu-lar format: they were designed in units or blocks reflecting particular skills or tasks. Trainees received only those modules relevant to their own work. Ten or 12 years after decimalization this approach has become so commonplace that it hardly seems worth mentioning, yet those who were involved in train-ing for decimalization may recall how prominently modularization featured in articles and promotional publications about the training packages. As we shall see, the modular structure is particularly suitable for administration by computer.

TASK ANALYSIS: GETTING STARTED

When the prospective course developer has identified a subject, procedure or other deficient area of performance for which a course of instruction seems called for, a useful first step is to summarize the topic in a brief synopsis. In occupational training this step is usually called the job description. The aim is to clarify your thinking about the topic. The synopsis should be written so as to explain the requirements of the job or the scope of the topic as if an entry in an encyclopaedia or similar work of reference.

Deficient performance varies greatly in scope. It may comprise a whole occupation or subject such as car maintenance or chess, or it may consist of a quite specific skill or ability such as adjusting the brakes or the 'en passant' play. Two examples of the job description or synopsis of the 'whole topic' variety are given in Figures 1.2a and 1.2b; two examples for more specific subjects are given in Figures 1.3a and 1.3b.

A radio and television service technician may be required to install, maintain, and service amplitude and frequency modulated home and auto receivers, transistorized radios, monochrome and colour television systems, high fidelity amplifiers, and tape recorders. He is able to read circuit diagrams and codes of values and to select component substitutes.

The radio and television service technician's work requires meeting the public both in the repair shop and on service calls. In order to service home receivers or equipment, he may be required to drive a car or truck. He must be able to tolerate heights, as antenna installations on rooftops are often an everyday occurrence. A service technician who establishes his own business may need to know how to maintain business records and inventory.

Figure 1.2a Job description: radio and television service technician
Source: *Developing Vocational Instruction* R F Mager and K M Beach, Fearon

Bridge is a card game played by two opposing pairs.

The game has two major phases. In the first, bidding, a player attempts to agree with his partner 'a contract' to win a number of tricks (seven or more) in each hand dealt. In the second phase the partnership bidding to the highest level attempts to win the contracted number of tricks. For every trick each player plays one of his 13 cards. The highest card played wins.

In the bidding phase, since each player's cards are concealed, partnerships must have a system of evaluating hands and indicating their likely strength through the bids made. In play it is important to remember the cards played and note other clues to the likely distribution of the opponents' cards.

Figure 1.2b Topic synopsis: bridge

The plug wirer is employed in the service department of a large departmental store which sells and repairs electrical equipment of all kinds. He connects plugs to the power leads of all new equipment and replaces faulty plugs on items returned for servicing and repair.

The power leads are two or three-core flexes coded to both the old and the new standards.

Figure 1.3a Job description: plug wirer

When an employer telephones a Job Centre to notify a vacancy the details are recorded on the *vacancy receipt form*.

The main purpose of the form is to generate a computer printed card to advertise the vacancy in the self service display and a second card, the order card, which records details of the vacancy in the Job Centre.

In translating the information about the job from the employer's description to the form itself, it is important to be precise in specifying the duties to be carried out and the characteristics and capabilities required in prospective applicants.

Order takers should have a good telephone technique and be capable of writing clearly and economically under pressure.

Figure 1.3b Job description: vacancy recording in a Job Centre

Reproduced by kind permission of Manpower Services Commission. Technical content is not necessarily 100 per cent accurate

Writing the synopsis of the course immediately precedes the process described by Galbraith of dividing and subdividing tasks into their component parts. That process may be presented in graphic form as follows:

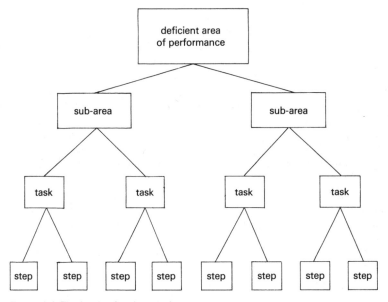

Figure 1.4 The levels of task analysis

Source: *Objective Objectives* J H Harless, Harless Educational Technologists Inc

The synopses we have just considered describe the top section of Figure 1.4 – the deficient area of performance. One must next determine the major sub-areas which comprise that performance. In the case of bridge for example, these will consist of bidding, the play of the cards, scoring and preparing to play (see level 2, Figure 1.5). For a supermarket check-out the sub-areas would include something like preparing the check-out, operating the till and cashing-up.

Specifying tasks

The next subdivision in the analysis process is critical – specifying the tasks which make up the sub-areas and the job. R F Mager has defined a task as 'a logically related set of actions required for the completion of a job. Thus a job includes a number of tasks. For example one of the tasks that must be performed by a vehicle mechanic is that of changing a tyre.' [1] Harless clarifies what is a logically related set of actions by defining a task as an activity having 'a beginning, an end and a product'. [2]

If we apply these definitions to our bridge example, we will find that the simplest area, preparing to play, comprises two basic tasks 'deciding the dealer and partners' and 'dealing the cards'. In the case of the supermarket check-out operator 'preparing the check-out' might include the tasks of 'loading the float', 'tidying the check-out' and 'getting the till ready'.

Tasks into steps

If you were briefing a tutor on an evening-class course for bridge or a skilled instructor of supermarket personnel it would probably be enough to give them the content of the course at the task level. The bridge tutor would only need to be told that he was expected to cover 'dealing' or 'making the open-ing bid' and so forth. However in preparing a course for individual study it is necessary to analyse carefully the steps that comprise the procedures to be learned and the understanding required to perform them.

When a trainee interacts with the course, the author must bear in mind that he will not be present to clarify or illustrate the little misunderstandings caused by inadequate examples or poor sequencing which can so easily be cleared up in the classroom, but can become insuperable obstacles to the student working on his own.

To ensure that nothing crucial is missed, every task that is identified in the job or area breakdown will itself need to be divided into the steps that comprise that task. We shall see that not every task or step needs to be taught; some may be excluded from the final course. But at this stage, it will be important not to overlook any detail. The steps which comprise the draw for dealer in bridge include 'each player takes a card', 'the dealer will be the player drawing the highest card', 'the second highest card will be the dealer's partner'. The full sequence of steps may be seen in Figure 1.5.

In recording the steps of a task one should aim to follow the sequence in which they occur. This is the case in our examples. Often, but not always, this will be the sequence one will follow in teaching the task.

When the steps of the task have been noted, no further breaking down

[1] *Developing Vocational Instruction* Mager and Beach, Fearon
[2] Harless *op cit*

Figure 1.5 Subject matter analysis: task and step level

will be necessary for many of them. How can one know when the subdividing process should stop? Harless' dictum is to 'divide tasks to the level where they are no longer deficient.' This may be rather more inelegantly paraphrased as 'if they could do what you told them to, then don't break it down any more'. Take the bridge example. The steps of the task 'dealing the cards' are all quite simple. No person of average intelligence who has handled playing cards should have any difficulty in carrying out those steps. But if we apply the same scrutiny to the steps of the 'draw for dealer' we cannot be quite so sure. The task, 'all players draw a card' surely needs no further explanation. But what about 'highest card sits as dealer'? That surely is not so self-evident. It so happens that in bridge, as in many card games, aces are high but that is not always the case. And what does one do in the case of a tie?

For most beginners this knowledge is bound to be deficient and further analysis will be required.

Performance unit analysis
One approach to this further analysis – the further subdivision one needs to make – is to break down the more complex steps into performance units. Where any kind of procedural activity with a strong element of continuity is concerned this can be a very effective form of analysis. In such cases the performance unit will consist of a cue or preceding situation (known as the stimulus), the reaction or activity prompted by that cue (known as the response) and the outcome of that response which becomes the stimulus for the next unit or stimulus ⟶ response ● stimulus. A simple example might be:

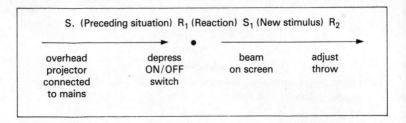

An S-R analysis for 'highest card is dealer' would be something like this:

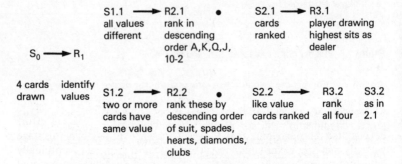

One value of this type of analysis is that it ensures that no step of a task is omitted (something which an expert in the subject is quite likely to do). The course designer can inspect every stimulus point for any possible variations. If for example, in the case of the S-R analysis of setting up the overhead projector he asked the question 'Could anything else happen at this point?' for each of the stimuli S_0 and S_1 he would find that for S_1 another possibility could occur, namely 'nothing happens'. Further useful analyses include the facilitation/competition analysis in which all responses may be checked and compared with any existing trainee capabilities, which may either facilitate or compete with (inhibit) learning of that unit. For example, in the above analysis of the bridge deal, R2.2 refers to a ranking of suits that is particular only to bridge. Those coming to bridge from whist (as many do) have learned a completely different suit ranking scale which may interfere with their learning of rankings in bridge.

This type of analysis may appear rather complicated and time-consuming. However, it is an invaluable addition to one's tool kit of training design techniques and, as we shall see later, it can be used as a spring-board to the lesson design procedures. More discussion and illustration of this type of analysis may be found in the work of Gilbert, Harless and Brunstrom.[1]

A flowchart type of analysis similar in scope to S-R analysis is described by Gagné and Briggs.[2] This analysis is called information processing analysis and would produce a flowchart of the bridge example like this:

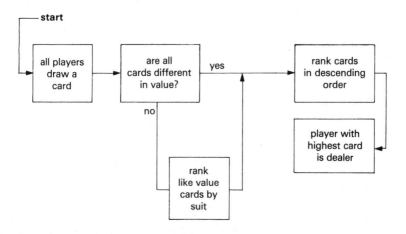

An information processing analysis of the draw for dealer in bridge

Intending authors of self-instructional materials will find the effort devoted to a thoroughgoing analysis well worthwhile; to skip over this stage will only cause problems later on. Authors who find themselves continually adjusting the wording and sequencing of their courses, adding new material and tinkering with exercises, are paying the price for neglecting or rushing the analysis process.

[1] *cf Human Competence* T F Gilbert, McGraw Hill, 1978; Harless *op cit; Developments in Training Design* C Brunstrom, APLET Yearbook, Kogan Page, 1974-5
[2] *Principles of Instructional Design* R M Gagné and L J Briggs, Holt, Reinhart and Winston, 1979

DEVELOPING TRAINING OBJECTIVES

'Instructional systems are effective only to the extent to which they qualify personnel for successful job performance.' [1]

What objectives are for

The training designer's principal aim should be to establish or enhance human performance. He is interested that the trainees who use his study materials should develop competence in a specific field. This competence may be something as precise as rectifying a fault in a chemical plant or as general as the ability to communicate effectively. In each case, if the trainer decides to develop a course in the subject, he can verify that the course has succeeded only by the trainees' ability to demonstrate their newly acquired capabilities. If they can now demonstrate understanding or mastery of some concept or skill previously beyond the limits of their ability, then we can say that they have learned. It seems appropriate therefore to describe a lesson or course in terms of those capabilities by which you would recognize that learning has occurred. To articulate such a description is to write an objective. As Susan Markle has observed 'Students learn what you cause them to do'. [2]

There is one area of screen or frame design which frequently troubles apprentice authors of computer-based or other self-instructional courses – asking the question. They may have superb graphics, imaginative simulations and new jokes, but the one thing they cannot do is set the trainee problems to exercise his understanding of the subject he is studying. As we shall see there are certain tactics which authors can employ to make their questions effective, meaningful and relevant. The most important of these is to write effective objectives and build courses upon them.

What objectives look like

Here are two objectives for teaching topics which might lend themselves to a CBT approach:

1. for a lesson on applying the single transferable vote form of proportional representation:
   'the student will be able to identify any candidates to be elected from the ballot after the first and subsequent counts, reallocate the surplus votes cast for the elected candidates to second preference candidates, and decide the candidates finally elected';
2. for a lesson for trainee croupiers:
   'given any number and combination of chips up to a maximum of 25, the student will be able to calculate their conversion value in coin of the realm within ten seconds'.

---

[1] *Instructional Systems Development* USAF July 1975
[2] S M Markle *op cit*

Why these topics may be particularly suitable for CBT is considered later in Chapter 2. For the moment it will be seen that in both cases the competence to be learned is clearly described in performance terms. These descriptions facilitate the specification of a question or exercise with which the student and his tutor can assess whether or not that competence has been acquired. Where a training objective does not readily suggest the problem or question which would assess learning then it could probably be improved.

From task analysis to objective
With many – probably most – course development projects you will already have structured the subject matter in your task analysis. You would naturally seek to define the tasks and steps that comprise the performance to be trained before writing the objectives which describe that performance. Consider one of those half-familiar jobs with which you have some superficial acquaintance – say a traffic warden or the security guard on the main entrance to a large office block. If you were asked to describe the capabilities necessary to perform such occupations (the objectives) you would first need to decide exactly what the tasks were which comprised them. Thus the training objective for a course or session is a summary of the task analysis. It defines the task in terms of the competence to be learned. The training designer can use this objective as the basis on which he can prepare a test or exercise by which, at the end of the course, the trainees can assess how much they have learned.

Working from the top
Objectives can be defined for different levels of learning – very specific (eg adjust brakes) or fairly general (car maintenance). The two objectives on proportional representation and roulette given above are clearly designed towards the specific end. The proportional representation task might well require a couple of lessons of one to one and a half hours. Counting roulette chips would be unlikely to require more than one 30 to 40-minute lesson, but very often the problem will require a series of lessons to produce the appropriate competence. Where should one start? One common approach, advocated by many authorities[1] is to write objectives from the top downwards.

Let us look at the task analysis for our example of playing bridge (Figure 1.5). The overall deficient performance is a complete inability to play the game (although this does not mean that most people starting to learn it will not have some relevant sub-skills such as the ability to recognize and name cards).

Such a deficiency can hardly be made good in one lesson. For many novices, learning bridge implies taking a one-year course of evening-classes. Thereafter they can aim to improve their play by joining a club, entering competitions and so on. An objective written at this level has been called a life long or continuing objective. A continuing objective for the bridge example is given in Figure 1.6. The objective for the level immediately below

[1] *cf* Gagné and Briggs *op cit*

relates to the overall course (in this case, as we have suggested above, one year). This describes the general capabilities to be learned as a result of formal tuition and supervised practice with feedback. Courses, like books, are more easily digested if divided into sections or units. The unit objectives given at level 3 in the figure reflect items at area level in our task analysis. Unit F relates to scoring, unit A to bidding and so on. Some units in a course may require several sessions or modules of study. Others may be covered in single sessions. The complexity of the subject matter will decide the term. In bridge, the unit on bidding will cover at least five or six sessions. On the other hand, scoring may be covered by the use of a simple job aid. Units usually comprise a number of closely related tasks or concepts. As a rough rule of thumb we can say that an objective for this level of performance will relate to a session of instruction. Thus in Figure 1.6 at level 4 the specific performance objectives will relate to specific sessions or modules of the course. A great number of CBT projects are developed as one-off task/topic modules of this kind such as operating Machine X or completing Form Y and so on.

SPECIFYING OBJECTIVES: THE BASIC MODEL

Specialist trainers will be aware of an extensive body of literature on framing objectives for instruction at the unit level. The best known work on the subject is by R F Mager.[1] One inadequacy of this text, as far as the field of occupational training is concerned, is that it is set largely in the sector of secondary and tertiary education. However, many writers have applied the Mager-type model, or similar approaches, to the adult, vocational training content.[2]

As we have seen, the objective is an essential planning tool for the course designer. It describes the capability to be learned and so enables the definition of an end-of-course test to measure the learning achievement. The examples cited earlier clearly indicate the desired capability; in the proportional representation example to decide how votes are allocated and in the roulette example to convert chips to coins. Guide books on objective writing never fail to stress the importance of couching the unit aims in terms of the performance by which trainees will demonstrate their understanding of the unit. This is easier said than done. Course descriptions for vocational training are replete with what Mager has called 'fuzzies'; that is, expressions which describe the trainer's aspirations or the teaching method he intends to employ – anything but the performance by which the learner can assess the extent of his learning. Thus we find the objectives for one course written as 'the tutor will lead a discussion on the Employment Protection Act' and for another 'students will have a knowledge of the main sections of the form X123'.

[1] *Preparing Instructional Objectives* R F Mager, 2nd edition, Fearon, 1975
[2] *cf The Engineering of Educational and Training Systems* R G Smith, Jr, Heath Lexington, 1971

Example: **Learning to play bridge**

1. *Continuing Objective* Students will continue to develop their bridge playing capabilities by joining a club and enrolling in a variety of competitions. They will experiment with a variety of bidding and playing systems and be increasingly able to adapt to the styles of unfamiliar partners.

2. *End of Course Objective* By the end of the course the students will have demonstrated their ability in competitive play to bid to a system and to play hands as declarer or defender.

3. *Unit Objectives* (some typical examples):
   Unit A: The student will bid or pass in any position, vulnerable or non-vulnerable, and be able to justify his decision by reference to his partner's responses, the strength and distribution of his hand, any bids by the opposition and the respective scores.
   Unit C: The student as declarer will play a hand of cards in trumps or no-trumps, demonstrating his awareness of the possible honour card distribution and length of suits in the opposition hands (by reference to the mathematical probability and inferences from any opposition bidding and discards), his timing for crossing between dummy and the closed hand and his ability to choose the appropriate discard.
   Unit D: The student will demonstrate his ability to defend against a contract in either second or fourth position by his choice of opening lead, his discards and his trick taking.
   Unit F: The student will be able to calculate the score of any contract in rubber bridge or competition play without the use of tables.

4. *Specific Performance Objectives for Unit A* (not-exhaustive)
   For hands at or near the ONE level:
   (a) Evaluate a selection of hands according to the ACOL Point-Count System and the Honour Trick System.
   (b) As dealer select and justify an opening bid for a selection of hands of 11 to 15 points, no hand having more than one five-card suit.
   (c) On a selection of hands respond to an opening bid by partner by passing or bidding.

Figure 1.6 Setting objectives to course levels

Thinking in performance terms

Mager and others have suggested that in specifying objectives the course designer aims to employ performance-describing verbs which clearly indicate how achievement may be observed. Examples include verbs like *locate*, *select*, *draw*, *calculate* and *translate*. Such verbs facilitate accurate measurement of the learned capability and are better than such 'fuzzies' as *understand*, *appreciate*, *familiarize* and so forth.

However, simply by using behaviour-describing verbs from the acceptable list does not necessarily guarantee useful objectives. Consider this example from a course for technician apprentices, teaching multiplying and dividing on a slide rule.

On completion of this instruction trainees will be able to:

1. *identify* the scales used for multiplication and division on a slide rule;
2. *describe* the steps used to carry out
   (a) multiplication
   (b) division;
3. *define* the type of scale marked on a slide rule and the principle of operation.

The three performance-describing verbs *identify*, *describe* and *define* are certainly open to fewer interpretations than *appreciate* or *understand*. Unfortunately the performances they describe do not reflect the desired capability, namely using the slide rule to perform calculations. The trainee might be able to perform all three of these activities without ever having mastered that process. When articulating the objective for a unit, course designers should ensure that they focus on the performance which demonstrates the competence to be learned as closely as possible to the content in which it is usually carried out. An objective from, say, a course unit for building society branch managers on deciding loan applications would be more effective if it requires participants to judge real or simulated applications rather than to 'state the rules for giving loans', an approach to objective definition which is common in many course descriptions.

CRITERIA AND CONDITIONS

In order to permit meaningful assessment of learning at the module (single session) level of instruction, an objective will include a reference to how well the performance described is to be carried out and, where appropriate, to the conditions affecting the performance. Often the objective will require the trainee to be tested on a number of examples. In this case, the number and range of examples chosen should adequately reflect the requirements of the job. Consider some typical sorts of occupational training for office or factory personnel, say for sales office staff replying by phone or letter to customer complaints or quality control inspectors looking for faults in finished products. In both cases the training objective will need to include a reference to a number of test items. For the sales office less than half a dozen examples will probably not be a reasonable reflection of the range of major complaints. The objective for the inspection task may specify dozens or even hundreds of items depending on the product, type and degree of fault which may occur.

Sometimes it will only be possible to verify a standard by receiving some kind of creative or physical response from the learner. For instance, a course for a drill operator might include a module on knowledge about types of drilling. One objective for this module might read 'discrimination between drilling, countersinking, counterboring and respective bits'. The standard for this objective would be 'for each operation, sketch section, view of hole and indicate bit without error'.[1] This would be the sort of task for which use of the computer in the marking procedure would be inappropriate, since an element of judgement would be required from an expert to assess the quality of the sketch. A similar problem might arise with the standards for an objective from a training officer's course, for example, 'select an appropriate instructional method to teach an objective'. The sort of standard set for this performance might be 'for each of three objectives the method selected must be compatible with all the following:

○ the objective
○ student characteristics
○ available time
○ available resources.'

This sort of assessment would be possible using the computer, but the high verbal content of the responses would not be easy to handle.

The third element of an objective, the conditions, applies where any apparatus, documentation, supplementary job details and so forth need to be included to simulate more closely the conditions of the task. It is not uncommon for course planners to use a conventional form layout to identify this and the other features of objectives as in this example:

What trainee will do	Conditions	Standards
State the total face value	of any combination of ten coins	(implied standard: without error)
Compute a standard deviation	given three sets of not less than 15 raw scores chosen at random	correct to second decimal place

OBJECTIVES AND TESTS

The measure of the success of learning will be the trainee's ability to solve problems relating to the subject he is learning when the course has finished. The tests which incorporate these problems will not be too difficult to devise if the training designer has developed well-written objectives. Indeed, it is the hallmark of a good objective that it immediately suggests a relevant post-test.

Let us consider two examples. The first concerns statistics for managers; it is a common feature of texts on statistics to explain how to compute

[1] Example provided by R J Le Hunte

standard deviation and Z scores. Less often is one given practical examples of how to interpret them in business or other industrial contexts. A test for this particular objective should therefore seek to place the capability to be learned in a plausible content for an industrial manager. So instead of a test saying 'calculate the standard deviation for these data', one would aim to have the learner apply that capability to a realistic case, as follows:

Objective	Ability to use standard deviation to compute Z scores and evaluate scores from different distributions
Test	The table that follows gives a record of defects detected by each of ten quality control inspectors on two shifts; decide whether Smith from shift A or Brown from shift B seems to be more efficient and by how much by calculating their respective Z scores

Here is the second example from the bridge topic:

Objective	Given ten hands of cards (five vulnerable, five non-vulnerable) bid or pass for each hand, sitting as dealer
Test	For each of the ten hands below say what you would bid as dealer

FACTORS AFFECTING TEST DESIGN

Course planners for CBT must bear in mind a number of factors when designing post-test questions and problems. It will be important not to ignore these and so impair the usefulness of the post-test.

1. Suitability for keyboard entry
As we have seen, a wide variety of post-test items will require responses quite difficult or inappropriate to enter at a terminal. These will vary from responses requiring a great deal of keying-in of words and numbers (unfair to trainers with no formal keyboard expertise) to responses involving the manipulation of apparatus and drawing of diagrams. Some variations to the normal keyboard may permit some types of exercise-testing discrimination skills to be administered with relative ease. The touch-sensitive screen and the digital pad are two examples.[1] But in large business applications which use the QWERTY keyboard the layout of the keys will be a constraint in test design.

[1] For more discussion on these see Chapter 6

2. Range and number of questions

Test items should be based on the requirements specified in the objective. The objectives and tests above on statistics and bridge illustrate the criteria of range and number. The objective on standard deviation says 'compute Z scores' and 'evaluate scores from different distributions'. The test includes one example entry. The course developer must decide whether this one question will be sufficient to verify that the understanding of the process has been acquired.

The bridge example illustrates a point about a range of questions. Clearly, by careful selection of the ten hands a test could be designed to guarantee a high score on the post-test. As even non-bridge players may be aware from glancing at the Christmas bridge competition in the Sunday newspapers, there is considerable scope for variation in bidding.

3. Nature of response

Think carefully how you would expect the trainee to give his solutions to the problem. In the test for the bridge bidding example, the trainee is asked to 'say' what his answer is. If tested at a terminal he could do this by typing 1C for 1 Club or NB for No Bid. But this should be made absolutely clear. In this test, for example, if he types P for Pass instead of NB (they are synonymous) will he be marked wrong?

CONCLUSION

A test should reflect the objectives on which it is based. Suppose an objective for a course for the office staff of a mail order company requires them to make decisions about crediting agents' accounts for returned goods. A post-test question for this course such as 'state the rules for giving credit on returns' will test a relevant aspect of the performance. But the test will surely remain incomplete unless trainers are tested on specimen cases of agents' letters.

Defining the post-test is the verification of the usefulness of the analysis process. An effective test usually signifies that the task analysis has been thorough; an inadequate test may suggest that further scrutiny is required.

2. Drawing up a learning plan

INTRODUCTION

Computer-based training tends to be more commonly used in large-scale business and industrial applications. Large-scale training operations are more easily handled in a segmented or modular format. In this approach, clearly-defined areas of activity may be learned only by those trainees for whom they are suitable. In developing a modular structure the course designer should identify the title of each module, an objective and the presentation method most suitable to it.

Using a computer terminal as the main vehicle for presenting the course modules does not preclude the use of additional presentation methods. In this chapter a variety of presentation approaches are described and there is a discussion of the criteria which may be used in their selection.

In order to enable courses to adapt to the needs of trainees of differing levels of knowledge and from differing backgrounds, authors should specify the level of achievement (prerequisites) they expect from those starting each module.

DEVELOPING A MODULAR STRUCTURE

As we have already seen, a large area of training concerns the learning of new systems and procedures. These innovations often require large numbers of trainees to attend many sessions of instruction. A new computer-based order-processing system or subscriber-accounting system may affect as many as 20 or 30 separate tasks in different combinations. For some staff, basic training in such a system may require hours of instruction. As in the case of decimalization training it will not always be necessary for all staff to receive precisely the same content. In these circumstances a common strategy to adopt, and one which is particularly suited to a computer-based operation, is a modular structure. Modular scheduling of a course is a natural corollary of the nesting of objectives from the top down in the manner described in the previous chapter.

We suggest that the reader regards the module as the equivalent of one or, sometimes, two sessions of individualized training of 30 to 45 minutes duration. Several modules will make up a unit or section. So the specific performance objectives at level 4 in Figure 1.6 will usually represent objectives for the modules that comprise unit A. Thus a modular schedule for this unit might begin:

Module	Scope	Objective
A.1	Hand evaluation, opening bid as dealer at level 1	(a) Evaluate a selection of hands according to Point-Count and Honour-trick systems (b) As dealer select an opening bid for a selection of hands of 11 to 15 points, no hand having more than one five-card suit
A.2	Response to opening bids of 1	For a selection of hands respond to partner's opening bid by passing or bidding

Note that the objectives (a) and (b) from Figure 1.6 have been combined for the first module. Objective (a) would only require five to ten minutes' instruction and is so closely linked to (b) that they are better linked into one module.

Modular scheduling enables the training designer to take account of differences in employee experience and work responsibilities.

A well-structured modular course can accommodate several levels of trainee. Figure 2.1 below shows the sort of progress a supervisor, senior clerk and clerk might respectively make through a unit of seven modules.

Evidently some mechanisms will be useful to enable these trainees with differing levels of need and knowledge to plan their learning. In a later section (page 35) we suggest how pre-testing can perform this function by assessing the readiness of individual students and routing them to appropriate parts of the course, depending upon their subsequent performance.

Modular courses can certainly be administered and presented in printed or audio-visual form without any intervention by, or support from, a computer. Excellent examples of modular courses in print and/or audio-visual form have been developed for a wide variety of occupational training applications including nursing, chemical processing and the construction industry. However, the computer is especially useful in the management of student progress and is crucial to the success of such a format. This question is explored more fully in Chapter 16.

SELECTING THE PRESENTATION METHOD

At the time that the training plan and modular schedule is produced, the presentation method to adopt for each module should be considered. Since

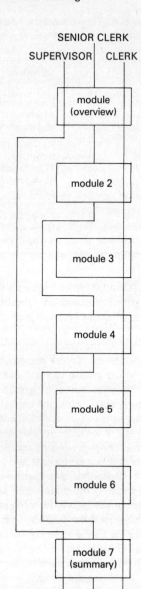

Figure 2.1 Different course levels

Reprinted by kind permission of IBM

this book concentrates on computer-based instruction it is not proposed to list and evaluate the whole range of instructional media. That is a subject well-reviewed in other books.[1] However, this chapter would be deficient if some reference were not made to such questions as the relative capabilities of computers and other media, and the factors which might affect the training designer's decision about the most effective means to present the content of his course.

Let us first note briefly four major factors which the course designer must consider when selecting media.[2]

1. The design of the environment for learning within the context of the overall training system constraints.
   ○ Thus in the context of a computer-based training (CBT) hypothesis one must consider questions like the existing use, if any, of computing facilities, their availability for training purposes and the type of work to which they are dedicated.
2. The nature of information presentation, practice and feedback required to learn the task.
   ○ some kinds of learning such as verbal interaction, manual completion of documents and so on are not suitable for demonstration on the screen.
3. The extent to which individualization would be cost-effective.
4. Which resources are available for developing and producing courseware and whether the equipment necessary to present courseware can be acquired.
   ○ are CBT authors and coders available? Can existing terminals be used?

Let us suppose we have taken these criteria into account and decided to consider seriously a CBT course. Let us consider the functions or roles for which computers have been used to perform in training. Figure 2.2 gives a list of examples. These examples represent an apparently remarkable variety of uses. Unfortunately, at present, a number of these functions are not readily available, or are not realistic possibilities for more than a privileged minority of trainers. Although the situation is changing rapidly for the better, the fact remains that of the functions listed in the figure, the most common is the first – using a terminal to present words and numbers as one might in books, programmed instruction texts or microfiches.

---

[1] *cf The Selection and Use of Instructional Media* A J Romiszowski, Kogan Page, 1974
[2] adapted from *Instructional Systems Development* AF Manual 50-2, US Air Force 1975

○ Presentation of text (including numbers)
○ Presentation of graphics
○ Record student responses
○ Print out hard copy
○ Perform calculations
○ Index resources
○ Control other presentation devices
○ Drive task-related apparatus
○ Present sound

Figure 2.2 Computer functions in CBT

CBT and programmed instruction

The desirability of developing instructional systems which correct or adapt themselves in response to a learner's inputs is discussed in Chapter 10. One such approach is programmed instruction. What has the computer to offer the training developer which could not be provided more cheaply with an attractive and effective self-instructional text? For some applications the simple answer to this question is 'nothing'! A combination of fear (of being thought outmoded) and ignorance (of what constitutes effective programmed instruction) may induce a trainer to waste resources by using the computer to present material which would otherwise be more effectively handled in print form. There will, however, be circumstances in which the computer may well prove to have positive advantages over the printed page, even where not much more than a simple presentation of words and numbers is required.

The following list presents some of the more valuable areas where a computer is more effective than print:

1. Presenting remedial sequences ('scrambled' texts are awkward to use)
2. Providing randomly selected problems
3. Giving help if the learner asks for it or his responses suggest the need
4. Giving more practice at the learner's request
5. Recording the learner's responses and comments
6. Not requiring 'written' responses
7. Amending 'published' courses more easily.

The reader will note that a number of these items contribute to that vital requirement of adaptability. Numbers 1, 3, 4 and 5 are all in that category. If these are going to be of particular importance, then the case for using a computer will be strong. However, in choosing the presentation method one must bear in mind the question of transferability. In order to facilitate transfer from training to job, it is usually good practice to have the instructional situation as similar as possible to the job situation. It is often said that there is no substitute for the real thing. There are exceptions to this rule of fidelity, two of which occur quite often. One of these concerns those tasks with abstract information-inputs requiring the production of abstractions. In training for this kind of ability it is less important to have the training environment resemble the actual task environment. Many desk jobs such as preparing financial estimates are of this kind, and this example might lend itself nicely to a CBT presentation.

The other circumstance concerns those situations where resemblance to the job is actually undesirable. For example, in a course on replying to customers' letters of complaint in a sales office it would probably be too distracting for trainees to start off with a variety of real letters. There would be too many variable inputs – not to mention illegible handwriting! A more effective strategy would be to start with some specimen letters from which much of the distracting cues and ambiguities had been removed. As the trainee advances in his training programme the letters will gradually become more realistic.

Opportunities for practice
Closely linked to the criteria of fidelity is that of practice. Each module should make provision for trainees to practise the competence they aim to acquire. For some skills, practice on the real thing may be difficult to arrange. This may be because it requires expensive equipment, is dangerous or something that only occurs rarely, unpredictably, or in circumstances where physical realism is hard to simulate in training. These constraints, either individually or in combination, affect training for a variety of industries. The training of process operators in chemical plants is an outstanding example of a situation where realistic practice of many tasks is not possible. But for such procedures it may well be possible to give trainees practice at a computer terminal. By following graphical representations on a visual display unit (VDU) of pipework, valves and other components of the plant, the trainee might learn to identify particular fault situations and learn which valve to choose to clear the fault.

Let us consider a project for office staff which illustrates some of these points. The task concerns the acceptance of telephone requests from business customers of a travel agent. While the call proceeds the clerk receiving the order completes a computer-processed form to which the client's requirements are transferred. Following computer-input, a summary of the client's needs is printed out on to a card used by a researcher to provide suitable accommodation or journey. The key capability of the task is the technique employed by the staff to establish the precise nature of the client's need. Since space is at a premium on the card, the order must be specific in detail without exceeding four lines of 52 characters. Supplementary detail is held by the order-taker to whom researchers can refer, but this takes more time. The order-taker also has to code certain sections of the form with such details as type of services, geographical area, carrier and so on.

Since mainframe computer terminals with VDUs are already available for this and other tasks it would seem sensible to use them as the main vehicle for course presentation. It would certainly be possible to simulate the telephone conversations on the VDU. Indeed the final package presents short excerpts of customer-clerk interactions on the screen. To keep the entire training environment in this form, however, would distance the simulation too far from the actual task environment. Hence an element of the module consists of audio recordings of the telephone order. These are used both to demonstrate effective and faulty questioning techniques and to present the post-test.

Another design consideration concerns documentation. Some trainers spend many hours reproducing printed forms on the screen so that trainees can 'complete' them by moving the cursor about from field to field. There are circumstances where this is useful, but very often it is far simpler and more realistic to provide printed specimens for demonstration and exercise purposes. This was done in the case of the travel agents. The presentation mix for this module is given in Figure 2.3.

○ **Coursebook**
- course overview
- demonstration order forms
- incorrect, incomplete and blank forms for appraisal exercises
- post-test element

○ **Audio tape**
- simulation of typical orders
- post-test element

○ **VDU**
- interactive sequences demonstrating form-filling procedure, questioning technique and assessing learning

---

Figure 2.3 Travel agent course: journey research package

TRAINEE CAPABILITIES AND CHARACTERISTICS

One of the most common and awkward constraints facing the classroom trainer is the range of knowledge, motivation and learning style among his student population. By grouping similar students for particular exercises and tutorials, the able instructor can sometimes mitigate the worst effects of these differences. Nevertheless the diagnosis of individual learning difficulties and the provision of suitable feedback in the confines of a group is at best a superficial process.

Many instructors in industry and teachers in higher education know little about their trainees' existing level of knowledge at the start of a course. Thus, much time and effort is wasted teaching them some of what they already know or presuming knowledge that they do not have.

While it is important to specify the objectives of the course in terms of the capabilities that the trainees are expected to acquire by the end, it is equally useful to specify their expected capabilities for the start. Otherwise it may well be that the course includes much redundant material. The substance of a course should be derived by subtracting the student's existing capabilities from the capabilities you want him to acquire.

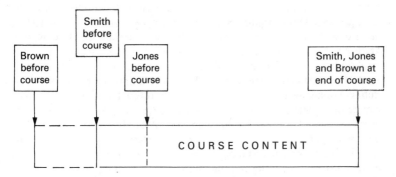

Figure 2.4 Basic course format

The basic format of a course is shown in Figure 2.4. The course will have maximum impact if it begins at a point immediately following the existing limit of the learner's knowledge of the subject and contains no material with which he is already familiar. This would be the case with trainee Smith. For Brown, this particular course falls short of the entry point for the course. Jones, on the other hand, possesses some knowledge of the early section and for him this point will be redundant. Thus developers must define as best they can the level of knowledge and skill expected of anyone starting a particular module. This is commonly known as specifying prerequisites. At the same time the course team must ensure that the modules they develop relate to prospective trainees. It will be of little use to produce beautifully packaged and well-designed courses with carefully specified prerequisite abilities for trainees who lack those prerequisites. An outline course plan taking account of these requirements is shown in Figure 2.5.

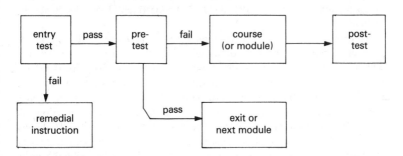

Figure 2.5 Trainee progress chart

The entry test

The entry test in Figure 2.5 is a test of prerequisites. It asks the question 'Do the trainees possess the necessary capabilities to start the course?'. If the test reveals a lack of the expected starting ability then remedial instruction must be arranged. If trainees score satisfactorily on the entry test then they are ready to start the programme. Before they do so it is often useful to administer a pre-test. This contains similar or identical exercises to the post-test. A good score at this point suggests not only that the trainee has the necessary knowledge to start the course but also that he knows so much of its content as to make it pointless for him to take it. He can therefore pass on to the next module or section, if there is one, or otherwise simply return to his normal duties. Trainees who fail the pre-test will pass through the course. On completing the course they can take the post-test. Their pre- and post-test scores can be evaluated and the learning gain computed. The computer is particularly well suited to performing these tasks. Indeed in some organizations simply substituting the computer for the human instructor for the purposes of administering, marking and analysing tests can produce quite remarkable savings in instructor time and provide more precise and immediate feedback to learners. In the Royal Navy, computer-based test marking in one project was estimated to have saved as much as 30 per cent of instructor time on one course. This is an aspect of computer-managed learning (CML) discussed in Chapter 16.

The discussion of modular scheduling has already illustrated the possibility of designing courses which permit the routing of particular trainees to particular modules depending on their varying knowledge and capability. The entry test to each module will permit this routing to take place. From Figure 2.5 one can see that where trainees fail to demonstrate that they are ready to start a course they may be given remedial or equalizing instruction. Clearly there is a limit to the extent to which this kind of provision can be made. In some cases remedial sequences may be developed which are used by only a tiny minority of trainees. For these trainees it might be more sensible to decide that these skills are not worth the expense of acquisition. Various sources of information are available about trainees' abilities. Personnel department records about academic and professional qualifications, previous employment, course attendance and departmental experience may be available.

Course designers are advised to inspect such data thoroughly. It may be that significant numbers of potential trainees have previous experience which could be exploited in developing the modular plan. For example, many large-scale computer-based training schemes based on mainframe terminals include sessions on keyboard skills for clerical staff who need to have access to terminals to obtain customer details or carry out transactions. A pre-course survey might reveal that a certain proportion of the staff already has keyboard familiarity. In this case a diagnostic test could be inserted near the start of the programme which could direct such trainees to skip the initial module or modules. If the proportion were larger one might even consider trimming the objectives to exclude that session from the course.

Trainees' personal characteristics

Besides surveying the trainees' current levels of knowledge and skill relevant to the subject area to be learned it will also be useful to review what is known about them as people. In particular any features of their background or make-up which the course author can exploit in deciding the cut and style of the module would be important. Any personal or experiential homogeneity, such as age, sex, geographical provenance, preferred reading matter and working environment could serve as a common point of reference in a learning unit.

Many organizations, such as banks and department stores, employ thousands of staff in hundreds of locations countrywide. In such cases it might seem that the personnel is so varied that individual members possess few if any common characteristics. But many modules relate to specific sectors or types of staff, and within these sub-groups common elements may well be detectable. These considerations should not be neglected. Courses have been developed which include questions framed in such a way as to require the learner to respond by writing or keying in a phrase or sentence. For trainees who normally write little if anything other than their name and address the question becomes as much a test of their literary skills as of their understanding of the subject. A course on job seeking for unemployed school-leavers in a Northern industrial town included an audio tape in which the principal narrative voice was that of the archetypal, well-to-do, southern gent. The incongruity of the presentation had simply not occurred to the authors.

Authors can use many devices to imbue text and graphics with local or sectional references designed to exploit trainee characteristics. These include local voice types in audio tapes, familiar geographical landmarks, buildings or historical allusions in text, the use of cartoons in adjunct printed materials and so on.

Humour is an ingredient with which most CBT lessons are not notably well endowed. Nevertheless students do seem to appreciate the occasional joke – as long as it is not at their expense!

3. Defining and ordering the content

INTRODUCTION

In learning programme development it is essential that the author does not hold back any of the content until too late. All the teaching points, concepts and rules which he regards as relevant to each module must be written down as a preliminary step to authorship. Otherwise the subsequent creative stages may proceed rather haltingly as the author decides which item comes first and as he recalls and inserts bits and pieces of the subject matter as he goes along.

This chapter deals with two important stages in structuring the content prior to writing the narrative and exercises for the trainees. First the process of recording all the factual content in a so-called rule set is described and exemplified. Some criteria for deciding the content sequence are discussed and a technique for sequencing rules is demonstrated. The second part of the chapter recommends that in modules of substantial length authors prepare students for the post-test by spacing review points or problems throughout the module to consolidate progress cumulatively.

The word 'frame' is used in this chapter to describe the presentation units authors employ to communicate with trainees. The word derives from the frame or window of the teaching-machines which presented the first programmed self-instructional lessons. The ensemble of pictures, words and numbers which the learner studied at each step of a teaching-machine programme acquired the name of the aperture through which they were viewed. At least one computer manufacturer has continued this convention by using the word screen with the same connotation.

In this book we tend to give the word frame a wider significance. In Part 1 particularly, the word is used as a concept meaning each unit of instruction or exercise comprising the lesson. The frame may include a description or example of the new material or procedure to be learned, some explanatory information, and, where appropriate, a title. There will always be some direction requiring a student response and feedback to the previous response. Often all the components of a frame (title, example, explanation, question and feedback) can be included on a single screen or part of a screen. In this case frame and screen are identical. But authors will often need to provide a demonstration or simulation involving audio-visual equipment, printed documents or even human interaction. Likewise the feedback may be wholly or partly tutor or supervisor administered. All these items should be regarded as components of the frame. Thus, in a course on letter writing, one sequence might include an example and explanation of a particular practice which is discouraged. The student could read this on the screen. The computer could then direct him to study one or more specimen letters in a folder accompanying the lesson, and identify occurrences of the malpractice in these letters. The letters form part of the stimulus material for the frame.

THE RULE SET

Drawing up the rule set is a stage in the development of self-instructional courses which has a long history. The elaboration of the content of self-instructional programmes in this form probably goes back as far as 1960. An example of a rule set is given in Figure 3.1. The individual numbered statements are the rules. They are very like the teaching points some teachers use in the preparation of classroom lessons. However, it will be noted that rules tend to have a far greater degree of specificity than the teaching points normally used by teachers.

Bridge: Deciding the dealer and partnerships

Rules

1. Bridge is played by four players
2. They play in partnerships
3. Each player sits across the table from his partner
4. To choose partners, the pack is spread face down on the table
5. Each player draws a card
6. The dealer has the choice of seats
7. The player with the second highest-ranking card partners the dealer
8. The other two players play as partners
9. Cards rank in ascending order 2 to 10, then J, Q, K, A
10. The player holding the highest-ranking card is the dealer
11. If two cards of like value are drawn, the higher suit rank wins
12. Suits rank Spades, Hearts, Diamonds, Clubs in order of precedence
13. This is reverse alphabetical order

Figure 3.1 Example of a rule set

The rule set serves as a bridge between the analytical phase of course design (the division and subdivision of the topic) and the creative process of authorship, whereby the words and pictures that the trainees will react to are elaborated in the first draft. The purpose of the rule set is to bring together in one sequence all the descriptive material about the topic. This will include descriptions of both what is done (if it is a procedure) as well as a record of what you need to know in order to carry it out. By comparing the example rule set with the task analysis for the same topic (Figure 1.5) it will be seen that the rule set includes all the steps of the procedure plus explanatory information and background detail.

Writing the rule set

Certain conventions are recommended in developing rules:

1. Make each rule a complete sentence. Some course-planners write rules in a kind of bureaucratic or abbreviated form, like an inter-office memo. But the earlier you begin to think about describing the topic in correct English the better. Otherwise you will find yourself tinkering with the wording of particular sequences when you are keying in the programme.
2. Restrict each rule to a one-topic statement. This means avoiding conjunctions like 'and', 'moreover', 'although' and so forth. Occasionally there may be some doubt whether to subdivide one or two rules. For example, rule 13 in Figure 3.1 could be written as four separate statements, each one describing the ranking of one individual suit.
3. Establish a sequence in which each rule shares a common theme with those immediately preceding and following it. (Further guidance on sequencing is given below in the section 'confirming the sequence'.)
4. Do not include examples. Rules are statements of fact or instructions. Naturally where rules describe unfamiliar concepts or procedures it will be necessary to cite examples. If a good example comes to mind as you are writing a rule, make a note of it in another column or separate sheet but do not let it get mixed up with the rules.

Functions of the rule set

Writing a rule set helps the author of the programme in a number of ways.

First, it enables him to fix the beginning and ending points of his topic. When he comes to write the lesson in the form in which the trainers will see it, he should not need to introduce any new material before rule 1.

Second, the complete rule set is the framework upon which the final programme is constructed. All that will be added are examples, exercises, graphical illustrations and stylistic embellishments such as humour.

Confirming the sequence

As the author writes his rules, he will be continually adjusting the order. Additional comments and steps may spring to mind which may have to be inserted. If he knows his subject well, or if it is fairly elementary, he can arrive at a reasonable sequence for teaching, by inspection and discussion with colleagues and experts in the subject matter.

Probably the simplest and most common order of instruction is the order in which the job is performed. This is quite adequate for most procedures which are composed of a series of fixed steps.

Some writers on instructional design give guidelines on sequencing. A few of these are summarized below. These apply as much to sequencing between modules, as to the sequencing of rules within modules.

General rules on order of instruction

1. Proceed from the simple to the complex.
2. Place procedural skills and knowledge in job performance order.
3. Introduce prerequisite skills prior to the time when they must be combined with other skills and then applied.
4. Incorporate the relevant knowledge or skills in the task in which they are most likely to be used.

The strategy of placing easily learned items early in the order of instruction is not always compatible with tasks where a more difficult step occurs early on. In such cases, the programme may arrange to 'talk through' the difficult early stage first, allowing the trainee practice on the subsequent simpler activities. At a later stage the trainee can return to learn the more difficult item.

USING A MATRIX

Various writers have suggested a procedure for checking the sequence of unfamiliar topics by using a matrix. The matrix is used to plot the relationships between each of the rules within the rule set and each of the other rules. Figure 3.2 gives an example.

Rule-set

1. All course modules should have objectives
2. Objectives include a statement of performance
3. The performance required is described by a verb
4. 'Doing' verbs best describe performance

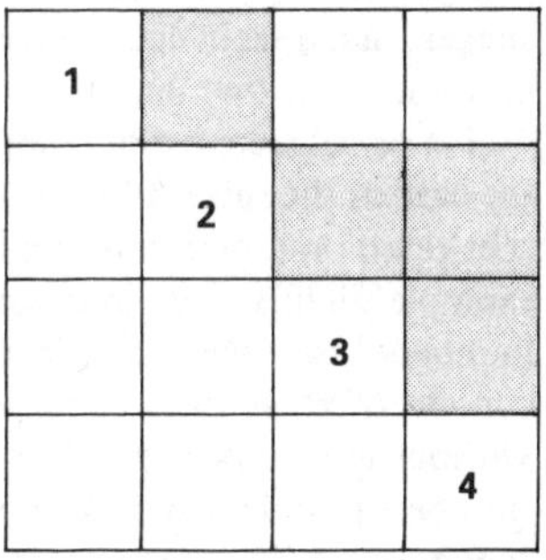

Figure 3.2 Four rules and their relationships plotted on a rule set

The four numbers across the so-called 'definition line' on the matrix represent the four rules. The author starts to complete the matrix by comparing rule 1 with each subsequent rule. Where, in his view, there is a strong thematic association between rule 1 and any subsequent rule, he will shade the box where the two rules intersect. He applies the same process to rule 2 and to all subsequent rules in turn.

In our example we see that rules 1 and 2 are closely related so the first box where they intersect is shaded. However the intersection of 1 and 3 and 1 and 4 is left unshaded since the author regards rules 3 and 4 as not strongly associated with 1.

The pattern that emerges on the matrix in Figure 3.2 may be considered desirable. It is an unbroken sequence of shaded boxes adjacent to the definition line and there are no isolated shaded boxes on the fringes.

Suppose we were to change the sequence slightly, transposing rules 1 and 2. This sequence, though clearly less logical than the first, is by no means absurd. The effect on the matrix pattern is remarkable (see Figure 3.3).

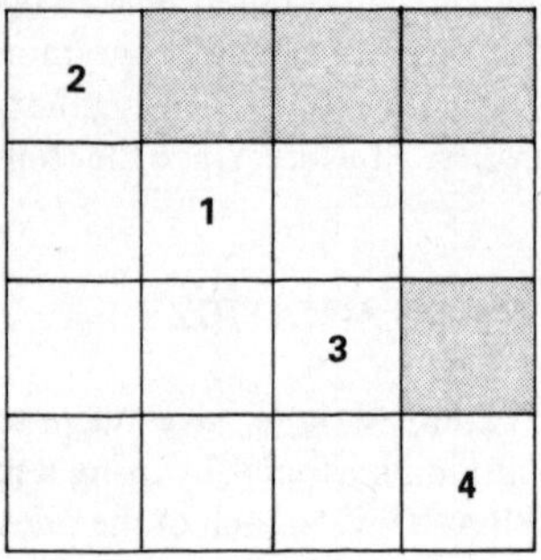

Figure 3.3 Matrix showing pattern achieved by transposing rules 1 and 2

The gaps along the definition line and the shaded box at the extreme right suggest that a sequence change may improve the flow. This is not a desirable pattern.

Let us consider a more substantial example of the use of the matrix. Take the case of the rule set for dealing in bridge in Figure 3.1. Suppose we are to plot these on a matrix to confirm the sequence for teaching. To make the example slightly more manageable let us first reduce the rules by excluding numbers 1 to 3 which are, in any case, serving a scene-setting function. The content of these rules could well be explained in an introductory passage without any student-programme interaction. The remaining ten rules, renumbered, and the matrix on which their associations are plotted are shown in Figure 3.4. The pattern that emerges from this matrix reveals two breaks in the sequence and a block of shaded sequences where rules 2 and 4 share common ground with the rules further along the definition line. Clearly rules 6 and 7 need promoting in the order and there is a problem with rule 3, which is not strongly related to any of the others. Moving up 6 and 7 and eliminating 3 from this sequence (it can be included with the previously discarded rules in an introductory frame) produces the pattern shown in Figure 3.5.

We can see that the gap has now been removed, leaving an unbroken sequence adjacent to the diagonal. This change also illustrates the third of the general rules on order detailed before, which advises the introduction of

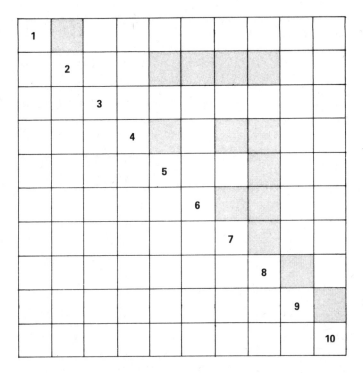

1. To choose partners, the pack is spread face down on the table
2. Each player draws a card
3. The dealer has the choice of seats
4. The player with the second highest-ranking card partners the dealer
5. The other two players play as partners
6. Cards rank in ascending order 2 to 10, then J, Q, K, A
7. The player holding the highest-ranking card is the dealer
8. If two cards of like value are drawn, the higher suit rank wins
9. Suits rank Spades, Hearts, Diamonds, Clubs in order of precedence
10. This is reverse alphabetical order

Figure 3.4 A matrix showing rule associations for bridge dealing example

prerequisite skills prior to their application with other skills. In this case, understanding card ranking (rule 6) will now come before the consequences of drawing the second highest card (rule 4).

More detail on the use of the matrix, not only for sequencing but in determining learning patterns, may be found in *Programmed Learning in*

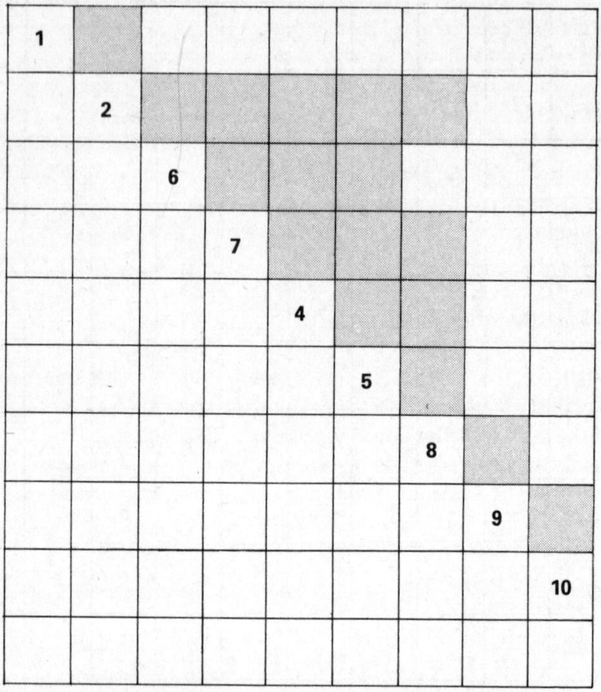

1. To choose partners, the pack is spread face down on the table
2. Each player draws a card
6. Cards rank in ascending order 2 to 10, then J, Q, K, A
7. The player holding the highest-ranking card is the dealer
4. The player with the second highest-ranking card partners the dealer
5. The other two players play as partners
8. If two cards of like value are drawn, the higher suit rank wins
9. Suits rank Spades, Hearts, Diamonds, Clubs in order of precedence
10. This is reverse alphabetical order

Figure 3.5 Rule set: bridge – the draw – revised sequences

Perspective by Thomas, Davies, Openshaw and Bird published by Lamson Press.

The rule set as insurance
One problem that often irritates the designers of both CBT and other self-instructional materials, occurs when the first version of the programme is

passed to the sponsor of the project – the user department for example. Occasionally the sponsor will seek to make changes in the content of the programme. Such changes can be expensive especially where they affect not one frame but many. Who is responsible? One insurance that authors can take out against this kind of complaint is to send the sponsor a copy of the rule set prior to authorship, inviting him to confirm the accuracy and completeness of the content and to suggest any amendments he would like. If subsequent changes are made to items previously agreed at rule set stage, then the sponsor should accept the consequential increase in costs and delay.

THE PROGRAMME STRUCTURE

As we shall see, the exercises, text and graphics with which trainees will react, can be fashioned from the rule set. Their form will depend on the author's view of the most effective approach to these particular learners. But, before looking at this process, it will be useful to pause to remind ourselves of the basic structure of a learning programme. The simplest lesson format is like this:

The post-test can take many forms as we have seen. It may be a conventional set of six to ten questions on a piece of knowledge or cognitive ability (eg what is the square root of each of these numbers?) or it may be a manipulative operation of some kind (eg set up and load the microcomputer). In the question-type test it is easy to see how the trainee can be assessed and given a mark as a percentage. Even in a hand-skill type of test there will often be clearly defined phases or aspects of the skill which are separately assessed and taught. Particular areas of success and failure can be identified and the weak spots relearned.

In a very short module – say ten minutes or under – the post-test may be the first unprompted exercise which the trainee receives. In modules of reasonable length, however, it will usually be necessary to prepare trainees for the post-test by giving them practice in listing all or part of the procedure or subject *before* they finish the module. If their responses suggest that they are not understanding the subject, they can receive remedial instruction at these stages.

Planning criterion frames

The whole programme is designed to enable trainees – through the post-test – to prove their new-found capability. The post-test should not be a lottery or a Pandora's box of unsuspected horrors. The problems to solve will already have been tackled during the interactive module prior to the post-test. In order to ensure that authors keep their targets well within sight, we suggest that they begin the creative phase of authorship by composing *first* those questions, problems or instructions which mirror the items the students will face later in the post-test. Such points in the programme test the students' mastery of fragments of the objective. They enable learner and tutor to verify whether the standard or criterion for that part-objective has been reached. Hence they are known as criterion or test frames. In the outline programme below we can see that three such points occur before the post-test is reached.

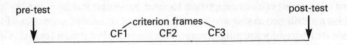

Consider an example of a module on avoiding wordiness from a course on report writing for managers. The first part of the post-test for this module might consist of a number of sentences for the learner's inspection and instruction:

> Identify any superfluous words you find in the following sentences:
> ○ Sentence A
> ○ Sentence B
>   etc.

Let us assume that the module has included references to three kinds of wordiness: redundancy (using words that unnecessarily repeat ideas), wordy constructions (use of subordinate clauses to link nouns and adjectives) and empty-word constructions (unnecessary use of 'there is, are, etc'). If the post-test is the first unprompted exercise trainees receive on this quite complex topic, then we can expect some variations in achievement – probably more than are acceptable. A more effective strategy would be to include criterion frames on the types of wordiness as they are introduced.

Here is the programme outline. Figures in parentheses indicate the number of criterion frames at each of the three points.

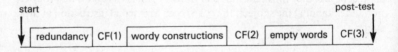

One of the three criterion frames on the redundancy section includes a sentence 'This report contains the basic essentials' and the instruction 'Cross out the redundant word in this sentence'. For the sequence on wordy construction one criterion frame presents another sentence 'The office systems department runs courses in computer programming' and the instruction 'Rewrite this sentence more economically'. These examples illustrate the crucial characteristic of the criterion frame – it sets a problem without giving any help with the answer. It is a mini-test preparing the learner for a similar test question in the post-test. Since the post-test already exists, it seems reasonable to suggest that the criterion frames are written before any other part of the programme.

Other kinds of frame
If we study the programme outline for the avoiding wordiness module, it is clear that we need some material to precede each of the review or test points (criterion frames) which concludes each of the three phases of the module. Since the criterion frame gives students no guidance or prompting with the answer, they cannot possibly respond correctly without guessing if this is an initial learning sequence.

The preceding material can vary greatly in specificity. Two basic forms are used. In the first the new material is introduced, worked or completed examples are given, and the learner is then required to solve a problem with the worked example still available. This is the so-called teach or demonstrate frame.

Here is an example of the teach or demonstrate frame from the wordiness module:

1 2	Using a clause merely to relate an adjective to a noun is generally too wordy
3	In the sentence
4	'The company prefers to employ drivers who are experienced'
5 6 7	The subordinate clause *who are experienced* is an unnecessarily wordy way to relate the adjective 'experienced' to the noun 'drivers'
8	By placing adjective and noun together we get –
9	'The company prefers to employ experienced drivers'
10	Re-write and shorten the sentence 'Reports which are hand- written are discouraged'

This is a typical teach frame which includes an example of a wordy expression and the improved version (lines 4 and 9), an explanation of what to do (lines 5 to 8) and an instruction on the problem to be solved (line 10).

If the student responds to the instruction by giving the correct answer, the author can employ two basic tactics. He can go straight on to the criterion frame ('Re-write this sentence'), or he can give the student more practice with a hint or clue as to the answer. He could, for example, follow up with something like this:

> Shorten the following sentences (look out for unnecessary subordinate clauses)
>
> (a) All the departments which were criticized in the chairman's report have greatly improved
>
> (b) ....
>
> (c) ....

In this case the hint in parenthesis turns a criterion frame into a so-called *prompt* or *practice* frame.

The original programme outline can thus be filled in with teach and practice frames, producing this kind of structure:

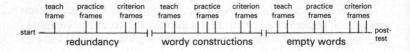

BRANCHING

In the example sequences of instruction we have considered so far, such as report writing and bridge, we have concentrated on the structuring of the programme. We have also looked at the ways in which the author can vary the amount of support he provides to learners to help them solve the problems they encounter en route to their goal.

Implicit in these examples is the assumption that the student's responses to problems are likely to be correct. This assumption is compatible with our earlier assertion that the scheme of learning should be so arranged that solutions to questions, calculations, discrimination exercises, etc tend towards correctness or mastery. Indeed, when one considers all the work of analysis, planning, sequencing and authorship it would surely be rather disappointing for a course designer to find that his students frequently demonstrated their lack of understanding of the subject. However, it would be equally unreasonable to suppose that all students will react similarly to the problem points they encounter in a lesson, which was the rationale of linear programmed instruction. But in reality students differ greatly, and in many ways. They differ in their rate of learning, their preferred learning environment, their motivations, their objectives, their pre-knowledge and their learning set.

Some learners respond better to an inductive approach, others to a deductive approach.

Thus, in CBT lessons, one is bound to reach points at which the author will have to deal with these differences. He will hope that at the final stage, the post-test, there will be a reasonable degree of common understanding among his students, however diverse they may be. But they may have arrived at this point only after frequent digressions.

The reader is invited to consider the structure of the CBT module as analogous to a railway network. A student who responds correctly to every question will travel on the main-line. Another who fails to solve problems or seeks help will at those points be routed to a branch line where he will receive feedback appropriate to his response.

Figure 3.6 presents a criterion frame on calculating the median for ungrouped data from a linear programmed text on statistics.

X	f
7	1
6	1
5	3
4	7
3	4
2	2
1	2

Determine the median using Formula 1.

Median =

3.79

Figure 3.6 A criterion frame from a linear printed programme

The preceding sequence has explained Formula 1, used for calculating the median of a frequency distribution. The majority of undergraduate students for whom this book is designed will no doubt reach the correct solution. However it is not unreasonable to suppose that a minority may not do so. For this minority there is no guidance – just the answer. We know of one case where a student achieved a solution of 6.79. Since this amount is exactly 3 more than the correct solution, the student supposed he had made a mathematical error. However his working was flawless; he had simply applied the formula to the wrong set of data – the f column. For useful feedback to be given to somebody making such an error, the linear format in Figure 3.7a (the original, linear structure) would need to be changed to something like Figure 3.7b, where differing responses receive differing treatment.

In Figure 3.7a all students get the correct answer (and no other feedback) regardless of the wording of their response. In Figure 3.7b those responding

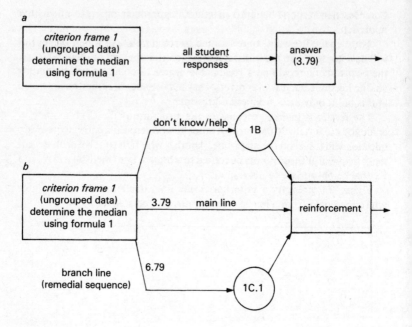

Figure 3.7 Linear and branching formats for teaching the same topic

6.79 receive the feedback in frame 1C.1, which might be something like 'You seem to have added the wrong column! Have another go'. Those expressing ignorance or seeking help will receive frame 1B, which might include a résumé of the procedure or some other clue. In the example, both the 1B and 1C.1 routes then go on to the feedback or the problem. This is a simplified – but not unusual – example to illustrate a branching operation. In many cases one or both of the branches will often include considerably more than one remedial frame.

Branching would normally suggest itself at the stages in a subject or procedure where a decision is called for which may vary even between experts. Thus two process operators of a chemical plant may take quite different remedial action to deal with a breakdown. Both may be effective but one more expensive or time-consuming. In bridge two players holding the same hand of cards may bid quite differently. Again one bid may be slightly more effective. For this sort of exercise, branching and intensive practice with a number of randomly-chosen examples will be useful, and the computer will perform these tasks with ease.

As we will see later in the book, branching in CBT can be very complex. This complexity greatly increases programme development time. Authors are advised to commit themselves to branches only when convinced of their usefulness. Wherever possible, it is advisable to ascertain typical errors made by students by trying out a draft module. This could be done usefully with a printed prototype programme, or even by classroom instruction. The branching structure will then reflect genuine student needs as opposed to the author's guesses. Methods of obtaining and assessing student data are discussed more fully in Chapter 16.

---

4. How frames are written

INTRODUCTION

This chapter describes the development of the instructional unit known as the frame. As described in Chapter 3, frames are used particularly in initial learning sequences and often include a simulation, specimen documentation or other elements. Frames represent the incremental learning steps that comprise modules. Depending on the complexity of the subject matter and the trainee's capability, frames will vary in the quantity of new information they convey. The course author's basic strategy should be to seek first to establish the review points (criterion frames) for the module. These enable students to demonstrate their gradual mastery of the subject. He should then write the minimum number of explanatory and practice frames to enable the trainees to tackle criterion frames with a reasonable expectation of success. At some points students will fail to solve problems, understand the questions or, for one of a number of other reasons, will not give or attempt to give the correct answer. This chapter discusses the ways these problem points offer the author the opportunity to provide branching to remedial sequences. On the whole, such flexibility is greatly facilitated by computer use but some kinds of question and feedback are more complex to process in CBT than in a printed programme.

A CHALLENGING APPROACH

Some years ago, in the heyday of small step linear programmed instruction, it was often suggested that the author's watchword be 'one frame per rule'. Indeed there is an introductory film on programmed instruction which is still being shown some ten or 12 years after its first publication and which asserts that the usual approach is to take several frames to teach one rule. While it might be an exaggeration to insist that this should *never* happen, a rule would have to be of significant importance or difficulty to warrant such treatment.

Modern practice in authorship for self-instruction is to present the content in steps of sufficient scope to challenge rather than spoonfeed. It is our hope that students will succeed with this method, but success should be accompanied by a sense of achievement. If early trials of the programme reveal that it is so challenging in places that students are failing to progress, we can insert branches or extra examples in teaching frames or some other adjustment to keep the student moving through the lesson.

Developing a frame

The example of frame development that follows carries to its conclusion the module from the hypothetical course on bridge. In the example the whole content will be developed so as to be presented on one page or screen. But, as we have seen, this need not be the case with every frame. Some may comprise adjunct printed or audio-visual components. The rule set has been written and, following the general rules on sequencing and drawing up a matrix, we have established a sequence for presentation (see Chapter 3).

Rule aggregation and criterion frames

In order to help develop the lesson in increments of learning within the trainee's grasp, two planning tools are already at hand. First, there are the criterion frames; second, there are the rules. Suppose the criterion frame for deciding the dealer in bridge is as follows:

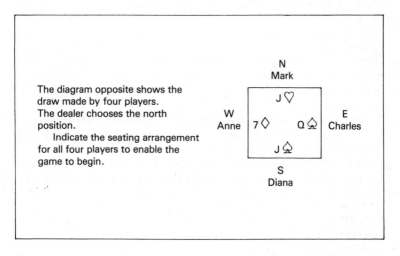

We now have to decide how to organize the content of the programme as contained in the rule set to give the student a reasonable chance of responding correctly to this question. Each rule should be inspected in turn and the question asked: 'does the information in this rule need to be explained and tested separately (as used to be the practice) or can I merge this rule with its neighbour and one or more subsequent rules?' One must decide how far to go in this process of merging or aggregating rules until a step becomes so large that it is likely to extend beyond the capabilities of the student, as described in our prerequisites. How will this approach work with our example?

The original rules for the bridge dealer example are given in Figure 3.1.

We have already decided to deal with rules 1, 2, 3 and 6 in our overview. Assuming that the overview has been written, we now have to present the remaining rules (see Figure 3.3). Using the rule aggregation method, what should be our rule grouping? There are three possibilities. The smallest meaningful grouping would be to combine the first four rules. It would be possible to explain all these points in one step to test the learner's understanding of the card rankings. Another option would be to combine rules 1 to 7, adding to the rule of card ranking the principle of pairings. Finally, one could present the whole set in one step. For many adult learners this grouping would not represent an unreasonably large learning step.

The decision to use a particular rule aggregation would depend on many factors. One would need to consider the preparedness of the trainees, their previous experience with similar topics and whether such experience is likely to facilitate or inhibit learning of the topic. As suggested, it will usually be worth the risk of leaning towards the more difficult approach. The lesson will be tried out in its developmental stage and if a step turns out to be too large then it can be subdivided, or a remedial branch can be inserted before the final version is published. If we took the cautious line and presented the topic in very gradual steps, all the trainees are likely to respond correctly to all the questions, but we will never know how much more challenging, shorter and probably more interesting we could have made the programme. In this case, for the purpose of demonstrating a procedure for frame design, let us suppose that we have selected the second of our three options: we propose to teach rules 1 to 7 in one step, leaving for the moment the procedure for breaking a tie.

The first step should *not* be to write the explanatory information at the top. Explaining information is wordy, and wordiness is contagious. Once an author begins writing he finds it very hard to stop. This may lead to lessons of great interest and literary merit. Unfortunately, computer terminals are not best suited to conveying large slabs of text and the latter leave little scope for student activity. Thus it seems to make sense to begin composing a frame by giving prominence to the activity, concept or rule to be learned. Next one should decide and write the problem or question to be answered. Third, a title or some other scene-setting phrase may be entered. Finally the words of explanation may be added. These steps are shown in the diagram opposite. According to the model frame types described in Chapter 3, we can see that this is a typical teach frame. There is a full explanation and a worked example as well as a question to test the learner's understanding of this topic.

On re-reading the first draft such a detailed explanation may strike the author or editor as unnecessary. In particular they may well question the inclusion of the worked example. In a CBT context one would probably go straight from the explanation to the question, eliminating the example completely. The example could be saved for the minority who respond incorrectly or ask for help. The example is called a main line frame and follows immediately after the overview. Those learners who respond correctly will proceed directly to the next main line frame, explaining and testing under-

1. Write example of knowledge/skill to learn

3. Write title

Bridge: The draw for dealer

To choose partners for a bridge game

○ spread the pack face down on the table
○ let each player draw a card
○ cards rank A, K, Q, J, 10 . . . 2
○ the players drawing two highest cards are
   dealer and dealer's partner
○ the other two are the opposing team

So in the draw

Smith K♣, Brown A♡, Robinson 2♠, Jones 7♢

Brown and Smith are dealer and partner

Who is dealer and partner in this draw?

Andrew

♢ 9

Leo ♡ J   ♠ A   Bernard

♣ 4

Sue

2. Write a question/ problem

4. Write description/ explanation

standing of the final three rules which explain the tie-break. The frame below shows also how one might include a slight element of inoffensive humour.

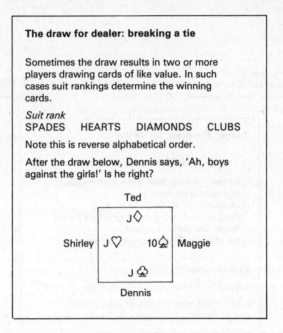

So the sequence we have covered is based on three main line frames:

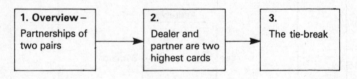

Inserting branches

When the author has composed the main line frames he can consider what sort of branches need to be provided. These will depend on the responses students are likely to make.

In the case of the first of the two frames we have just developed (on identifying the highest card) the responses might appear to be fairly simple – just entering two names. If this were a printed text, a simple way of controlling the response would be to round off the frame by completing the question with multiple-choice alternatives, for example:

Who are dealer and partner respectively in this draw?
(a) Bernard (dealer) and Sue

(b) Andrew (dealer) and Sue
(c) Bernard (dealer) and Leo
(d) Leo (dealer) and Bernard

This type of question is also common in a computer-based lesson and (or because) it is easy to control. If the author decides to pose only the original question, leaving the trainee to enter his response at the keyboard, his branches may become a tangled web of possibilities. The likely responses to this question include any one of the four names (entered by those who think they must first give the dealer's name only), and any one of six pairs of names in any order. A student might also enter three or even four names, either through change of mind or simply to muddy the waters. He might also type 'help', 'I don't know' or something like 'which order?' To forestall some of these problems, the author can qualify his question by adding some instruction on the form of response such as 'Please enter two names giving the dealer's name first'.

Some idea of how complicated a branching pattern can become may be imagined by adding to the main line pattern just the branch required to deal with those students who enter the dealer's name only at frame M2 – they type 'Bernard' instead of 'Bernard and Leo'. In this case one might reply 'Yes, you got the dealer but what about his partner?' If now they give 'Leo', they can proceed to M3, but if they give another name or type 'I don't know' or something else, you must decide whether to give help or whether simply to tell them the answer. Here is one possible format:

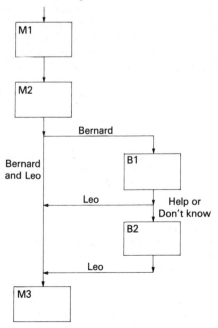

Even this one branch has been greatly simplified, no provision being indicated for responses at B1 other than 'Leo' or 'help'.

Providing feedback

Once the learner has made his response, he should receive feedback on the adequacy of his performance. Where the performance is deficient there should be the opportunity, through remedial exercises, to make good that deficiency. In drill and practice – say on mathematical skills – an infinite store of examples graded by difficulty level may be accessed so that the trainee may gradually move upwards through varying levels of skill. In a very simple piece of instruction, like our bridge dealer example, it is often unnecessary to tell a student who responds correctly more than that he has done just that. While it is normally good practice to follow up confirmation of a correct response with some reinforcing material, designed to enhance retention of the newly acquired knowledge, this reinforcement can be overdone.

In the context of a CBT module, where the feedback does not consist of much more than 'Yes – you're right', it can appear as the first line of the next screen. If rather more discussion of a response is required, this feedback may need to be presented on a screen immediately preceding the next main line frame.

In Chapter 12 we discuss the development of a brief extract from a module for receptionists in an employment bureau for office personnel. One question from this module asks the trainee to list the sort of duties expected from the caretaker of an office block. The purpose of the section is to underline the importance of specifying duties precisely, and the difference between duties (work done) and qualities (personal attributes). Caretakers perform a wide variety of duties but for the purposes of this exercise it will be sufficient if the trainee identifies any three acceptable items. So a response like *'locking/ unlocking doors, security checks, cleaning'* will receive the feedback:

> Yes, you have identified three of the duties performed by care-takers.
> Here is my complete list . . . .
> . . . .
> Maybe you thought of some others. The important thing to bear in mind is that you will help an employer to meet his staff requirements by helping him specify those requirements as accurately as possible.

This is useful reinforcing material and will occupy an amount of screen space sufficiently large as to preclude continuing with the next main line frame on the same screen.

THE STAGES OF INSTRUCTION

The steps of training design outlined above correspond closely to the stages of instruction as outlined by Gagné and Briggs.[1] These are:

1. Gaining attention
2. Informing the learner of the objective
3. Stimulating recall of prerequisite learning
4. Presenting stimulus material
5. Providing 'learning guidance'
6. Eliciting the performance
7. Providing feedback about performance
8. Assessing the performance
9. Enhancing retention

Our bridge sequence reflects most of these stages. The overview and the title will include stages 1 and 2. In our example frames, there is no explicit reference to prerequisite learning but in the main line frame on page 55 the rule of card rankings could have been expanded to read 'Cards rank A, K, Q, J, 10...2, as in whist' if it had been expected that most students would have had previous knowledge of that game.

'Presenting the stimulus material' is the centre section in the example, written first. Stage 5 on 'learning guidance' is the explanatory information which follows the title. Stage 6 is reflected in the question which rounds off the frame. Stages 7, 8 and 9 would be covered in the feedback which in this case need only be an intermediary screen of one or two lines confirming the correct response.

COURSE DESIGN CHECKLIST

○ In task analysis break down procedures into steps within learners' capabilities
○ Define clear objectives
○ Obtain test examples as soon as post-test is drafted
○ Sign off content at rule set stage
○ Obtain go-ahead for objectives from sponsor
○ Relate programme content to objectives
○ Write test questions (frames) first
○ Get students to solve problems rather than recall verbal statements
○ Test new information
○ In multiple-choice questions give plausible options
○ Give answers to problems and discuss alternatives

[1] *op cit*

○ Ensure students understand nature and mode of response
○ Include periodic reviews in long modules
○ Provide an overview (but write it last)
○ Use a variety of presentation
○ Make treatment appropriate to learners' backgrounds
○ Use illustrations and diagrams to explain concepts and procedures

Part 2

Computing systems for the trainer – aspects of computing generally relevant to computer-based training

INTRODUCTION

The word computer conjures up different images and thoughts in people's minds depending upon their experiences. Some view computers as powerful, intelligent machines that can maintain a 'big brother' watch over everyone. Others are staggered and fascinated by the marvels achieved by the space programmes of the superpowers, where computers play an important part. Whether we have this slightly mystical wonder, or whether we merely regard them as objects that produce our electricity bills and bank statements, their power and complexity tend to be daunting.

Computers do not have intelligence in the way humans do. They cannot think for themselves. What they are good at is carrying out arithmetic operations and making logical decisions at phenomenally fast speeds. But they only do what humans program them to do. (This spelling of 'programme' is invariably used when referring to computer programs; 'programme' is used to describe training courses.)

Apart from the speed at which computers execute instructions, two developments in particular have contributed to the growth in the use of computers – efficient storage of large amounts of data and diminishing cost. Today, computers can store huge amounts of information on magnetic media and any item of this information can be obtained in a few milliseconds (thousandths of a second) and displayed or printed for the user. Technological developments have led to large-scale integration where thousands of electrical circuits, which a few years ago consisted of transistors and wiring, can now be fitted into a microprocessor chip the size of a thumb nail (see photograph overleaf). Chips are designed for specific purposes. They are then combined and mounted on printed circuit boards to produce computers. Parallel developments with data storage have led to powerful systems being available at prices unthinkable only a few years ago. They are also very reliable.

These developments have led, among other things, to microcomputers becoming widely used in schools and at home where one can be bought for less than the price of a video recorder or colour television. For the generations going through school now and in future years, the mystique and fear of

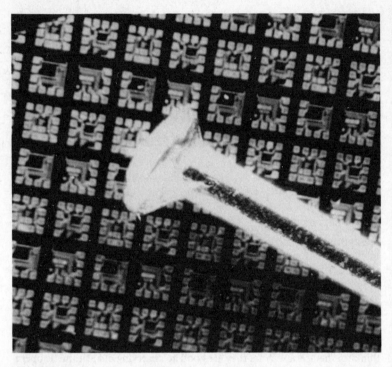

the computer will not exist, but the excitement of using its power effectively will remain.

This section aims to give readers some appreciation of the concepts involved in computing. It is written with the student of CBT in mind. To this end Chapter 6 describes visual display screens, keyboards and printers in some detail, as these devices are very significant to the presentation of CBT material.

5. The components of a computer – the hardware

INTRODUCTION

In discussing the elements of a computer system, it is difficult to know what to include and what to leave out, particularly when giving a fairly brief overview. It is not necessary for the trainer to know everything about the workings of the computer, so this chapter attempts to give enough insight into the general principles and the components that make up a computer system, to allow the trainer to understand, for example, the differences between mainframe, mini- and microcomputers, and to know what the computer specialists mean when they discuss bytes, megabytes and floppy disks, etc.

Computers range in price from a few pounds to several million pounds and, in general, you get what you pay for. However, the principles behind what goes on in the kernel of the machine are the same. Today's computers carry out instructions given to them at very high speeds – rated in millions of instructions per second on larger machines. The main purpose of a computer is to take information, process it and then produce some sort of output (see Figure 5.1).

Figure 5.1 The information processing cycle

Let us consider a few examples:

1. The most common form of input into computers is rapidly becoming the operation of entering information via a keyboard that is often connected to a visual display screen. The person sitting at the keyboard, a student on a computer-based training course, for example, types answers to questions displayed on the screen. The *input* is the answer which is *processed* very rapidly by the computer to give an almost immediate response on the screen – the *output* (see Figure 5.2 and page 8).
2. When our electricity meters are read, the data is keyed in by clerks using a screen and keyboard. They will key in the customer number and the meter reading. Certain checks will be made on the information

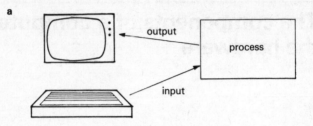

b   **OUTPUT** (on screen)→What do the
     initials F D stand for in F D Roosevelt?
     INPUT (via keyboard)→FRANKLIN DANIEL
     OUTPUT (on screen)→Well, Franklin is
     correct, but the D stands for DELANO.

Figure 5.2 A visual display screen and keyboard

keyed in and errors will be displayed on the screen, for example, if the
latest meter reading appears to be lower than the last. When the input
data has been checked and passed (processed) another output, the bill,
will be printed and sent to the customer (see Figure 5.3). Not only that,
but if the customer does not pay promptly, he will get a reminder. If he
still does not pay, the Electricity Supply Cut-Off Department will get a
note, also from the computer, telling them to do their duty.

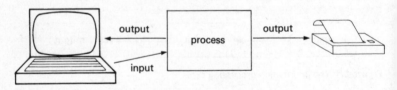

Figure 5.3 The printer as an output device

3. Traffic management in cities is increasingly being assisted by the use of
   computers to control the phasing of traffic lights. The input is provided
   by sensors that continuously monitor the traffic flow on the various
   streets in the management scheme. The time of day is also input by a
   clock held inside the computer. By monitoring (processing) all this
   information day and night, the computer system can control the traffic
   lights (the output) to keep traffic flowing. For example, traffic heading
   into the area of high daytime employment will be favoured in the
   morning, the traffic lights being phased to keep traffic flowing steadily
   at about 25 mph. In the evening, the drivers going home will be
   favoured. During busy shopping times the traffic lights in shopping

areas can give pedestrians more opportunities to cross (see Figure 5.4). In the 1970s Glasgow developed a successful scheme covering part of the city centre where the use of computer control generally kept traffic flowing very smoothly while still permitting pedestrians to cross in reasonable safety.

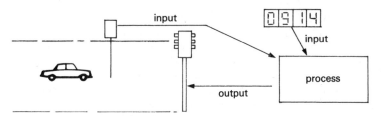

Figure 5.4 Computer control of traffic lights

Thus, in each case there is some form of input, a process and some output. The input may be very small. In a microcomputer-controlled paint spray, a single input from a detector will set the sprayer off on a programmed path (the process) held within the computer, so that it sprays all the necessary parts of the item to be painted. The output, in this case, is the paint and the path taken by the sprayer.

We shall discuss inputs and outputs later in this chapter and in the following one, but let us first discuss the processor or central processing unit.

THE CENTRAL PROCESSING UNIT (CPU)

The central processing unit can be divided into three main components: the control unit, the arithmetic and logic unit (ALU) and the memory (see Figure 5.5).

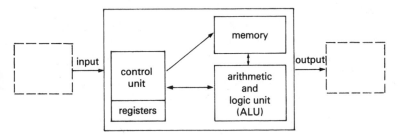

Figure 5.5 The central processing unit (CPU)

The CPU receives information from an input device. This information can be instructions to the computer – the computer program – or it can be data – the information upon which the instructions will operate. Both types of information need to be stored in the computer memory.

The computer memory

The computer memory consists of a large number of locations each of which can hold a piece of information: a character (A,B,c,d, etc), a number (0,1,2, etc) or part of a coded instruction to the computer. There may be a large number of memory locations; large computers have several million, while microcomputers usually have several thousand. Each memory location has a unique address so that the information can be accessed directly. Data can be stored in or read from memory very fast. The memory on modern computers is often termed random access memory (RAM). RAM retains all the coded information set up in it while power is switched on, but when the computer is switched off the information is lost and the memory needs to be loaded again when the computer is switched back on.

The arithmetic and logic unit (ALU)

This unit carries out the standard arithmetic operations – addition, subtraction, multiplication and division. It also carries out the logical operations of comparing values so that switches can be set that cause the execution of a program to follow different sequences, depending on the results of these comparisons.

The control unit

The control unit co-ordinates all the functions of the central processor by interpreting and executing instructions held in the computer memory. A sequence of instructions may tell the control unit to read data from an input device and store them in memory, starting at memory location 2735. The control unit would do precisely that, assuming that there were data waiting to be read in. If there were no data, an error routine would be entered which might involve waiting and doing nothing until something was available. (Multi-million pound computers are not usually allowed to do this, but many microcomputers spend most of their time waiting for the user to key something in.)

Another sequence of instructions might tell the control unit to read two numbers from two memory locations, add them and store the result in a third memory location. In this case, we can consider precisely the instructions the control unit would interpret and carry out, and the inter-reaction between the control unit, the ALU and the memory (see Figure 5.6).

From this example you can see that the computer does precisely what it is told and it has to be told nearly everything. In this simple case, it was not told what the values in locations 359 and 360 were. This is important because you could use this piece of program time and time again, knowing that by storing

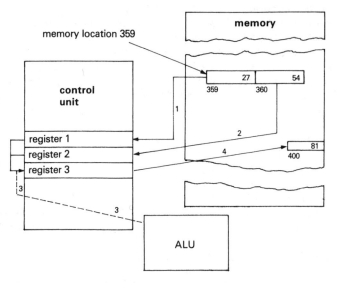

Instruction to Control Unit

1. Load number in memory location 359(27) into register 1 (registers are convenient temporary locations for data which ease the work of writing programs and speed up program execution).
2. Load the number in memory location 360(54) into register 2.
3. Add the numbers in registers 1 and 2, and put the result into register 3 (done by the ALU).
4. Store the number held in register 3 in memory location 400(81).

Figure 5.6 A simple addition within the CPU

two numbers in locations 359 and 360 you would always get the sum in location 400 after executing the four instructions.

You may well be thinking that this sounds difficult, tedious and certainly not the thing an experienced trainer should be doing. If so, you are right. A computer system consists of hardware – the CPU and input/output devices – and software. Software makes the computer do what the user wants it to do, at least good software does. Our four instructions to add two numbers are examples of software. Software is provided either by the computer manufacturer or by specialist companies to avoid all the users having to write at the lowest level. The software consists of such things as operating systems, compilers, accounting systems and author languages. These are discussed in Chapter 7.

Before leaving the discussion of the CPU let us consider briefly how numbers and characters are represented in the memory of the computer.

Bits, bytes and words

When we see the number 562 we normally assume that it represents five hundred and sixty-two. This is because we are conditioned to the decimal system where the base is 10. School children nowadays are taught to handle numbers with different bases such as octal (8) and binary (2), much to the confusion of many parents. With the number 562 we understand this to mean that we have 5 hundreds, 6 tens and 2 units (5 x 100 + 6 x 10 + 2 x 1) so each digit has a meaning represented by its value and its position.

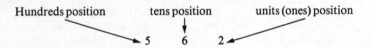

Computers work by using the binary system where the base is 2. This means that each position can have a value of 0 or 1. Instead of going up in powers of ten (10, 10 x 10, 10 x 10 x 10) the positions go up in powers of 2 (2, 2 x 2, 2 x 2 x 2, 2 x 2 x 2 x 2, etc).

Thus the binary number 1001 can be represented as:

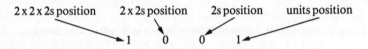

This number can be converted to decimal:

$$
\begin{array}{llr}
2 \times 2 \times 2 \times 1 & = 8 \times 1 & = 8 \\
+ 2 \times 2 \times 0 & = 4 \times 0 & = 0 \\
+ 2 \times 0 & & = 0 \\
+ 1 & & = 1 \\
\hline
& & = 9
\end{array}
$$

So 1001 in binary has the same value as 9 in decimal.

It has already been explained that the memory of a computer consists of a large number of locations, each of which is uniquely addressable. In most modern computers these locations are called bytes. They consist of eight positions and each position can be set to 0 or 1. These positions are called bits.

One memory location (a byte)

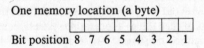

The maximum number that can be stored in a byte is:

$$2^7 \quad 2^6 \quad 2^5 \quad 2^4 \quad 2^3 \quad 2^2 \quad 2^1 \quad 1$$

1	1	1	1	1	1	1	1

That is

$2^7 =$	$2 \times 2 \times 2 \times 2 \times 2 \times 2 \times 2$	$=$	128
$+ 2^6 =$	$2 \times 2 \times 2 \times 2 \times 2 \times 2$	$=$	64
$+ 2^5 =$	$2 \times 2 \times 2 \times 2 \times 2$	$=$	32
$+ 2^4 =$	$2 \times 2 \times 2 \times 2$	$=$	16
$+ 2^3 =$	$2 \times 2 \times 2$	$=$	8
$+ 2^2 =$	2×2	$=$	4
$+ 2 =$	2	$=$	2
$+ 1$		$=$	1
			255

Since the smallest number is 0 (no bits set to 1), there is a total of 256 different bit combinations possible in an 8 bit byte (0 to 255).

255 is not much use as a maximum number to be held in the computer, and there are various methods of treating more than one byte as an entity to hold numbers. A group of contiguous bytes that can be manipulated together is called a word. A word may be 2 bytes (16 bits) or 4 bytes (32 bits) or other combinations. 16 bits can hold numbers up to 65,535. You may hear or read about 8 bit and 16 bit (or even 32 bit) computers. Basically, 16 bit microcomputers are more powerful than 8 bit microcomputers for a number of reasons, the most important of which is that 16 bit microcomputers can easily address a lot more random access memory than an 8 bit microcomputer. However, there are various factors, particularly in the area of software, that may make an 8 bit microcomputer the better choice. This overview of how numbers are stored is somewhat simplistic but demonstrates how combinations of bits are used in the computer memory to represent numbers.

So far we have discussed how memory can hold instructions that the control unit acts upon, and how it can also store binary numbers on which arithmetic operations can be carried out. A large number of business operations, and computer-based training in particular, do very little with numbers. They are mostly concerned with accepting as input, manipulating and presenting as output, large quantities of character information – names and addresses, product descriptions and, for CBT, training material and questions. Character information is stored in the bytes in memory. If one character is stored in a byte, there are 256 possible characters that the different bit patterns can represent. That is quite adequate for all the alphabetic characters in upper and lower case, the numbers 0 to 9 and the various punctuation and special characters that are found on a typewriter keyboard. One widely-used coding convention is ASCII (American Standard Code for Information Interchange), pronounced as the two words 'ass' and 'key'.

Part of the ASCII code is tabulated below:

Character	%	&	'	(	)	*	+	,	-	.	/	0	1	2	3	4	5	6	7	8	9
ASCII Code	37	38	39	40	41	42	43	44	45	46	47	48	49	50	51	52	53	54	55	56	57

Character	A	B	C	D	E	F	G	H	I	J	K	L	M	N	O	P	Q	R	S	T	U
ASCII Code	65	66	67	68	69	70	71	72	73	74	75	76	77	78	79	80	81	82	83	84	85

Character	V	W	X	Y	Z
ASCII Code	86	87	88	89	90

Thus, if we wanted to hold FRANKLIN as part of the correct answer to the question posed in Figure 5.2b, it could be held somewhere in memory (say, location 5390 onwards) as the following ASCII codes:

Letter	F	R	A	N	K	L	I	N
Code in memory	70	82	65	78	75	76	73	78
Memory location	5390	5391	5392	5393	5394	5395	5396	5397

TYPES OF COMPUTER

The general business executive, whose company uses computers for accounting, payroll and information retrieval, knows about one or more of three types of computer. These are mainframe, mini- and microcomputers, which shall be considered in turn before a discussion of one or two other types.

Mainframe computers
The dividing line between mainframe and minicomputers is becoming increasingly blurred and rather meaningless, but the terms are generally used and apply to machines that fit within general cost bands.

If you buy a single computer for several hundred thousand pounds, you have a mainframe computer to which you must add on the input/output devices (discussed in the next section) that are needed to run it. Your bill for hardware is likely to be over half a million pounds. For this you get a computer with a large amount of memory (several megabytes, where one megabyte equals one million bytes), a very high processor speed (millions of instructions per second) and very sophisticated error detection and correction incorporated within the computer (see Figure 5.7). It is also possible, where appropriate, to attach large numbers of terminals to mainframe computers, so that a hundred or more people may use the computer simultaneously. With some of the largest computers you also need a plumber because water cooling is needed to remove the heat generated. Mainframe computers usually require air conditioning.

The world computer industry is dominated by International Business Machines (IBM) which is often stated to have approximately 70 per cent of the world market. The company has been highly profitable and thus has enormous resources to pour into research and development as well as marketing.

The mainframe computer market is very expensive to enter, but a number of American and Japanese companies have developed mainframe computers that can run the programs from IBM computers without substantial change. They are called 'IBM look-alikes' and try to keep just ahead of IBM on performance and price, by capping each new IBM announcement as it is made. Amdahl is the best known of these companies. Some European companies (BASF, Olivetti) are also selling Japanese computers that are IBM look-alikes.

Other mainframe manufacturers who produce their own ranges of computers include Honeywell, Burroughs, Univac and Control Data Corporation (CDC). In the United Kingdom, International Computers Limited (ICL) has a substantial share of the UK market, keeping IBM well below 50 per cent.

Minicomputers

The prices for minicomputer systems range from £15,000 to at least £250,000. The marketing men have dreamed up the name 'superminis' for computers which are very similar in performance to mainframes, having the 32 bit word length that is the IBM standard, and which gives the processor more power than smaller 16 bit computers but adds to the cost.

Minicomputers were designed to work in normal surroundings and do not normally require special air conditioning, although small air conditioners are often installed to maintain a pleasant working environment. They are widely used in process control, which was an area where they were first installed. Their performance is suited to that sort of application and for commercial use in small businesses or sections of larger companies. Minicomputers are also widely used in networks where computers can be linked together. This is discussed further in Chapter 8.

Most of the manufacturers of mainframe computers also supply minicomputers, since they consider it necessary to provide all the customers' computer needs whenever possible. Many minicomputer users today will be potential mainframe users tomorrow.

Digital Equipment Corporation (DEC) manufactures mainframe computers, but is primarily known as a minicomputer manufacturer. It is a very large and successful company with its VAX and PDP range of minicomputers. Hewlett-Packard, widely known and respected in the instrumentation field, entered the business computer market fairly late, but has a very successful range of minicomputers. Data General and Prime are two other big names in the field. The market is crowded with manufacturers on both sides of the Atlantic. Modcomp is an established company with an authoring language (SIMPLER) for computer-based training. Others include Computer Automation and Wang in the USA and Rediffusion, Computer Technology, Systime, Digico, Philips and Nord in Europe.

Microcomputers
Microcomputer systems range in price from £200 to £20,000. They provide a fast processor with limited capability to support input/output devices but generally a fairly high level of user-friendliness when the relatively inexperienced user is sitting at a terminal – a topic that is discussed more than once in this book. They do not have the same level of error checking and correction found on more expensive computers.

At the cheapest end of the range, microcomputers are used largely in the home, for education, or for very specific purposes – fairly simple process control or repetitive calculations, for example. In the £2000 to £6000 range systems can be purchased which are capable of doing a large number of jobs in a small company, research department or director's office; there is some very good software available to help anyone use the microcomputer for useful purposes.

The microcomputer system market place is very overcrowded with a large number of enterprising young companies striving to get a secure foothold. There are a few basic designs of microcomputer chips that form the basis of the systems built. These include the Intel 8080 and 8086, Zilog Z80, Motorola 6800 and 68000 and the MOS Technology 6502.

The large companies are Apple, Commodore with the PET range, and Tandy. They have all sold large numbers of microcomputers mostly at the cheaper end of the market. They are now trying to consolidate their positions in the business market. The UK manufacturer, Sinclair, has been very successful with the ZX80 and its successor the ZX81 at well under £100, and the BBC computer project has given an enormous boost to Acorn Computers who designed the BBC Microcomputer. Probably the most significant recent development has been the somewhat belated entry of IBM into the microcomputer market with the IBM Personal Computer; this has drawn superlatives from many reviewers for its overall design, documentation and general presentation.

Other names from a long list include Cromemco, Superbrain and, among UK manufacturers, Research Machines, Rair and Cifer. Add to the above nearly all the mainframe and minicomputer manufacturers together with a string of Japanese companies, and you will agree that there are a lot of people vying for a share of the market.

Word processors
Word processors are used instead of typewriters when reports, letters, etc need to be produced in draft form for correction and amendment before final copies are produced. They consist of a visual display, a normal type-

writer keyboard, a printer, a means of storing the data and a microcomputer.

It is not appropriate in this book to describe word processors in detail. However, since they use the same technology and components as microcomputers, it is not surprising that word processing, of a sort, is available on microcomputers, and that computing facilities are becoming available on word processors. With the two systems converging, it is quite possible that word processors will soon be able to run general computer-based training courses. In fact, some can do so now. This trend is discussed further in Chapter 9.

INPUT/OUTPUT DEVICES

We have considered the central processing unit of a computer and mentioned input and output. In this section we shall look first at the very important subject of backing store and then at some devices used for feeding information into the computer, and for presenting information from the computer. The items of most interest in computer-based training are covered in more detail in Chapter 6.

The computer memory consists of tens of thousands of bytes in a microcomputer and perhaps a few million bytes in a mainframe computer (see Figure 5.7). Instructions are carried out very rapidly, in the order of a million

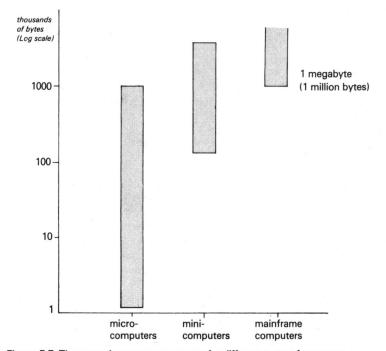

Figure 5.7 The approximate memory ranges for different types of computer

instructions per second, but memory is relatively expensive and also volatile; it loses its bit settings when switched off. Thus, any information stored in the main memory of the computer must be saved in a more permanent place and for less cost.

Backing storage

Disk drives
The standard method of storing data permanently on all mini- and mainframe computers is the disk drive. (This spelling of 'disk' is commonly used in computer terminology.) The current capacity of a single disk drive ranges from about five million characters (bytes) of information to several hundred million, and more in the future. To set this in context, a typical page of text in this book is about 3000 characters. Any piece of information on the disk can be found and read into computer memory in a few milliseconds, provided the computer program knows where to find it.

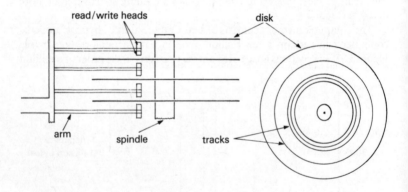

Figure 5.8 A disk pack and the read/write mechanism

Disk drives consist of one or more circular disks (see Figure 5.8) that rotate at high speed (2400 revolutions per minute) round a central shaft. The surfaces of the disk are coated with a magnetic layer and data can be written on to the disk by recording a bit pattern on to the magnetic surface. This is done by arms that can move in and out between the surfaces. There is a 'write head' and a 'read head' that float very near to each surface of the disk. The read head can read back the stored data as many times as necessary. The principle of the recording technique is similar to that of an audio tape cassette where a write head writes music or speech on to the tape and the read head reads it back. The cassette can be played again and again. When writing computer data for storage, it is only necessary to write a series of 0's and 1's to represent the characters stored.

Each disk surface is composed of a series of concentric circles called tracks, and the read/write heads move from track to track as instructed by the computer. Because they can access directly any track of the disk and thus read any piece of data on that track in a short time, disks are called direct access storage devices.

The quality of manufacture of disk packs and the drives in which they run is very high, and the risk of contamination by microscopic dust particles is such that the units are increasingly being manufactured as an entity within the disks with the read/write heads permanently sealed into a clean environment.

Diskettes

Another type of direct access storage device is the diskette, or 'floppy disk'. It is a relatively cheap device and is extensively used in small microcomputer systems for business and education, as well as in word processors. Diskette drives have capacities of 80,000 to over two million characters on a single floppy disk.

The storage principle is similar to that for disk storage except that the data are stored on a flexible plastic disk coated with a magnetic film. This diskette is permanently enclosed within a square cardboard case (see Figure 5.9) which holds it fairly stiff. The diskette in its case is inserted into the diskette drive. When the drive door is closed, a cone comes out to align and grip the

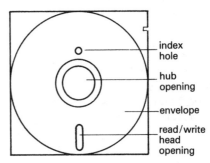

Figure 5.9 A diskette or floppy disk

diskette in the centre, and a read/write head is pressed on to the diskette which rotates inside the cardboard. The head can move back and forth across the tracks on the diskette. This rather crude system is slower at finding and reading data but can still access them in less than a second. The diskettes and drives are manufactured in two sizes – 8-inch and 5¼-inch – but, particularly with the smaller drives, the storage of data is often organized in different ways by different suppliers, so diskettes that can be read on one make of microcomputer will probably not be readable on a microcomputer from a different manufacturer. Diskettes should be readable on the diskette drives of two different microcomputers of the same make and model.

Diskette storage is not as reliable as rigid disk storage, but the floppy disks are cheap (£1 to £2 each) and it is easier to produce and keep back-up copies.

Magnetic tape
Magnetic tapes are reels of polyester film, coated on one surface with a magnetic coating. Tapes may be as long as 2400 feet (or sometimes more). Information is again stored a byte at a time as a bit pattern across the tape. Thus, there are eight tracks for the data (see Figure 5.10).

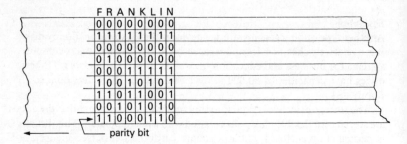

Figure 5.10 Data storage on magnetic tape

There is also a ninth bit, called a parity bit, that is written at the same time and is used to check for accuracy when data is read back. (There are many checks for accuracy, particularly in mini- and mainframe computers that cannot be covered in this book.) The tapes are called 9-track tapes and can store data at densities of up to 6250 bytes per inch (bpi). A 2400-foot tape could thus, in theory, store 2400 x 12 x 6250 = 180 million characters of information. In fact, it is always considerably less because of the gaps that are left on the tape between blocks of data. The principle behind the method of recording and reading back the data is similar to that for disks.

There is, however, one significant difference between magnetic tape and disk storage. With disks, the read/write head can move straight to the track that is needed, even if it is near the highest address on the disk. With a magnetic tape, reading or writing can only be done sequentially. If you want to access a piece of data at the end of a magnetic tape you can only wind through the tape to that point, which may take several seconds. Magnetic tapes can still be of value, however, as information is often accessed sequentially; they are also very useful to provide back-up storage of data from disk, as magnetic tapes are cheap and do not take up a lot of space.

Magnetic tape drives are usually found on mainframe and minicomputers. A similar device found particularly on cheap microcomputers is the tape cassette.

Magnetic tape cassette

Cassette tape drives, which are, in some cases, audio tape drives plugged into the microcomputer, provide the same facilities as magnetic tape drives, but at a much cheaper and less sophisticated level. The data are stored on the cassette, often an ordinary audio cassette, as a series of bit patterns along the tape. The amount of data that can be stored depends on the length of the tape, but a normal tape with 30 minutes of playing time on each side will take 30 minutes per side when attached to the microcomputer. Cassettes are useful for loading programs into the computer memory and for storing new programs. They can also be used for storing small quantities of data, but they are sequential devices and their use is limited. Because the overall system can be very cheap with a cassette drive (£200 to £400), there are occasions when such systems may be worth considering for teaching purposes.

Input devices

There is a wide variety of methods for entering information into the computer, but all of them depend on making the information available to the computer in a form that it can interpret accurately. Information is fed into computers from forms – cheques, orders, gas bills, etc – but also automatically and continuously from devices that measure pollution, temperature, position, pressure, etc. If information has to be entered by hand, there is always the risk of error because of the transcription process from the form to the machine-readable state. Not only that, there is the cost of the personnel involved. Effective methods of accepting information as it is written by hand or from voice input are developing, and these are discussed in Chapter 6, but we shall look here at some of the more common methods that are widely used today.

Punched card and paper tape

For many years, a mainstay of almost all substantial computing sections of businesses (data processing departments) was the punched card. The most common design was 80 columns long (see Figure 5.11) and a rather noisy machine, called a card punch, punched holes in the card according to a code. It was thus possible to get 80 characters-worth of information into the computer on each card if it was filled. The risk of error with keying is significant, so for most data it is necessary to key-punch and verify. Verification involves a second key-punch operator entering exactly the same information into a verifier; this is a similar device to the card punch. The verifier reads the cards punched, checks that the data being keyed in are identical to those on each card and gives a warning whenever a difference is detected. This method reduces the risk of error in the data processing department to a very low level, but it has no control over the information fed in which may have been copied from a variety of forms on to a coding sheet for the punch operator.

This may sound complicated and it is (see Figure 5.12). The next stage is to feed a deck of these punched cards into a card-reader; this detects the holes

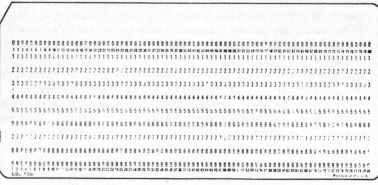

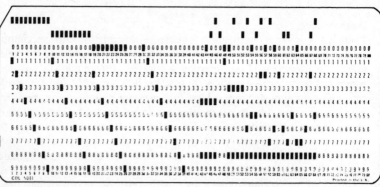

Figure 5.11 An example of an 80-column punched card before and after the code has been punched

punched into the cards and sends the code to the computer. Card-readers are mechanical devices which feed each card through sensors and stack them on the other side. They usually operate at speeds of up to 1000 cards a minute.

There are thousands of data processing departments using cards today, but card input is waning and being superseded by a variety of methods, primarily keyboard input using visual display units (VDUs). VDUs are very important in computer-based training and a large part of Chapter 6 is dedicated to a discussion of VDUs.

Punched paper tape is similar to punched card in that a code is punched on to a roll of paper. It is not limited by the 80 columns of a punched card, but the process of punching and verifying is the same. Paper tape is also produced by some machines such as X-ray diffractometers and pollution monitoring equipment, where the continuous nature of a large reel of paper tape means that the equipment can run unattended for long periods.

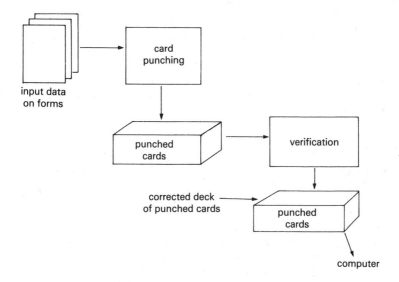

Figure 5.12 Card punching and verifying

Magnetic ink character reading (MICR)
This is a method of input which uses a highly stylized set of letters and numbers which are printed on documents in magnetized ink. These magnetized characters can be read by a special reader. The line along the bottom of a cheque contains standard information about the customer's branch code, account and cheque number. When a cheque is paid into a bank, the value of the cheque is added to the line, again in magnetic ink, before the cheque is fed into the MICR reader. One particular advantage of magnetic ink character reading is that even though the numbers on the cheque can be obscured by writing or dirt, the characters are still legible to the MICR reader.

Optical character reading (OCR)
Optical character reading depends on a light beam scanning letters and numbers which can then be recognized with a high degree of reliability. With all the different typewriter styles and special characters that can be included in printed material, the problems in producing a very flexible system are huge. Although the advantages of reading typed documents and diagrams into the computer are great, it is tempting to think that the saying 'garbage in – garbage out', might really come into its own should uncontrolled use of such devices become widespread.

OCR devices have also been designed to read handwritten data. They are used for meter readers (who can quickly be trained to write the stylized numbers accurately), order handling, etc.

Monitoring

The examples of traffic management and automatic paint-spraying cited at the start of the chapter depend on direct input of information to the computer from sensors or instruments on the job. This is an important area of use for computers and they are extensively used in the chemical and process industries for monitoring and control, control being the output decided on as a result of the various inputs. They are also used in hospitals for patient monitoring in intensive care units. The computers used for these purposes are often dedicated to monitoring and control and do nothing else.

Many computers have an internal clock that can be monitored by users' programs. This can be important in the management of computer-based training when it may be useful to know how much time was spent on part of a course and the overall time spent at a terminal.

Other input devices

The devices most relevant to CBT are discussed in some detail in Chapter 6. These include visual display units and typewriter terminals, without which a survey of input devices, however brief, would not be complete.

Magnetic tape, cassettes and floppy disks have been described previously under 'Backing storage'. They are all used extensively as methods of distributing programs and data either commercially or between organizations or parts of a company.

Two other methods of input are worth mentioning because they are both becoming commonplace in the high street. They are bar codes and magnetic stripes.

Bar codes are appearing on most packets of groceries. The pattern of bars in a bar code is arranged to represent numbers when it is read and translated by the computer. Groceries are marked with a unique code for each product from each manufacturer, indicating the size of the packet or tin. This is called the Universal Product Code. The information can then be read at the supermarket check-out point using a bar code reader which may be a laser wand or a light pen. The price of the product can automatically be displayed and stock records updated. There are not many supermarkets in Britain using the system yet. Similar systems with different codes are used in libraries and other industries (see Figure 5.13).

Magnetic stripes are used by some retail chains to mark their products. They are also to be seen on bank cash cards. The relevant information is stored in the magnetic stripe and can be read by a suitable reader. The same principle is used in some security systems and can be used in building society pass books so that a deposit or withdrawal can be recorded directly at a terminal.

Output devices

The section, 'Backing storage', covered the magnetic storage media that are used for input and output. The most important output devices – screens, printers and plotters – are discussed in Chapter 6 because of their specific

Figure 5.13 A bar code label for a book

relevance to CBT. This section covers a few specific output devices and can be omitted by those who are only interested in output devices which can be widely used, or which have potential for use in CBT.

Card and paper tape punches
Information from the computer can be punched on to cards or paper tape for storage or to be sent elsewhere; this method of storage and distribution was once extensively used. There is one area where punched paper tape, or the stronger polyester tape, is still widely used and this is in the control of automatic machine tools. The punched tape and the readers seem to be able to withstand the hazards of a machine shop better than most alternatives.

Computer output on microfiche or microfilm (COM)
COM is an alternative to the printed page. A COM system takes output from the computer, sets it up as a page of information, photographs it and at the same time reduces it to postage stamp size. There are various designs and it is a fairly cheap form of producing a lot of information that users may only wish to view selectively. In the order of 100 to 200 pages of information can be stored on a postcard-sized negative (microfiche). These negatives can then be reproduced and posted cheaply around the world. Microfiche are extensively used in libraries and bookshops. The British Library provides a service where libraries can get their book titles on microfiche together with standard information about them.

Microfiche viewers are necessary to magnify the pages on to page-sized screens. It is then easy to slide the microfiche around to find the information required. Some viewers can print any pages that the user may wish to take away.

Microfilm works on exactly the same principle except that the images are produced on a roll of film instead of a sheet. Microfilming is extensively used to store old information that cannot be destroyed for legal or company reasons, or which takes up vast amounts of shelf space, but is unlikely to be needed on the computer again.

Direct output

Direct inputs are received from monitoring devices in industry and hospitals and the computer analyses all these inputs very rapidly so that immediate action can be taken if abnormal situations arise. The action, when taken, is often a direct output such as opening a valve, raising a temperature or sounding an alarm. Some remote safety monitoring systems are programmed to dial a telephone number and play a recorded message if certain valves go outside limits. If that number is engaged, the computer either tries again or dials another number, and so on. In patient-monitoring systems, the computer only monitors, but there may still be direct outputs as warnings either because the patient's condition has changed or because a piece of equipment needs attention. Systems of this type, where signals must be analysed and acted on at once if necessary, are called real-time systems, because their response is, in human terms, immediate. In fact, a hundred or so computer instructions may have been carried out since the alarm signal was given, but that only leads to a delay of a fraction of a second.

Direct output has a use in training when specialized simulations are written for process plant control or flight simulations, but any detailed discussion of this is beyond the scope of this book. There is, however, a lot of potential for the use of direct output in CBT, in simpler fashions, such as controlling apparatus and monitoring.

6. The man-machine interface – how you communicate with the computer

INTRODUCTION

This chapter discusses the means of computer communication that are currently used in computer-based training and looks at others that are beginning to be considered. The vast majority of trainees interact with the computer using a computer terminal. This consists of a keyboard, usually like that of a typewriter, and a screen. The screen may occasionally be replaced by a printer or there may be a printer in addition (see Figure 6.1).

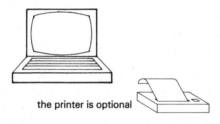

the printer is optional

Figure 6.1 A computer terminal

The terminal is very significant in CBT as the choice affects the quality of the material that can be presented to the student, the time it takes to design the layout of information to be presented on the screen, and the ease with which the student enters responses to the computer.

KEYBOARDS

A keyboard is the standard means for the user to input data into the computer. Other methods are discussed below. Unfortunately, it is not a very satisfactory means of input because most people have little or no knowledge of the layout of a typewriter keyboard which is the layout that has been adopted and added to for computer terminals (see Figure 6.2).

Figure 6.2 A typical typewriter style keyboard with numeric keypad for use in a computer terminal

This lack of knowledge means that students may be slow at typing their responses and liable to make errors. These factors may need to be taken into account when timing student sessions and analysing responses. (See Chapter 13 on response analysis.)

Some keys are added to terminal keyboards to fulfil special functions. The most important of these is the RETURN or ENTER key. This is pressed by the user to indicate to the computer, by the sending of a special code, that the typed line is complete and that the computer can now analyse it. Other keys that may be present include a delete key which when pressed deletes the character just typed, special function keys that can be used for special purposes by different programs and one marked CONTROL or CTRL which also has a particular function when used with other keys. The training officer will not normally need to worry about these odd keys. Some keyboards may also have a numeric keypad to the right of the typewriter keyboard. This may be of help when entering numeric data. The numeric keypad is used by data entry operators who have large quantities of numeric data to enter.

Most keyboards nowadays provide upper and lower case letters. Upper case is obtained by using the SHIFT and SHIFT/LOCK keys. This also gives access to the special characters – %, &, (,), # etc – that come above the numbers along the top line of the keyboard. Some terminals also have a CAPS LOCK key that locks all the alphabetic characters into upper case, but leaves the other keys (eg the numbers) in their unshifted state. Some or all of the keys may repeat if held down for a few seconds. This can be useful for lining up columns when entering programs.

Keyboards are attached to a screen, a printer or a microcomputer. The keyboards designed for professional use in industry generally feel similar when the keys are pressed. They have been designed to 'feel' like an electric typewriter even to the extent of 'clicking' when pressed. Some of the keyboards used with the cheaper microcomputers, designed primarily for home use, are touch-sensitive: the letters are marked on a flat surface and finger pressure over the correct position causes the character to be transmitted to the microcomputer. They look and feel nothing like a typewriter keyboard.

The quality of the keyboard is not generally as crucial as that of the screen used, but it is important. If people are being trained to do a job that uses a keyboard – data entry or on-line enquiry for example – it is important that the terminal (the keyboard and screen) used during training is the same as the one they will use when doing the job.

SCREENS

Just as the keyboard is the standard means of data input for CBT, the screen is the standard output device. The screen may be a television, a television monitor, a screen as part of a screen/keyboard combination (a visual display unit (VDU)), a screen incorporated into a microcomputer or a special purpose display. Screens may display about 32 to 80 characters per line or even more, and up to 25 lines or more at one time (see Figure 6.3). The use of graphics is discussed later in the chapter.

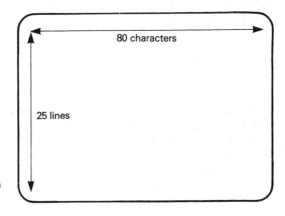

Figure 6.3 An 80-column screen

Televisions are capable of displaying 40 characters per line but beyond that the definition is likely to suffer. Television monitors vary considerably in quality and price and those sold for attachment to microcomputers are just capable of displaying 80 characters per line. The quality, however, is not adequate for extended viewing, whereas 40 or 64 characters per line is.

VDUs are sold in large numbers for attachment to terminal and computer networks (see Chapter 8) and directly to some microcomputers. They are designed to present character information in a very readable form, generally as 24 or 25 lines of 80 characters per line in upper and lower case. There is nothing mystical about the 80 characters. It has taken over from the

80-column punched card which used to be the standard form of data input. However, it is quite a good number and there is no great demand to go higher, although some screens go up to 132 characters per line.

Most screens are made using technology similar to that for television. This leads to bulky devices with high voltages inside. It is possible to get plasma displays that use a flat screen. They are more expensive, at present, but have a stable flicker-free display and are compact.

Character information

Characters can be represented within a dot matrix as shown below. If a matrix of seven rows by five columns is used, a capital Y could be represented as

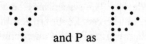

and P as

It is, in fact, quite easy to represent all the capital letters well within a 7 x 5 matrix. Problems arise with lower case letters that normally 'hang down' below the line. They are g, j, p, q, and y. Using a 9 x 5 dot matrix gets over that problem quite well, eg

It follows that the larger the dot matrix available for the characters, the better the character quality. It is now becoming common for good VDUs and some microcomputers to have dot matrices of 9 x 7 which allow very well-defined characters. With a screen that can display 80 characters per line there are 80 positions defined on each line, each of which can display a character within the (9 x 7) dot matrix. To avoid the characters touching, each character is framed by a small unlit box (see Figure 6.4).

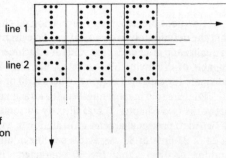

line 1

line 2

Figure 6.4 The arrangement of
character matrices on
a screen

Ergonomic factors

The design of the layout of screens and keyboards is the subject of much current research. It is, of course, important to make the environment for training as pleasant as it can reasonably be, but trainees do not usually spend extended periods at the terminal without a break; in fact, this is not to be recommended. So, for CBT, the ergonomic factors are not so crucial as they are for people working with screens all day. They should be considered, however, and in some cases may have to be considered because of agreements that have been signed with the trade unions.

The ergonomic factors include:

1. Character quality or readability – this is determined by a number of factors, but mainly by the dot matrix available for constructing the characters, the quality of the screen and by the colour (see 3 below);
2. Flicker – a screen that is not very stable, although the eyes may make allowances for it, can lead quite quickly to the user developing headaches or eye strain;
3. Colour of display – initially displays were primarily white characters on a black background. Tests have shown that green on black is considerably better, in that it produces less fatigue and strain, and it is suggested that amber on brown may be the most restful;
4. Non-reflective – the lighting is important to avoid glare on to the screen. A non-reflective surface helps;
5. Adjustable intensity – it should be possible to increase or decrease the brightness of the characters on the display to allow for changes in the room lighting.

Since not all people are of the same height and build, the design of the working area is important. Screens are designed for viewing at about 18 inches to two feet away and it may be possible to tilt the screen up or down for the optimum position. The keyboard is an integral part of the system but it may be attached to the VDU or microcomputer by using a cable, so that the operator can move it to the most comfortable position. Most students will also have some additional printed material that should be conveniently to hand.

Presenting information on the screen

When using CBT, it is necessary to present the information in an attractive manner. This is made much easier with a screen that displays 24 lines of 80 characters per line in upper and lower case, than if you are restricted to less. However, costs may dictate something less. Figures 6.5a and b show the same information as it might be displayed on a screen capable of displaying 24 lines of 40 characters and one with 24 lines of 80 characters. The effective use of the screen in CBT is discussed fully in Chapter 13.

Whatever size of screen you have to use, the method of use is similar. When a VDU or microcomputer system is switched on, you may be presented

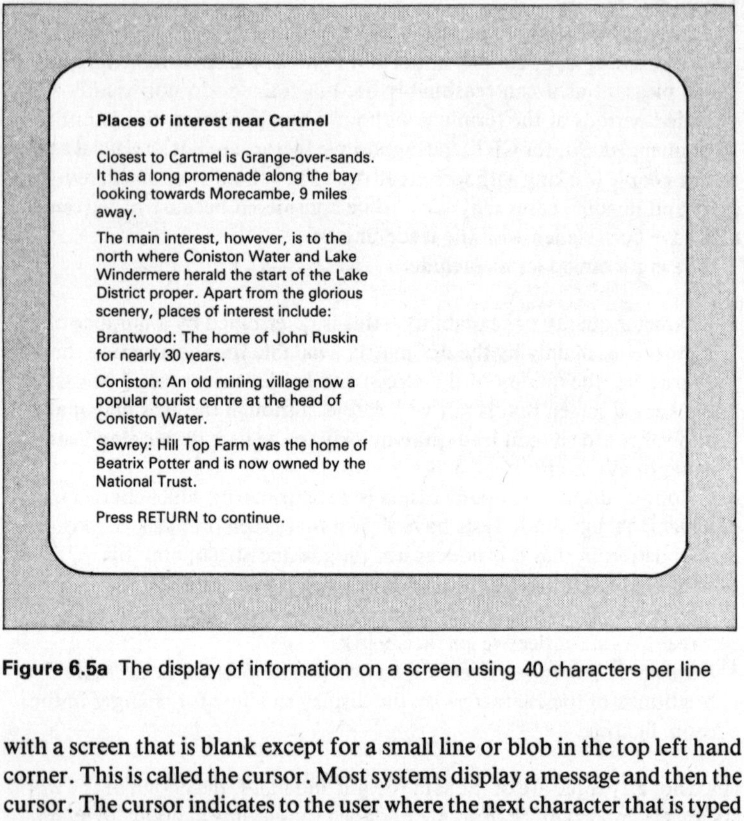

Places of interest near Cartmel

Closest to Cartmel is Grange-over-sands.
It has a long promenade along the bay
looking towards Morecambe, 9 miles
away.

The main interest, however, is to the
north where Coniston Water and Lake
Windermere herald the start of the Lake
District proper. Apart from the glorious
scenery, places of interest include:

Brantwood: The home of John Ruskin
for nearly 30 years.

Coniston: An old mining village now a
popular tourist centre at the head of
Coniston Water.

Sawrey: Hill Top Farm was the home of
Beatrix Potter and is now owned by the
National Trust.

Press RETURN to continue.

Figure 6.5a The display of information on a screen using 40 characters per line

with a screen that is blank except for a small line or blob in the top left hand corner. This is called the cursor. Most systems display a message and then the cursor. The cursor indicates to the user where the next character that is typed on the keyboard will be displayed. As a key is depressed, the character is displayed and the cursor moves to the next position. The cursor is important for authors of computer-based training courses so that they can see how they are laying out the information.

If the information to be presented to the student is displayed line by line on a blank screen the first line appears at the top of the screen and each subsequent line appears below until the bottom of the screen is reached. The next line then causes all the other lines to move up the screen by one line. The top line is lost and the new line appears at the bottom. This is called scrolling and is useful in that the previous few lines are available for the student to refer to. It is, however, rather disconcerting to see the lines continually rolling up the screen. Paging is the common alternative to scrolling. When paging, the author can issue a command to clear the screen and place the cursor in the top left-hand corner of the screen. Successive lines of text then display from the top. Thus, each new screenful of information is displayed on a blank screen. Ideally, the author should be able to use scrolling and paging as necessary during a module, and this is usually the case.

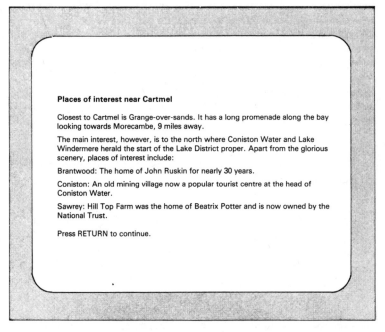

Figure 6.5b The display of information on a screen using 80 characters per line

The author has more flexibility if the whole screen is available and he can decide exactly where to display the information and accept replies to questions. Direct addressing allows any character to be displayed in any position on the screen. It may be essential to do this when writing CBT courses for people who are going to use the terminal for data entry or enquiry, and where the screen layout for the course must echo that for the actual job (see Figure 6.6).

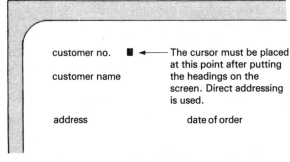

Figure 6.6 Use of direct addressing

Whether using direct addressing or not, it is possible to display a screen of information, perhaps a little at a time, until you wish to clear it and start again. To do this there is a 'clear screen' command that blanks the screen and places the cursor in the starting position.

With screen addressing it is possible to split the screen into different areas so that a part of the screen is static while others change. Some systems make it easy for the user to do this by effectively dividing the screen into several smaller screens. This can be useful when a diagram or form is being displayed and several questions need to be asked about it.

Special features of screens

It is often possible to do more than display characters on the screen in white on black or green on black:

1. Reverse video changes the characters from white on black to black on white and may be used for individual characters, words or the whole screen;
2. Flashing causes specific characters or words to flash on and off;
3. Highlighting (high intensity) permits characters or words to be displayed at a higher intensity than the rest of the characters on the screen.

All of the above should be used with caution, particularly flashing. It is not usually possible to underline words on the screen in the same way as on a printed page. If you need to underline, it is necessary to put the dashes on the line underneath. Highlighting can be a very effective alternative.

With the more sophisticated VDUs, it is possible to protect fields. This means that the cursor cannot go everywhere on the screen, but only in areas that are unprotected. This can be used to prevent the novice getting completely lost through pressing the wrong keys on the keyboard and getting the cursor in the wrong place. Its more important general use, however, is to help data entry clerks to work rapidly by moving the cursor automatically to the next area for data to be entered. For example, the customer number in Figure 6.6 might be only six digits long. The operator would only be allowed to enter six numbers; the rest of the line would be protected. When the customer number had been entered and checked, the cursor would move to the beginning of the next unprotected field.

Screen graphics

Screen graphics provides the capability to display graphs, diagrams or even reasonably good pictures on the screen. The quality of the graphics depends primarily on the resolution and whether there is colour or grey scaling.

Character graphics

The character screen recommended earlier has 24 lines of 80 characters per line. It is possible to construct diagrams, histograms, etc using the characters that are available, eg dashes and asterisks. The quality is not very good and the scope is limited. Nevertheless, it can be useful.

Some microcomputer systems add a graphics character-set to the normal characters (see Figure 6.7). By combining these with ingenuity and patience, reasonable shapes can be produced. This form of graphics may be useful where, for example, a histogram is presented to the student but the exact shape depends on how well the student has understood the previous material. Unless the diagram is varying, it is better to put anything that is at all complex on to the accompanying printed material. Character graphics can be used effectively for boxing titles, headings, etc if its use is not overdone.

Note that the graphics characters can use the full 8 x 8 dot matrix. The letters only use a 7 x 6 dot matrix. This permits continuous lines with the graphics characters.

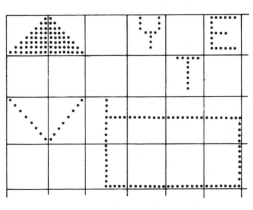

Figure 6.7 Some graphics characters

Character graphics are not provided on many microcomputer systems and are rare on VDUs.

True graphics

It has already been explained how the characters on a screen are generated by lighting points in a dot matrix. If these points could be lit individually in any position on the screen, it would be possible to draw shapes with a resolution of up to the total number of horizontal by vertical dots on the screen. This is, in fact, how graphics are displayed. There are commands available to the user that permit him to draw a line between two points on the screen. The resolution of a small microcomputer with true graphics is likely to be in the order of 280 points horizontally by 192 vertically. This permits some very good graphics, provided they do not get too complicated. It is quite adequate for sine curves, graphics for break-even analysis, simple circuit diagrams, etc.

Some of the more expensive microcomputers provide better resolution, while special purpose terminals provide resolutions of about 1500 x 1000 or better. Largely because of the quality of the screen needed to display so many dots, these high resolution graphics terminals are expensive (several thousand pounds each). They are widely used in the fast expanding area of computer-aided design.

Colour

The use of colour can enhance the presentation of teaching material if used purposefully. Some systems permit colour to be used in the display of text (eg Prestel) or text and character graphics. The ability to use colour with true graphics presents a lot of scope for making the training system very attractive. It is quite often the case that only a few (two or four) colours are available at the highest resolution, and more colours become available as the resolution decreases. Good graphics, whether black and white or colour, are time-consuming to produce, so be sure it is worthwhile before you start.

Video output

VDUs are designed to be viewed by one person situated about 18 inches from the screen. Large televisions and television monitors can be viewed from further away but not by large numbers of people. Computer-based training is generally run by a seated individual facing a screen, but it is possible, in the training department, for instructors to display information on the screen so that a class can view it. Perhaps the best way to do this is to link a number of television monitors together, so that the output from the computer is displayed on each. To do this a video output socket is needed on the back of the screen. Many VDUs and microcomputers with built-in screens do not have this facility, nor do ordinary televisions. If a video output socket is likely to be needed it is important to check its availability before purchasing. Some manufacturers, eg Sony, have developed large screen monitors (54 or 72 inch) for group viewing.

PRINTERS

There are three common situations where the use of printers may be appropriate for CBT: it is sometimes necessary to produce the training course on a printing terminal; it may be important for the student to have a printed copy of some of the material to take away, eg test results; the supervisor may need to print course statistics, or authors may require a printed copy of the teaching material to enhance or modify it.

Printing terminals

In the early days of computing, a printing terminal, called the Teletype, was almost universally used to link into computer systems. It printed at ten characters per second in capital letters only and was noisy with poor print quality. It included a built-in keyboard. A lot of computer-assisted instruction material for colleges and schools was written for these terminals, and is still used today.

Printing terminals today are faster (30 to 120 characters per second), quieter and very reliable. They use the dot matrix principle for forming characters, as described when discussing character representation on screens. With the printer, a head moves across the paper. It consists of a vertical line of fine needles that are fired at the paper through the ink ribbon in a pattern to represent the required letters (see Figure 6.8).

```
An example of text printed
on a dot matrix printer.
This printer uses a 9X5 dot
matrix, allowing true
descenders.
The character set includes:
ABCDEFGHIJKLMNOPQRSTUVWXYZ
abcdefghijklmnopqrstuvwxyz
1234567890
.,!"#$%&'()*:=-+;@/?><
```

Figure 6.8 Typical printed output with a dot matrix printer

With a printing terminal, the student is offered a lesson with the whole session – the information displayed and the student's input – recorded on paper for him to take away. One possible advantage of printing the whole session is that the student can refer back if he wishes, or take the print-out away for further work. If screens are being used, it is not always possible to refer back, although the author may provide such a facility.

A printer attached to the work station

If it is necessary for the student to have a printed copy of some parts of the course, it may be desirable to connect a printer without a keyboard to the VDU or microcomputer. The student on the course may then control what is printed out. The actual printer will be a dot matrix printer, similar to the one described earlier, but lacking a keyboard since that is already part of the VDU or microcomputer (see Figure 6.1). This arrangement is probably the optimum for general CBT, but it is often questionable whether the cost is justified. It may be possible to share the printer between several users if there is a group of work stations together.

A central high speed printer

When CBT is being developed and run on mainframe or minicomputers, there is likely to be a fast line printer (200 to 1000 + lines per minute) attached to the computer. Fast printers do not use the matrix principle but embossed characters on a belt, or even lasers. It is not necessary to describe them in any detail here, but they are major output devices for most data processing departments. They can be used for administrative purposes during the running of courses, to collect statistics of usage, users comments, test results, etc. They can also be used by course authors to provide printed listings of the courses they are developing. On smaller systems a printer without a keyboard would be adequate, although slow for long listings.

Printed graphics

Some matrix printers have a graphics feature so that they can be used to 'dump' a picture, shown on the screen, on to paper. It is a slow process to print a picture of the whole screen but the quality can be quite good and it is now possible to buy printers which 'dump' a colour picture on to paper (see Figure 6.9).

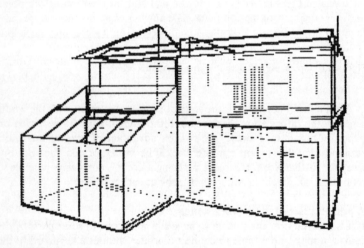

Figure 6.9 A screen drawing of a building 'dumped' to a dot matrix printer
Reproduced by kind permission of Datron Micro Centres

PLOTTERS

Plotters are used to draw diagrams, plot graphs, histograms, etc on paper. The techniques used for plotting vary with the size of plot and accuracy required. A small plotter for A4 drawings consists of a flat bed upon which the paper rests and a mechanism to move a pen in the X and Y directions simultaneously. The pen can also be 'down' so that it is drawing, or 'up' to move to a new point. There may also be several colours of pens, any of which can be selected. Plotted output is generally of a high standard and plotters are used to produce engineering drawings, plans and street layouts, as well as high quality graphs, pie charts, histograms, etc. Plotters are not often used in CBT but they could be appropriate in specialized areas, for example, in teaching statistics, circuit design, seismology and urban planning.

DIGITAL PADS AND GRAPHICS TABLETS

When discussing the keyboard at the beginning of the chapter, it was pointed out that this is not a very satisfactory means of input for the general user, since the layout of the QWERTY typewriter keyboard appears strange and illogical. In the next few pages we shall discuss some other possibilities that are available although not widely used as yet.

The digital pad (see Figure 6.10) consists of a rectangular board on which diagrams, charts, pictures, etc can be placed. The pad is constructed so that the user can press his finger on to the pad and the position of the point pressed is fed back to the computer. The number of points that can be indicated is fairly small and it is quite a crude device, but for training the young and unskilled it has potential. It is also quite cheap (£100 upwards).

The graphics tablet or digitizer adopts the principle of feeding back details of a point indicated to a higher level of refinement (see Figure 6.11). Rather than use a finger to indicate the point selected, the graphics tablet uses a pointer or cross-wires, depending on the make. If, say, a map was placed on the graphics tablet and the student was asked to indicate a church with a spire, he would either move the pointer or slide the cross-wires to the point on the map where he thought the church was marked. To transmit the co-ordinates of that point to the computer, he would either press the pointer firmly on to the surface of the tablet or press a button on the cross-wires. The computer could then evaluate the co-ordinates and respond accordingly. The graphics tablet appears to offer some exciting opportunities in the CBT area. Large graphics tablets are used in computer-aided design, cartography, urban planning and civil engineering. The large-sized graphics tablets cost several thousand pounds but small ones, that could be useful in training, cost only a few hundred.

TOUCH-SENSITIVE SCREENS AND LIGHT PENS

Touch-sensitive screens are similar to digital pads except that the user touches the screen at the point selected. The point is recognized in one of two ways. First, by shining a grid of lights horizontally and vertically across the screen, very close to the surface. The finger then breaks some of the light beams (see Figure 6.12). Second, by pressing a flexible cover on to the screen;

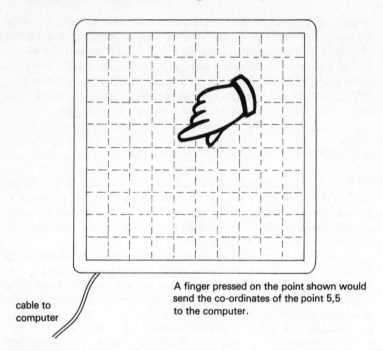

A finger pressed on the point shown would send the co-ordinates of the point 5,5 to the computer.

cable to computer

Figure 6.10 A digital pad

in both cases the co-ordinates of the point indicated are fed back to the computer. Since the finger is used as the means of input, it is a fairly crude method. The touch-sensitive screen may be used with the PLATO and SIMPLER computer-based training systems and thus is quite popular in training.

The light pen is more sensitive and is akin to the graphics tablet, except that again it is directed at the screen. It is a pen-shaped device connected by a cable to the terminal and a thin beam of light shines from the end (see Figure 6.13). When the pen is pressed on to the screen, the co-ordinates of the point are fed to the computer.

CURSOR CONTROLLERS AND GAMES PADDLES

The screen cursor has already been described above. It is possible to control the position of the cursor by various means. Some terminals provide keys with arrows pointing left, right, up and down, others provide small thumbwheels, so that by turning one, the cursor moves left or right and by turning the other, it moves up or down. A third method uses a sphere which is partly exposed above the keyboard. By rotating it in any direction the cursor will move accordingly.

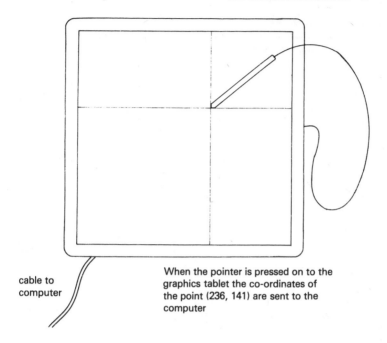

cable to
computer

When the pointer is pressed on to the
graphics tablet the co-ordinates of
the point (236, 141) are sent to the
computer

Figure 6.11 A graphics tablet (digitizer)

Games paddles use a similar principle of moving a cursor of some sort on
the screen. As amusement arcades show, the effective use of such means of
input, together with quite good graphics (and noise) can be highly motivating. Perhaps, if the same money could be made from a training course in
industrial relations or accounting practice as from space invader games,
there would be some high technology courses in these areas.

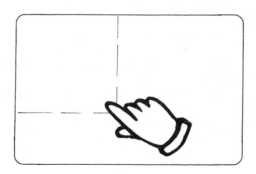

Figure 6.12 A touch-sensitive screen

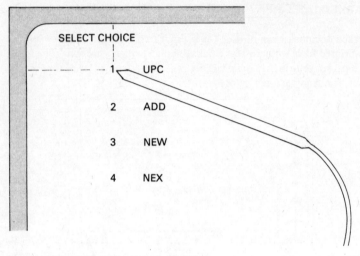

Figure 6.13 A light pen

SOUND AND VOICE

Many microcomputer systems can produce sound and fairly crude music. Sound can be used effectively as a prompt and, to a limited extent, to enhance parts of a course. In general though, it has very little place other than in the games area. Of course, the use of educational games for training less able youngsters is important.

The use of voice, on the other hand, offers many possibilities; voice can or will be capable of acting as an input as well as an output medium. It has been possible for several years to make a tape recorder play certain parts of a tape under computer control. Microprocessor chip manufacturers are now producing voice chips that can produce words and sentences. The technique has been used in pocket games that speak words that the user then has to spell. This technology is still in its early days, but is developing very rapidly.

Voice input is more complex still, because no two people speak in the same way. Voice input devices can be designed to recognize, for example, the numbers 0 to 9 where 'one', carefully spoken, cannot be confused with another of the numbers. This can be used for taking orders. The computer would use voice output to confirm the numbers it had received. The design of systems to allow flexible use of voice input is enormously complicated but the potential that it offers over a wide range of applications is such that large sums are being spent on research.

MARKED DOCUMENT READERS

Marked documents can be used for test marking. Students mark boxes on a pre-printed form with crosses or ticks to indicate their selections. The forms are most suited to multiple choice questions, but can also be used for numeric input, for example (see Figure 6.14).

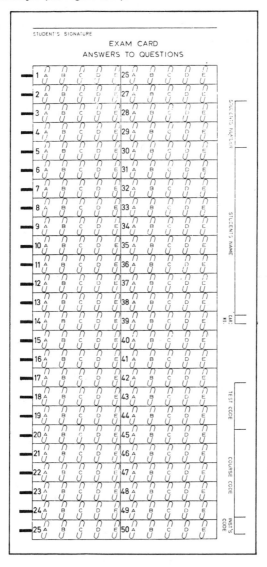

Figure 6.14 A marked card for multiple-choice tests

The marked documents are fed into a marked document reader, connected to the computer. The marks are sensed as the documents pass under a row of small lights. Marked documents are only used in fairly specialized areas, but they do have the advantage that the information entered by the user can be entered directly into the computer without anyone else transcribing the data with the concomitant cost and risk of error. Examination and test marking is one of the major areas of application, but the number of documents being fed through needs to be quite high to justify the cost of the reader and the special documents. Marked documents can be used in the computer-managed learning area of CBT. This area is discussed in Chapter 16.

7. Making the computer work for you – the software

INTRODUCTION

In this chapter we shall consider how the hardware of the computer – the CPU, disk storage, VDUs, etc can be transformed from a series of boxes to a computer system of use to industry and commerce. The essential intermediary between man and the computer hardware is the software. The term software refers to programs written by computer manufacturers, computer experts in companies, or computer-based training material written by a trainer using an author language. (Authoring systems and author languages are discussed in Part 3.)

Different types of software are like the layers of an onion surrounding the central core, ie the computer hardware (see Figure 7.1). We shall work from the inside out.

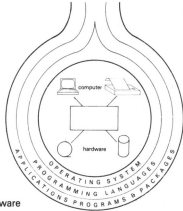

Figure 7.1 The different types of software

OPERATING SYSTEM

The operating system is the control program that keeps a finger on the pulse of the computer hardware. It decides which jobs should run on a priority basis, depending on the facilities needed by each one, and the importance attached to the job when it is submitted. Some of the operating system remains in part of the computer memory all the time the computer is running, while other parts are loaded from disk storage as they are needed and over-written when not required until later. The purpose of the operating system is to help management make efficient use of the overall system. The operating system is a collection of programs that combine to carry out a wide variety of functions, most of which can be included under one of the following:

1. Input/output
2. Operator communication
3. Error handling
4. Use of computer memory.

Input/output

The operating system must have overall control of the input/output devices, so that a print-out for one user does not get lines for another user mixed up in it. A second user who needs the printer must have his output held in a queue until the printer is finished with one job and ready for the next. The operating system must also recognize which terminal has sent which message so that the replies go back to the correct user.

The operating system also includes routines to support all the standard input/output devices that can be attached to the computer. These routines carry out the normal input/output functions without the user's programmers having to know in detail how the devices work. They can give commands such as PRINT to print a line, or GET to get a record from a disk file, and the operating system input/output routines do the rest including error handling.

Operator communication

On microcomputers the operator and the user are often the same person, but on mainframe computers there will normally be one or more operators running the system. The operating system will communicate with the operators from start-up in the morning when they will be asked to enter the date and time, and throughout the day when they will receive messages on the operator's console telling them to mount specific tapes on tape drives, mount or remove disk packs, or put more paper, or special stationery for payslips, say, into the printer. The operators will also be able to monitor the system to see how it is being used and, possibly, link to remote users at certain times for special purposes. The operating system will produce a log during the day and will report any malfunctions of the system that are detected to the operators.

Error handling

Computer equipment is generally very reliable. However, devices do not need to break down for errors to occur, and the more sophisticated the operating system is, the better it will be for handling error conditions. As far as the operating system is concerned, an error has occurred if a user program needs to print some data on a particular printer and that printer is not switched on. The operating system will display a message to the operator of the type 'PRINTER 001 NOT READY'. That job will then wait until the operator switches on the printer or cancels the job. If the operating system were not very good, it might cause the program to stop at the point when it needed the printer, without any message appearing. Nothing would then happen unless and until the operator realized what was wrong or gave up and cancelled the job.

Some error handling may be taking place unknown to the operator. For example, the operating system software may detect, by certain checks that are made, that an error has occurred while reading data from a disk. The error handling routine may then retry the operation several times. If this is unsuccessful, it may move the head away from that track and back again and try several more times before giving up and telling the operator. If this sort of error recovery takes place, it is important that the operating system stores away information on a disk file to tell the operator at a later time what errors have been detected and when, so that the engineer can repair the fault before it becomes too serious.

Use of computer memory
The operating system needs to keep an ever-changing map of exactly what is going on in the computer memory so that, if a new program needs to be loaded, it knows whereabouts in memory there are enough memory locations to hold the program. On large systems supporting many users, the map of memory will be changing many times each second and the operating system must be constantly up-to-date.

The better the operating system, the better it will manage the use of the computer memory. There is, however, a point at which the time the operating system spends trying to use everything efficiently puts such an overhead on the processor that the amount of processor time available to the users becomes reduced to an unacceptable extent. It may then be cheaper to add memory and use it rather less efficiently.

TYPES OF OPERATING SYSTEM

Batch processing
Early computers were single-user systems (called batch processing systems), and most small microcomputer systems run on the same principle today. CP/M, a well known microcomputer system, is of this type. A small modern microcomputer system for business purposes typically consists of a type-writer keyboard for input, a screen for temporary output, diskette drives for data storage and retrieval, and a printer for permanent output (see Figure 7.2 a and b). The company using this system may wish to do three things with it during the morning:

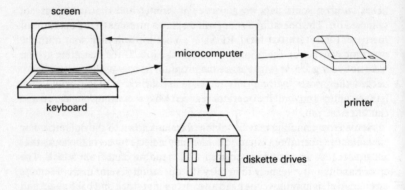

Figure 7.2a A small microcomputer system for business purposes

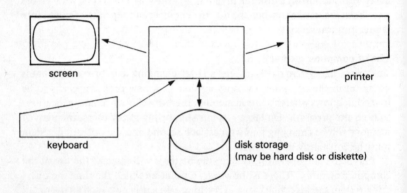

Figure 7.2b Diagrammatic representation of 7.2a

1. Enter the day's orders and get reports on sales, stock, etc
2. Print some address labels
3. Enter some quality control data and produce reports.

Since this is a single-user system, the manager must decide the sequence in which the jobs will be run; once the first job has started, it will have to be completed before the next job can start (see Figure 7.3).

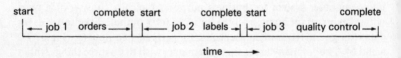

Figure 7.3 Batch processing

This is not a very efficient way to run a system since most of the parts are idle almost all of the time (this may not be true of the printer which can be heavily used) and the processor itself is probably working for less than 1 per cent of the time.

Let us consider what happens when printing on a slow printer attached to a computer. A dot matrix printer that can print at 120 characters per second is typical for low volumes of printing and for microcomputers. The computer has to send a character to the printer every 1/120th of a second, which is approximately one character every eight milliseconds. A typical microcomputer can execute about a quarter of a million instructions per second and it might take 20 instructions to send a character to the printer. The time that the processor is busy when printing is thus 20/250,000 seconds (= 80 microseconds) in eight milliseconds. This is 1 per cent of the time. What does the computer do the other 99 per cent of the time? Nothing. Of course, mini- and mainframe computers, which execute more instructions per second, are kept even less busy while printing.

To overcome this problem, the writers of operating systems developed multi-programming systems. The memory of the computer is divided into a number of regions and a different program can run in each one (see Figure 7.4).

COMPUTER MEMORY

operating system	program 1	program 2	program 3	temporarily unused

Figure 7.4 Multiprogramming

The operating system then sees that each program has some processor time according to various rules, but if one program is doing some input/output which, remember, is relatively slow, the operating system gives the processor time that would otherwise be wasted (more than 99 per cent of it when printing on a terminal) to another program in memory. As a program is completed, the operating system looks for the next job and loads that. Of course, programs vary in size, so things can get quite complex, but the principle of using the processor more efficiently still holds.

Timesharing
It may not matter too much that a microcomputer costing a few thousand pounds sits doing nothing for 99 per cent of the time while it prints a report or you scratch your head and look at the keyboard. It may be able to earn its keep very handsomely in this way. Firms spending hundreds of thousands of pounds on computers expect more, however, and they run operating systems

that can support dozens or even hundreds of terminals linked in by telephone lines, each doing something different. These systems are called timesharing systems. If you are connected into the system and have given your code and password (a form of security controlled by the operating system), the computer will not wait while you think what to do, but it will see which of the other users have pressed the ENTER keys on their terminals and want the computer to respond, or it may give a user program that involves a lot of computing a small amount of time (perhaps half a second) before putting it back to the end of the queue. Users are serviced in sequence. As seen above, the difference in speed between the processor doing something and the user entering information at, say, ten characters per second, is so great that effectively each user gets an immediate response from the computer when entering data or making enquiries. When CBT is run on larger multi-user systems, a timesharing system is almost invariably used (see Figure 7.5).

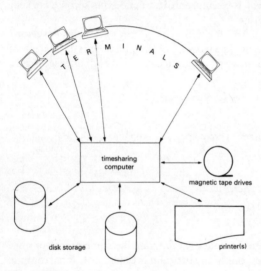

Figure 7.5 A timesharing system

PROGRAMMING LANGUAGES

The next layer of the 'onion' is composed of programming languages. The operating system provides the user with standard methods of accessing various input/output devices. In a similar way, programming languages help programmers to communicate with the computer by using a number of rules built into each language, without having to know the details of the hardware of the particular computer they are using. Before taking a brief look at some of the more common programming languages, we shall outline the procedure that must be gone through in turning an idea in a department into a successful computer application (see Figure 7.6). As we shall see, this process resembles the stages in the design of a computer-based training course quite closely.

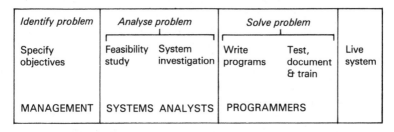

Identify problem	Analyse problem		Solve problem		
Specify objectives	Feasibility study	System investigation	Write programs	Test, document & train	Live system
MANAGEMENT	SYSTEMS ANALYSTS		PROGRAMMERS		

Figure 7.6 Turning a business problem into a computer solution

The stages may be represented as follows:

1. *Specifying the objectives.* The scope of the problem must be established. This is a management decision although advice will be given in most cases by staff with expertise in the area under consideration.
2. *Feasibility study.* Before extensive detailed work is carried out on the solution to the problem, a feasibility study must be made to establish the likely cost, duration and benefits. It will also decide whether a computer solution is the most appropriate. This is particularly relevant with computer-based training since the cost equation is only now swinging quite dramatically towards using computers. In the past, CBT has only been justifiable in a fairly limited number of areas.
3. *Systems investigation.* If the feasibility study concludes that a computer solution is appropriate, a detailed systems analysis is carried out to specify precisely what information is fed in and what the outputs are. Much of the skill, and also the time-consuming part, of a systems analyst's job is in predicting and providing solutions to all the things that can go wrong when running the system.
4. *Program writing.* The job done by programmers involves taking the system design produced by the analysts and turning it into a system that can run on the computer. To do this they write statements that obey a set of rules and these are translated into machine code instructions by the computer. We shall discuss some of the programming languages that are available when we have completed the stages in implementing a system. Packages are sometimes used to solve the problem that has been identified.
5. *Testing, documenting and training.* This stage overlaps stage 4 since some parts will be written and tested before others are started. It is standard practice nowadays to write systems as a collection of modules,

each of which has a specific job to do. This makes rigorous testing and 'debugging' easier. (Debugging is computer jargon for removing errors from programs.) Documentation is very often inadequate since it is both time-consuming and difficult to write high quality material. However, good documentation is essential, both for the computer department and for the user department. Training is also crucially important to ensure that users understand what has to be done and why certain actions are necessary. Trainers will not need reminding of the importance of this, but are they involved in this area in their organizations at present?

6. *A live system*. When everything and everyone is ready, the system can go live and become part of the operation of the business. Where a computer system is replacing an existing system, it may be possible to run the two in parallel for a period, but this may not be practical.

There is a wide variety of programming languages available and academic computer specialists enjoy inventing new ones and pouring scorn on most existing ones. However, the pragmatists of business and commerce only use a fairly small range of languages, all of which are abhorred by most academics. We shall consider three of the most common – COBOL, FORTRAN and BASIC. We shall also touch on PASCAL, which is growing in popularity and actually quite liked by the professors. These are all examples of so-called high-level languages.

What is a high-level language?
In Chapter 5 we discussed how the control unit interprets instructions and executes them. These are machine language instructions and consist of a series of bits. To make life easier for programmers, mnemonic codes were developed, whereby a series of letters signified an instruction and memory locations could be represented by symbols, eg LD 2, LABEL1. Here LD is a mnemonic code for the LOAD instruction whose machine code might be the bit pattern 11001. The rest of the instruction indicates that register 2 is to be loaded with the data in the memory location indicated by the name LABEL1. This forms the basis of assembler languages which are much easier to write than machine code, but are long-winded and difficult to modify and debug. The writing of assembler language programs lies very much in the realm of the specialist programmer.

People's time is expensive but computer time is becoming less so. Therefore, anything that makes programmers more effective is likely to be valued. High-level languages were developed for this reason. The coding has an approximate English meaning to it. For example,

```
INPUT  HEIGHT, LENGTH
AREA = HEIGHT X LENGTH
PRINT  ''THE AREA OF A RECTANGLE OF HEIGHT
       ''HEIGHT'' AND LENGTH''
PRINT  LENGTH ''HAS AN AREA OF '' AREA
```

could be valid lines of a program in a high-level language. Because of this clear connection to English, high-level languages are easier to learn than assembler language or machine code, they are quicker to write, easier to understand, being partially self-documenting, and therefore easier to maintain.

But why have more than one high-level language? Attempts have been made to produce universal programming languages (IBM tried with PL/1) but the requirements of business and the science and engineering fields are quite different, as will be discussed, so a language to cover both areas becomes large and complex. There are also other factors such as whether programs are interactive or involve data collection and batch processing. No programming language is perfect – far from it – so there are continuous attempts at improvement. A few get beyond the research project stage.

COBOL (COmmon Business Oriented Language)
COBOL or its derivatives, is the most widely-used programming language. It is particularly good at handling alphabetic information which is what most business computing is concerned with, where names, addresses, product codes and descriptions are manipulated extensively, but any mathematics is fairly simple. It is therefore a business language. It is verbose but designed so that, when well written, it is self-documenting to some extent. It is, however, not easy to learn rapidly. Because COBOL was designed with well-defined standards, the language tends to be the same on different computers or, at least, the differences are known and small. Trainers who are not involved in computer education are most unlikely to need to know any more about COBOL.

FORTRAN (FORmula TRANslator)
While COBOL is extensively used for business applications, FORTRAN is popular with scientists, engineers and statisticians. It is a compact language which can handle complicated calculations efficiently, but is inefficient for handling complex reports and tabulations. There are clear standards for FORTRAN, so, like COBOL, it is usually fairly easy to transfer programs from one machine to another. FORTRAN is often used for simulations and may, therefore, be used for some aspects of training.

BASIC (Beginners' All-purpose Symbolic Instruction Code)
FORTRAN and COBOL date back to the days when card-readers were the main input devices and line printers were the main output devices; they are not ideally suited for use by a programmer sitting at a terminal. BASIC, however, was developed at Dartmouth College in the United States for use on a timesharing system for undergraduates. It was designed to be easy to learn. Because it has proved to be just that, it is now an extremely popular language on timesharing systems and most microcomputers. A student can learn to write a surprisingly useful program with less than a day's tuition and can become quite competent in a week. BASIC is very widely taught in schools

and is one of the first introductions most pupils have to a programming language. It has, however, several drawbacks. Unlike FORTRAN and COBOL, it has no standard and is rather a limited language in its original form. To make it useful for general purposes, many computer companies have enhanced the language. This, of course, means that programs written for one computer will probably be incompatible on another without changes which could be extensive.

A host of computer-assisted learning programs have been written in BASIC for use in schools and colleges and there are circumstances where BASIC may be appropriate for CBT, for example, where the organization has a computer that supports BASIC but not a suitable author language. Development time, and therefore cost, will be higher using BASIC than it would be to produce the same material using a suitable author language, if available. Some results obtained by the authors are given in Chapter 13.

PASCAL

This is a modern language from the mid-1970s which encourages the programmer to write 'well structured' programs. This fashionable phrase means that the logic of the program is clear from the way in which the program is coded, and the program is therefore more likely to be correct and, if incorrect, more easily debugged. The language is becoming popular and has a well-defined standard. Input/output is not very well handled with some versions. It is, however, likely to grow in importance. There are several implementations of PASCAL on microcomputers.

Other languages

Among the high-level languages that are quite widely used, one should include PL/1, which was produced by IBM for use both sides of the commerce-science divide (PL/M is a derivative for microcomputers), APL which is a very concise interactive language using its own symbols for its instructions, ALGOL which is claimed by some to be superior to FORTRAN, but which never caught on because IBM stuck to FORTRAN, and RPG (Report Program Generator) which is used in commerce primarily, as its name implies, for producing reports.

APPLICATION PROGRAMS AND PACKAGES

We now come to the outside layer of the 'onion'. It is at this point that we get a program or suite of programs that the person in the user department, who may know little and care even less about computers, has to run to enter data and receive output. Application programs are the end results of the design process outlined earlier in the chapter. They are produced by programmers usually using high-level languages.

Part of the feasibility study carried out in most computer projects will include an evaluation of packages that may be available to do the job, or part of it, more cost-effectively than writing the programs within the company. In the 1960s, when computer hardware was very expensive, the software supplied by the manufacturers was included in the price and programs were exchanged at little cost. As hardware prices dropped, companies like IBM could see their income being hit, so they started to charge for software. At the same time 'people costs' for programmers were increasing in data processing departments. It thus became economic for entrepreneurs to develop packages that could do standard things reliably, eg payroll, accounting, critical path analysis and engineering design. These packages are designed to be tailored with a small amount of effort to each customer's specific needs. The package market has developed a high turnover and is a vigorous and exciting area of computer activity, stretching from the largest computers to microcomputers.

There are two types of application package of particular interest to the trainer who is likely to use CBT. These are: 1. author languages and computer-managed learning, and 2. actual training programs. There are several author language systems that may include some computer-managed learning and these are discussed in Chapter 15. Good training material is not widely available although some is available on the PLATO and other systems. Several firms have also produced CBT material for training computer personnel. There is a vast amount of teaching material for schools and colleges covering dancing, music, foreign languages, geography and the more traditional areas of science, engineering, mathematics and statistics. Some of the material is highly imaginative and very worthwhile. Trainers who are thinking about CBT should not spurn opportunities to see what is being used in the classroom, but they should remember that only some of the material is good.

STAFFING A COMPUTER INSTALLATION

Figure 7.7 shows the sort of management structure that may exist in a medium-sized computer installation with 20 to 30 staff.

Systems analysts provide the interface between the user and the data processing department. They may have come from the ranks of programmers but the training they need is different from that of programmers. Programmers are responsible for the software. Systems programmers are responsible for the operating system – sorting out bugs, mounting modifications, improving the operating efficiency of the system. Applications programmers are responsible for writing systems defined by the systems analysts, mounting applications packages and maintaining all current applications.

Operators run the computer and control its operation. They mount tapes and disks, remove printed output from the line printer, and are responsible for taking back-up of the system and files of data, according to rules laid down by management. The numbers of operators employed will depend on whether the installation runs a shift system.

Data preparation staff enter and verify information sent to the data processing department by users. At one time they used devices such as card punches and verifiers, but nowadays they tend to use VDUs linked on-line to the computer. One result of this has been to move the data entry function from the data processing department back to the user departments that create the information. Responsibility for accuracy then rests with the generating department.

Users of smaller systems may have a small department of up to half a dozen people who design and write the programs, maintain them and operate the system. They can probably call on professional expertise from the computer supplier or consultants when they have specific problems outside the area of their expertise.

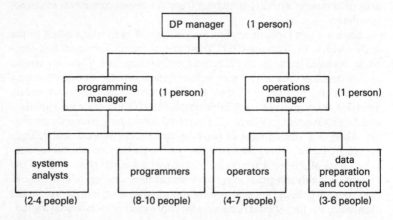

Figure 7.7 A possible management structure in a medium-sized computer department

Many firms run systems, called 'turnkey' systems, that are provided as a hardware and software solution specifically for that firm. The applications programs are provided by a 'software house' that usually buys the hardware and delivers a complete solution to the customer. At least that is the theory. There are many successful installations of turnkey systems but few are achieved without trials and tribulations and the burning of midnight oil. The common idea behind such systems is that the firm does not need to acquire extensive computer knowledge; the systems house will train the firm's personnel to run the computer reliably and effectively. Nevertheless, they usually have a supervisor and a deputy who spend a substantial amount of their time working with the computer.

The growth in the use of microcomputers has resulted in computers appearing in places where they have never been seen before. In many cases they are used as needed by engineers or designers and have little or no strict supervision, the users being responsible for their own diskettes. In small companies where a microcomputer is used to do the firm's accounts, and possibly payroll, much more careful supervision is needed to ensure that the firm's accounts are not corrupted or irrevocably lost; many a microcomputer user has been disillusioned by the errors he has made through poor advice, unreliable software and lack of training.

8. Communicating between computers

INTRODUCTION

The last two chapters of Part 2 of the book cover areas of some technical complexity but it is useful for the people involved in training to have some grasp of the direction in which developments are going, as the implications for training are extensive and constantly changing. This chapter discusses some of the more important ways in which computers can link together as networks. The next chapter looks at a variety of new and specialized areas.

WHAT IS A NETWORK?

A network, in computer terms, is a series of links between a computer system and a number of devices remote from the computer. If the devices are terminals then it is a terminal network; if the devices are other computers, it is a computer network (see Figure 8.1).

A Star Network

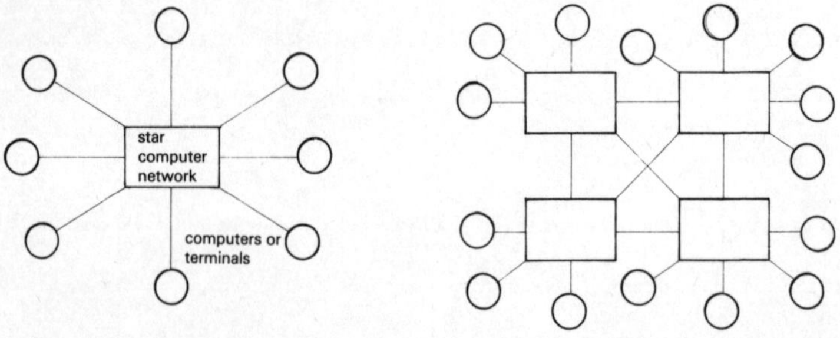

Figure 8.1 Some examples of networks

Terminal networks

In Chapter 7, we discussed timesharing systems where a number of terminals can link into a central computer and, because of the relative speeds of the terminals and the processor, each user appears to have the computer more or less to himself. This is a terminal network. The terminals may be in the same room as the computer or in another continent, but only a telephone call away. It is, of course, not quite so simple. If it is necessary to link a terminal into the computer using telephone wires, which is usually the case if the connection is across a public highway, it is necessary to use 'modems' at each end of the telephone line (see Figure 8.2). This is because telephone wires are designed to carry conversations. These are analogue signals; they will vary in a continuous manner (see Figure 8.3a). As has been described, computers are interested in information in the form of bits which can be 1 or 0. These bits must be converted into an analogue signal to go over the telephone lines and then revert again into bits at the receiving end (see Figure 8.3b).

The analogue signal is 'modulated' to carry the data to the receiving end and there are several ways that the signal can be modulated to transfer the digital data. The modems do this. Modem is an abbreviation of *mo*dulator-*dem*odulator. A special type of modem is an acoustic coupler. This device allows the user to telephone in to the computer using an ordinary telephone handset. When a connection is made, the user hears a steady whistle, which is the carrier signal. If he now pushes the telephone into the acoustic coupler, the terminal is linked to the computer (see Figure 8.4). Acoustic couplers are used when the user only needs to make occasional contact with the computer, or to link in from different places. Salesmen, for example, often demonstrate

A Ring Network

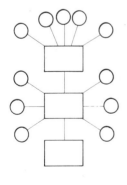
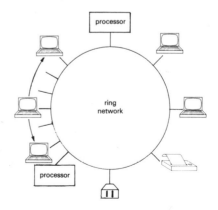

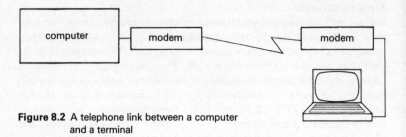

Figure 8.2 A telephone link between a computer
and a terminal

terminals or application programs like that. Where usage is likely to be substantial, it is cheaper to lease a telephone line from the post office and have it always available. This obviates the need to dial each time you wish to use the computer.

Terminal networks have been provided for several years by universities,

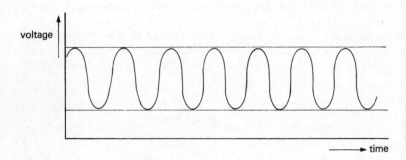

Figure 8.3a An analogue signal

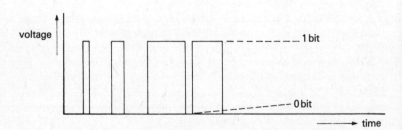

Figure 8.3b A digital signal as 0 and 1 bits

colleges, and commercial bureaux as well as by companies. All universities and polytechnics in Britain provide a timesharing service using a terminal network. They may be able to support a hundred or more terminals simultaneously, all linked to the computer. Users can do a wide range of things. Many use the computer to learn to program, but others do statistics, engineering design, survey analysis, graphics, textual analysis, documentation, etc.

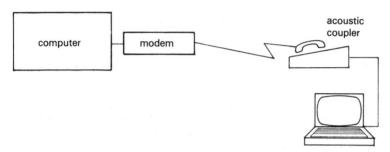

Figure 8.4 The use of an acoustic coupler in a network

Basically, the commercial bureaux make money by selling computer time to their customers. The customers rent or buy a terminal, and telephone in to the computer when they need to use it. Heavy users may lease a line. The advent of microcomputers is causing many bureaux to rethink their role and some are supplying microcomputers to carry out some of the functions originally performed by the central computer. This is an example of distributed processing (see pages 119-120).

A major use of terminal networks today is for data base enquiry. Data base is a piece of computer jargon that refers to any organized collection of data held on a computer system to meet the specific information needs of a company or institution. Some collections of data need to be vast to be generally useful, and it is therefore beyond the resources of most companies to create and update such data bases. Common examples are bibliographic details of publications, references to articles in journals and information on chemical compounds. Most academic libraries and many companies are able to link into the relevant data base wherever it may be in the world. It is not always easy to make effective use of these enquiry systems. The search is often made by specifying keywords to the computer which then responds with the number of references found. For example, a search carried out by linking to a data base in the United States gave the information overleaf. The required references were selected, printed in the USA and mailed to the enquirer in Britain. What came back demonstrates the power of the system, but also the problems. We requested items 1, 3 and 4 – a total of 125 references. When the list arrived, there were, for example, references to 'Partons

Search Words	Number of Occurrences
1. computer-based training	10
2. computer-aided instruction	2481
3. PLATO	109
4. IIS	6

Note: PLATO and IIS are author languages for CBT
(see Chapter 17).

in antiquity' in which some theories of the philosopher Plato were mentioned. What we should have asked for were references that included computer-aided instruction *and* PLATO. Virtually all extraneous references to Plato, the philosopher, would thus have been eliminated. Of course, with these data bases, a key factor is how up-to-date the references are. One search option usually permits you to exclude references prior to a certain date.

Computer networks
It is not surprising that computer users who started quite happily on time-sharing systems should occasionally find that they would like to use another computer, for one of several reasons; there might be unique output facilities on one machine or a special software package, or a particularly powerful machine for scientific work. It thus became attractive to link the computers together so that, in theory at least, the most suitable computer was used for any major piece of work. These networks have developed particularly in the universities and the scientific and engineering research areas. The links that are set up between the computers can usually transfer data at high speeds. There have been parallel developments in the commercial world that will be discussed later under distributed processing.

Another form of network that has developed with microelectronics and is still in its infancy, although babies grow fast in this industry, is the local area network (LAN). The LAN uses some form of cabling – wires or optical fibres – to link together any suitable devices that may connect into it. It is rather like plugging into the electricity ring main. These LANs are likely to have a significant impact on the areas in which computer-based training moves.

The cost of installing cabling for LANs can be low enough for firms to consider installing it, along with the other services, when building or refurbishing offices. The LAN can then be plugged into, as and where needed. Potentially this brings powerful computing facilities to every office. Systems are being used today where word processors and microcomputers are used in offices, linked via the LAN into one or more service machines that have the more expensive and specialized devices attached to them. For example, it is economical to buy hard disk storage instead of floppy disk drives, and provide it centrally for each unit on the network. This improves security and response times as disk drives are more reliable than diskettes, and much faster for reading or writing data. The speed of the network is such that the transmission delay is very small. Similarly it may be economic to install better quality or faster printers for the production of documents, or a high quality plotter that could not otherwise be justified due to the expense.

Apart from their obvious potential for CBT in the office and factory, local area networks can be used when a number of computers are in use in classroom training (see Figure 8.5).

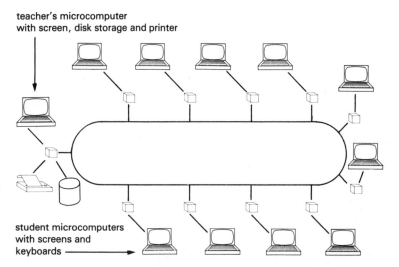

teacher's microcomputer
with screen, disk storage and printer

student microcomputers
with screens and
keyboards

Note: The students can use the printer and disk storage, if the teacher permits it

Figure 8.5 A local area network (LAN) in the classroom

The trainer operates the master computer with its control facilities such as disk storage, but each trainee can load the programs and data needed for his individual requirements from the central disks into his microcomputer. In addition, the trainer can monitor what each trainee is doing from his central point.

DISTRIBUTED PROCESSING

The concept of distributed processing is that the computing power should be farmed out to the various parts of the concern using it, in proportion to their needs. But, instead of having a lot of autonomous data processing departments, these distributed computers link into the next computer on the chain and require little or no local data processing expertise (see Figure 8.6).

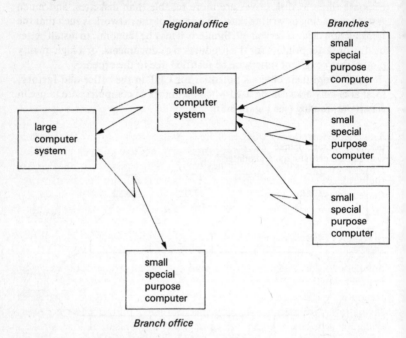

Figure 8.6 A distributed system

There can be several benefits in having such an arrangement instead of a large central facility: communications costs may be reduced as less data need to be sent back and forth; availability is enhanced since most of the system can continue to function even if one of the component computers is out of use; acceptance of the system may increase if the local computer can be shown to provide up-to-date information better and more quickly than a centralized system. There can also be some disadvantages, particularly in support by the data processing department and in hardware costs. However, as most specialized terminals, whether banking, point-of-sale, eg the modern electronic tills in some department stores, factory data collection or on-line enquiry, have microcomputers built into them, elements of the job that were previously done on the computer they linked into are now being built into the terminals themselves. These are so-called intelligent terminals and can be programmed to carry out data verification and other checks, and to store data for onward transmission later. This is an example of distributed processing.

9. Developments relevant to CBT

INTRODUCTION

This chapter mentions a number of areas, most of them fairly recent developments, where there is a clear or potential relevance to computer-based training. They are areas that do not fit neatly into the general picture that Part 2 of the book set out to draw; they are nevertheless topics to be considered by those interested in CBT.

SIMULATORS

Simulation is discussed at various points in Part 3 of the book and is an important part of CBT. Simulators are special purpose devices, of which a computer or computers are integral parts, and are built for the purpose of simulating a process or activity, to appear as though the trainee were actually doing the job. The best known examples are in flight simulation. An exact mock-up of the flight deck of an aeroplane is built, supported on hydraulic rams, so that during training pilots not only work the controls exactly as they would in an actual flight, but feel the effects of their actions. Such systems are expensive to build, but are extensively used as the alternatives are also expensive and less satisfactory.

In the chemical and related industries it may be desirable to build a mock-up of part or the whole of the main control panels of a production plant or power station and have the plant simulated by computer. This can be used as an important training tool but it also helps to optimize the layout of the instrument panel.

A less spectacular application, but one within both the technical and financial capabilities of many training officers, is exemplified in the Royal Navy. One important task, which is difficult to teach, involves training radar operators in the use of a keyboard (not a QWERTY keyboard) to record movements of the objects they are monitoring on a radar screen. The Royal Navy School of Educational and Training Technology (RNSETT) devised an ingenious solution to this problem. First the RNSETT training designers substituted a complete radar keyboard for the normal keyboard of a mainframe terminal. Then they used a commercially available authoring system (of the type described in Chapter 15) to present a series of screens on the VDU similar to those the operator would encounter in the 'live' system. The simulation can vary the complexity of the signals transmitted and provide sufficient practice in speed and accuracy of interpretation. Transfer difficulties are virtually eliminated since the trainees respond to problems by using a keyboard similar to that they will operate on the job.

Simulators are not very common because they are usually only worth having for complex systems and are, therefore, expensive to build.

PRESTEL AND VIEWDATA

Prestel is a public service which allows people with suitably modified televisions to phone in to a post office computer, using a simple keypad, and request information from a large data base. Once a company or organization has decided to use Prestel to publicize its wares, a specialist information provider will enter their material into the system for them. Shops can advertise their products and take orders via Prestel. Users can access train timetables, ferry availability, the latest share prices or get the weather forecast. The information made available can cover virtually any area, except pornography and official secrets. Prestel has been very slow to develop as a home service, but in the business area the same technique is developing rapidly in the form of private viewdata systems.

Private viewdata systems use the same principle as Prestel but have a private computer and data base. Either way, the post office benefits because people use the telephone network. Private viewdata systems are run by companies for information dissemination within a company, and possibly outside. Used extensively and effectively, they should reduce paperwork and help to ensure that people are working with up-to-date information. For example, if a price list is stored on a viewdata system, updates can be made and new prices are then immediately available for every authorized user to see.

Viewdata is in its early stages but is developing steadily and will have uses in training. Already a major bank is using such a system to train branch personnel. Prestel is planning to provide pictures so that firms which advertise via Prestel can include photographs of their products or facilities. There is also the future possibility of transmitting computer programs via Prestel.

VIDEODISC

Videotape and slide or tape/slide are widely used and are effective tools for training. It is not difficult to control these by computer if desirable. However, neither videotape nor slide lends itself particularly well to computer control. Videotape is read sequentially, so it is not very easy to move rapidly to different parts of the tape. Slide systems, on the other hand, are slow, mechanical and liable to get out of sequence, or be difficult to set up for automatic operation.

Videodisc is an exciting development which combines the quality of videotape film, the ability to stop, play back, etc, with the ability to jump to any specific part of the film and display a frame or sequence. The whole technology of the videodisc is developing rapidly but certain general principles can be identified. A videodisc is a platter about the size of a long playing record upon which enough audio and video information for between half an hour and an hour's viewing is stored as microscopic pits in the disc. The recorded data are usually read by a low-powered laser (see Figure 9.1). Since there is no mechanical contact, the discs do not deteriorate. There are various methods of creating and reading discs, so there seems to be little immediate hope of standardization. The random access capability is a major requirement for CBT; not all systems provide this.

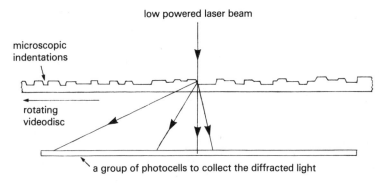

Figure 9.1 An optically transmissive videodisc system

Videodiscs are played on a player that feeds the picture and sound through a home colour television. Those produced for home use will be similar to the video cassette players widely sold today. Superior systems controlled by computer can be purchased, and this is an area where exciting possibilities arise. Any part of the disc can be accessed in a matter of a few seconds and a single frame or a sequence of film can be displayed at normal speed or in slow motion. There is much research being carried out into the effective use of computer-controlled videodisc for education and training, where the potential to repeat frames, and branch through the course giving real self-paced instruction, can be realized.

As already stated, computer graphics often leave much to be desired even for fairly simple diagrams, so that videodisc can offer much, even as a massive slide carousel (50,000 slides or more). But the use of motion pictures adds another dimension.

We shall consider two areas out of an infinite range. Training in negotiating skills, for both management and trade unions, could use film of a potential conflict and lead the student through different scenarios, depending on decisions taken, with the possibility of reviewing material or seeing addi-

tional material such as the home situation of an employee whose performance deteriorates.

In many areas of science education, botany, zoology, climatology, for
example, accurate name association is important. In botany, different types
of plants can be displayed and the student asked to identify them. The rate of
progress and difficulty would depend on the level of knowledge of the
student. An erroneous answer could lead to the plant incorrectly suggested
being displayed, so that the student could identify, and enter, the differences.

A typical videodisc training system might consist of the items shown in
Figure 9.2.

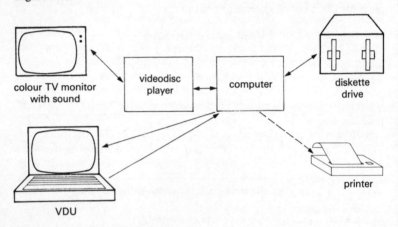

Figure 9.2 Typical videodisc training system

Lest this became a eulogy for new technology, there are a few disadvantages
of videodisc. Most of the disadvantages are associated with the cost: it is
expensive to plan and create the film (16mm or videotape); it is also expensive
to create the master disc. However, once the master has been produced for
£1000 or so, copies are cheap at a few pounds each. The film industry likes
the idea of videodiscs because it is not easy to duplicate them, thus making
copyright easier to protect.

One important criterion for a large-scale training operation is that the
courseware should be capable of rapid updating. Computer-based training
material should be readily updated – videodisc is not. Thus a careful evaluation needs to be made of how to use videodisc and what to put on to it.

EXPERT SYSTEMS

Any detailed discussion of expert systems and artificial intelligence is beyond
the scope of this book, but it is an area of growing importance, and expert

systems are going to be used increasingly in the education and training field, for model building and as tutors – the so-called intelligent tutoring systems.

An expert system is defined by Michie as

> a computing system which embodies organized knowledge concerning some specific area of human expertise, such as medical diagnosis, chemical identification, economic geology, structural analysis, number theory, etc sufficient to be able to do duty as a skilful and cost effective consultant.[1]

One example will give an idea of the practical benefits that expert systems can provide. A lot of work is going on in the area of medical diagnosis. A computer-based body of knowledge is built up about an area of medical interest, heart problems, respiratory difficulties, etc. Much of the data collected is significant when combined with other factors, and inferences have to be drawn when the information collected from the user is analysed. The user, in this case a doctor, will have a dialogue with the computer and provide all the available information he has about the case. The expert system that has been written to collate and analyse this information will come up with conclusions based on the data that were originally fed into it. These conclusions may not be enough for the user who may wish to delve further at certain points to know why the system is asking specific questions or drawing particular inferences. The user can therefore ask the expert system to explain itself at any point. Thus, such an expert system can come to a useful conclusion, given sufficient information, but also show the user how it reached those conclusions. The tutorial possibilities for training are there but the difficulties and costs of providing comprehensive systems are usually extensive.

THE OFFICE OF THE FUTURE

We have already discussed or touched upon a number of developments that will form part of the office of the future. Computer suppliers are desperately trying to pull these and other products together to make a coherent whole. Why? The cynical answer must be that the office is the largest untapped area of business left for the computer to move into.

Nobody has a clear idea how the office of the future *will* develop, although a number of vested interests are quite clear as to how they would *like* it to develop. However, one trend is clear: more and more information, whether data (text, graphics or numbers), pictures or voice, will be carried over networks. To make effective use of these networks, office staff, from the manager down, will increasingly have to become familiar with using VDUs – a training challenge in itself. As staff become familiar with terminals, they will send messages, letters and make appointments via the network, and will tend to file this information on disk storage rather than in filing cabinets. We thus get electronic mail, electronic filing and the paperless

[1] *Expert Systems in the Microelectronic Age* edited by D Michie, EUP, 1979

office, perhaps more accurately called the less-paper office, which will rely instead on the same information accumulating in a huge data base accessible only from the terminals.

The telephone switchboard may well become the hub of the network, connecting computer to computer as well as person to person. Many experts regard viewdata (fairly recently espoused by IBM) as a key element in communicating between offices via the telephone network because it is relatively cheap and quite easy for the layman to use.

Secretaries will use word processing systems to produce reports and documents. Word processors will generally be linked into the network and the finished product will often be transmitted to the recipient and printed at the receiving end, or it may be read from a screen and electronically filed without ever being printed.

Telex is a widely used method of cheap transmission of printed data, and the principle will continue in improved form as teletex, which gives higher speed, both upper and lower case letters, editing of text, etc.

Pictures need to be sent around the country and facsimile transmission (fax) is now a proven technology. A picture is read at the transmitting end and printed at the receiving end, providing a remote copy. The method can be regarded as similar to photocopying, with the scanning at one end of a telephone line and the printing at the other. In fact, it has been found that fax is mainly used for transmitting text. Storing pictures on the computer takes up large amounts of disk storage and is expensive, but with developments like videodisc, picture Prestel and image processing using the computer, the office of the slightly more distant future will handle pictures along with data and voice. Person to person conversations may be carried on using vision-phones where speakers can see each other as well as talk. The technique that is available today of holding remote meetings over television links, will also develop. Add to all the above the capability to control the building environment – heat, light, lifts, etc and to control access using security systems, and the term 'office of the future' is fairly all-embracing.

This, then, is the theory and certainly some of the above will come to pass – indeed it is already happening. But there are problems. With word processors from a multiplicity of manufacturers being installed in the office, new telephone switchboards being bought, and computer terminals spreading, there is the problem of equipment from different suppliers. Each piece probably does the job it was purchased to do, but there is little or no chance of linking them together to form an integrated system. To plan for an integrated system covering much of what has already been discussed means tying the firm to one equipment supplier for many years and no supplier yet has the whole strategy for the development of office systems clearly mapped out.

There are considerable costs involved in installing a sophisticated office system not only for equipment, but also as a result of changed procedures, attitudes, and methods of working generally. Not least of the problems is that of office staff who may have seen or experienced the changes in working methods that have been brought about by the increasing use of computer terminals. Word processors are often seen as a threat not only to jobs but also to working conditions and job satisfaction.

From this picture of opportunity and confusion, one thing emerges quite clearly for the trainer. More and more people are going to have terminals at, or close to, their place of work. In many cases they will be wholly appropriate tools for training and, in most cases, they will be useful adjuncts for substantial parts of training. The office of the future thus provides opportunities for trainers, provided their attitudes can change as well.

THE HOME OF THE FUTURE

The developments of home computing, Prestel, and the wiring of Britain for multi-channel cable television are paving the way for substantial changes in the home. These developments mean that it will be possible to order goods from the home, review the holiday offerings and vacancies of various firms, book and pay for the selected holiday and read up-to-date news on the television at any time selectively. They will also provide home banking, so that payments can be made directly using the home terminal. This is another step towards the cashless society.

The Open University has been very successful in using television and radio for parts of its courses. With many channels available, the possibilities for home education expand considerably, and the capability of two-way communication provides for interaction.

With improved data communication over the telephone system and compact portable terminals becoming available, it will become easier for employees to send information to the office, receive messages and request information held in the office system. It should become possible for people to work from home most of the time. Some people who frequently work from home, such as salesmen and service engineers, will be able to do so more efficiently and executives will be able to communicate with the office system without rushing in after a business trip or meeting. Programmers, some typists, and many office personnel could do some of their work from home, which might mean working at the office for only half the time. So, perhaps the office of the future will be partly in the home. (Such exotica as talking ovens and automatic vacuum cleaners are considered to be beyond the scope of this book.)

THE CHANGING ROLE OF WORK

This topic is under continuous discussion and is highly political. In the space available here, we can only touch on some of the factors relevant to, or caused by, the rapid development of uses for the computer and microprocessor.

Some investigators argue that espousing computer aids and developing indigenous expertise in building and programming systems will lead to the creation of as many jobs as are lost. Others point to substantial job losses already experienced due to automated production techniques, and higher productivity in some cases where word processors have been introduced into the office. They conclude that, if uncontrolled, these trends will cause catastrophic unemployment and civil strife.

It seems clear that job losses will occur among the less skilful and less well-educated. Assembly lines are being automated; some clerical jobs in banking and insurance, for example, are being eliminated. But skilled jobs are also being lost. One modern signal-box on British Rail, run by a handful of people, replaces dozens of the old type spread along the track. Modern electronic circuitry is highly reliable with the result that fewer maintenance engineers are required for computers, telephone equipment, radios, etc. The level of skill of the service engineer is often less, because repair is a matter of replacing printed circuit boards and sending the faulty boards back to a workshop. Computer-aided design (CAD) is developing rapidly and will reduce the number of draughtsmen who are needed. Computer typesetting of national and local newspapers has caused considerable strife between unions and management.

The examples mentioned above are all occurring today. Some of the developments mentioned earlier in this chapter have yet to have a marked effect. A few can be itemized:

1. videotape and videodisc – on the already embattled cinema industry;
2. shopping from home – on traditional shops, travel agents, and insurance brokers, particularly the small corner shop business;
3. working from home and video conferencing – on the need for offices and commuter and business transport;
4. home news information – on the daily newspapers and the technical press;
5. home education – on the traditional structure of evening classes, etc for vocational study, and further education in general. The Open Tech is an interesting concept or group of concepts that will impinge on this area. The Open Tech is currently being established in Britain and aims to provide tuition for men and women seeking technical skills. The tuition will be provided not by a formal course of instruction leading to a conventional qualification, but in a variety of individualized and other study methods. The existing network of colleges of further and higher education will be used along with other organizations. There are obvious parallels with the Open University, but the organization of the Open Tech will be quite different;
6. better electronic communications – on the traditional postal delivery service.

The way in which we work is going to change and will almost certainly mean increased leisure for the majority through a combination of a shorter working week, longer holidays and earlier retirement. What we do with the extra time is a matter of considerable interest to the (expanding) leisure industry. Some of that time will be spent learning new skills. Distance learning is a phrase that is currently in vogue and describes methods of learning where the student is separated from the instructor. It covers computer-based training and computer-assisted learning as well as audio-visual and videodisc teaching, printed study packs and correspondence courses. As the market for such courses expands, so will new and improved methods of presentation. As is stated elsewhere, the cost equation for using CBT is coming right in more and more circumstances, so developments are likely to be rapid.

COMPUTING CHECKLIST

You may be in a position where you have to use existing computing equipment or you may have to select a complete system purely for training purposes. Whatever your circumstances, use this checklist selectively as not all points will be relevant in every situation. Some of the items will be more meaningful when you have read Part 3.

Which CBT system(s) are we considering?
What training is going to use CBT?
Where is the training going to take place?
How many trainees will there be?
How many hours training?
   course hours
   student hours
What is the time scale?
Is the computer system decided for us?
What computer systems do the CBT systems under consideration run on?
What machine facilities are required?
   computer memory
   disk or diskette storage
   processor (CPU) speed
   terminal support
   (these may be additional if using an existing machine)

Screens
Are screens to be used?
What sort of keyboard?
Is a printer necessary?
   If so, is one needed for each terminal?
   What speed?
   What quality of print?
How many columns and lines on the screen?
Do we need graphics?

What sort?

What resolution?

Is colour needed?

What other features (touch-sensitive, light pen, etc) are necessary?

Are any other devices needed (plotter, graphics tablet, etc)?

Are any special connections needed (interface to machines, video-disc, etc)?

Are all the devices you want to attach supported by the computer operating system and the CBT system?

Which rooms are the terminals going into?

Is there room for study material and terminal?

Is the lighting adequate?

Are there restrictions on access?

Have we a data processing department?

Can/will it provide support?

What level?

On what basis?

For how long?

Do the computer experts need special training?

Who pays?

How much does the training department need to know on the computer side?

How is it going to get that expertise?

What training does the CBT system supplier provide?

What other support can we expect from the CBT system supplier?

Is it in writing?

What other firms use the CBT system we are considering?

Have we visited any of them?

What did we find out?

Are their systems directly comparable with ours?

What is the documentation like?

What are the costs? Are they one-off, lease or rental?

New system?

Additions to existing system?

Are there telephone charges for the terminal network?

Training of DP personnel?

Training of trainers?

CBT system?

People?

What maintenance costs are there?

What consumables are there (paper, diskettes, cassettes, graph paper, etc)?

Do we plan (hope) to expand the system?

How (add new computers, expand existing system, LAN, etc)?

Will the CBT system still run?

What will it cost?

Do we qualify for an educational discount?
   Have we got it?
Have we shopped around where appropriate?
   If one supplier is much cheaper, why is he?
   Is his maintenance adequate and reliable?
Does the company have agreements with the unions about types of
   screens, working conditions, etc?

Part 3
Computer-based training

INTRODUCTION

Computer terminology abounds in acronyms and we have used several in Part 2. We have talked about computer-based training (CBT) already, without attempting to define clearly what we mean. We have rather left the reader, if he is not already familiar with the term, with his own picture of CBT. As well as CBT, we have computer-assisted (or aided) instruction (or learning), CAI or CAL, computer-assisted (or aided) training (or teaching), CAT, and computer-managed learning (or instruction), CML or CMI. So, what do we mean by CBT and the rest? We plan to limit ourselves to three acronyms from among the list: CBT, CAT and CML. They are related as shown:

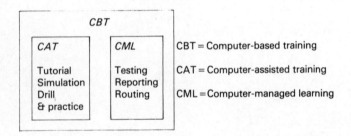

Computer-based training (CBT) is a generic term that covers both computer-assisted training and computer-managed learning. Computer-assisted training (CAT) means using the computer as an interactive training medium through tutorials, simulations and drill and practice. Computer-managed learning (CML) means using the computer to direct the student through a course which may, or may not, be computer-based. The path the student follows is dependent on the results of tests and measures of performance taken during the course. Reports of various kinds are also produced. We have attempted to describe the other acronyms in the glossary but they frequently mean what the user wants them to mean.

At this point, it is also appropriate to explain what we mean by author languages and authoring systems. Author languages are special purpose languages to enable trainers to produce tutorial training material for students working at a terminal. Authoring systems consist of an author language as well as a number of aids for the author, to make his life easier. The most important aid is a good screen editor that permits the author to modify his courses easily.

So, this part of the book describes CBT. We describe how it fits into the training spectrum and when it may be appropriate. A major problem in designing solutions to training problems using CBT is the transfer of the design from paper to screen, and the screen design itself. This transfer problem is discussed at length in earlier chapters. To help readers understand the scope of, and problems with, an author language, we have developed a hypothetical author language. A chapter is devoted to testing and evaluation – an area which is too often overlooked because it comes at the end of the project and is time-consuming and tedious to do properly. It may, of course, also cast doubt on training material that you have burnt the midnight oil to produce. Chapter 16 discusses computer-managed learning as a topic, although aspects of CML are intrinsic to any authoring system. Part 3 ends with a chapter on commercially available authoring systems and indicates the computers on which they run. A problem with discussing authoring systems is that they can vary from £50 to £100 for a diskette and a manual, to a hundred thousand pounds or more for a system that is sold to include the computer and terminals. We have tried to indicate the extent of the facilities provided in a brief overview of the more well known systems.

10. CBT in the spectrum of training technology

INTRODUCTION

A computer, particularly a micro, is an extremely seductive acquisition. There are so many attractions: the great range of applications, the easy portability, the rapid programme implementation capability and the relative ease of use – all these are powerfully appealing to the neophyte training designer. All other possible training methods are soon relegated to the status of yesterday's newspaper.

THE COMPUTER AS A TRAINING AID

Any organization introducing the computer to its training programmes must be constantly aware that the trainers' view of their profession is not affected by what one writer has called 'media myopia'. Symptomatic of media myopia is 'the belief that a single medium will provide the answers to all educational problems'.[1] In recent years such a belief has been expressed by advocates of teaching machines and educational television. Teaching machines have now virtually disappeared; they are the dinosaurs of education. The reasons for the extraordinarily short life of the teaching machine are many and not entirely pedagogic. As we shall see, the fate of teaching machines was not totally irrelevant to the future of computers in training applications, where self-instructional lessons are envisaged.

Unlike teaching machines, television is remarkable for its ubiquity. However, in many organizations the medium seems to be rarely used as a means of acquiring or enhancing competence – more as one of the many tools available for conveying information or stimulating interest. While these are undoubtedly vital stages in the learning process, numerous devices other than the television are capable of performing this role. On the other hand it would be quite misleading to discuss the computer as a training aid on the same terms as the blackboard, the slide projector or the television set. The question 'Which of these media teaches best?' is the wrong question. More helpful would be the question 'How can these media contribute to an effective training system?'

Training systems can be classified and described according to many cri-

[1] *Toward Defining The Role of CAI* M Dence, Educational Technology, Nov 1980

teria. The criterion which seems to us to have greatest value to the training designer is that of adaptability.

In Figure 10.1 we can see how this criterion applies to a variety of educational strategies. The figure shows educational and training devices grouped into two main categories. The first category includes uses of the media to transmit information from the teacher to the learner, in a one-way communication system. The other grouping comprises methods or devices which function as two-way communication systems; that is they make some provision for student responses. This provision may be 'fixed' or 'flexible'. Flexible presentations include strategies which, one way or another, arrange for the teaching sequence and content to adjust to the learner's progress, as indicated by his responses to questions, problems and other stimuli. Strategies reacting to learner feedback in this way are known as adaptive or correctable systems. The computer, in which cybernetic principles are axiomatic to its design, is an ideal basis on which to develop adaptive teaching and studying methods.

	One-way[1] communication systems	Two-way[2] communication systems	
Fixed presentation[3]	Radio Tape recordings Film – loop 　　　– strip 　　　– radio vision 　　　– moving 　　　– silent/sound Television (open) Television (cctv)	Films　with TV　　students' Radio　responses Language laboratories Linear programmed 　instruction	A systems approach　Team teaching[5]
Flexible presentation[4]	—	Programmed instruction Adaptive mechanisms Computer-assisted 　instruction	

Key:
1. No interaction between communicator and receiver.
2. Interaction between communicator and receiver.
3. Presentation order does not alter (despite 2).
4. Presentation order depends on student responses.
5. Methods integrating 'appropriate' techniques.

Figure 10.1 Teaching methods considered as communication systems

Extract reproduced with kind permission of the author from Hartley, J (ed)
Strategies for Programmed Instruction, London, Butterworths, 1972

Clearly there is no way that the teacher or trainer in the classroom can adjust and develop his lesson to the learning disposition of each individual member of the class. Group work, team teaching, proctors and many other strategies have all contributed to mitigating the worst effects of this problem. But the difficulties remain. All learners have different rates of learning, prefer different approaches to learning, have different objectives, are motivated differently, and so on.

Programmed instruction

Programmed instruction (PI) was the first major effort to find a solution to this problem. Programmed courses are designed for specific categories of learners. They are interactive. They develop new knowledge and skills in trainees through a sequence of exercises, presented so as to lead the vast majority of learners to mastery of the chosen topic of study. The well designed programme steers a course between frequently losing the student in blind alleys and spoonfeeding him every step of the way towards his goal.

The aspiring author of self-instructional programmes must pay constant attention to three fundamental principles of course design. First, he must ensure that the learners are active. Students learn what you cause them to rather than what you tell them. Thus, effective courses tend to include frequent questions and problems testing understanding at successive stages of learning. Second, the learners should be able to check the correctness and relevance of their responses to questions and solutions to problems. In other words the programme should provide knowledge of results as the trainee progresses towards mastery. Finally, the scheme of learning should be so arranged that solutions to questions, calculations, discriminations and other problem-solving activities, tend towards correctness or mastery. It may be true that we learn from our mistakes, but if we begin to make too many it is likely that all we will learn is to avoid the error-prone activity in future. The drop-out rates for the learning of Latin and the violin demonstrate this very well.

The design system for programmed instruction is a microcosm of the design system known as training technology. Unfortunately, the methodology of PI has usually tended to give second place to the more easily recognizable product – the programmed text and, at one time, the teaching machine. The curious little books with missing words, the pages in strange sequences, and the expensive and complicated machines, alienated and disillusioned many teachers and trainers who sought Thorndike's famous 'miracle of mechanical ingenuity...', which would arrange for a student to receive page two of a book only when he could demonstrate understanding of page one.[1]

For some, a teaching machine like the Auto-Tutor Mark II, embodied just such a miracle. The Auto-Tutor seemed to be capable of providing the crucial characteristic of individualization of instruction claimed for the

[1] E L Thorndike, Education, 1912 cited in *Programmed Learning in Perspective*, Thomas, Davies *et al*, Lamson Technical Products, 1963

branching or 'intrinsic' system of PI by its progenitor, Norman Crowder. Crowder called his method 'intrinsic' because the student controls his own progress through a lesson, by the responses he makes to the questions or problems he meets. These questions are couched in multiple-choice form to enable him to select the route or branch appropriate to his understanding of the material. As Crowder observed, 'a programme with multiple-choice questions is not an intrinsic programme unless each separate answer choice in each question leads the student to material prepared especially for the student who has made that particular choice'.[1]

In practice this principle is not easy to follow. A brief inspection of a few branching programmes in print form will soon reveal that, very often, despite the use of multiple-choice questions, students who make particular choices do *not* receive material appropriate only to that choice. Often, when a student has made an incorrect response, he is simply told that he is wrong and asked to choose another option from the original set of three or four. A programme based entirely on such a strategy will permit its students to progress from beginning to end, by trial and error, without ever demonstrating a genuine understanding of the topic in question. The programme never adapts to the individual learner's response.

A genuine element of learner control can only be provided by inserting remedial sequences of frames for all incorrect responses. Yet how complex is the resulting maze of paths the author must design in order to permit even a modest element of individualization. The danger still remains that among the remedial material by-passed by the student, who by skill or good fortune selects the correct response, there may be some content of value to all. This problem arises because, as Anderson has observed, 'any single item in a branching programme is a fallible basis for branching decisions, often yielding false positives'. He concludes, 'when more elaborate and less error-prone procedures, such as those that presumably could be implemented with computer-assisted instruction are used to make branching decisions, then there may be an advantage to branching techniques'.[2] One also recalls Skinner's observation that posing multiple-choice questions offers the student the opportunity to make an error he might not otherwise have made.

A computer-based training course
In CBT, by storing lessons in a computer rather than in the pages of a book, many of the drawbacks of the intrinsic programme in print form may be removed. CBT offers a clear gain over printed materials in three major areas: the first of these, the area discussed by Anderson, concerns the process by which the student is routed through the lesson. In Chapter 3 (pages 38-51) we have seen that when students respond with reasonable but unexpected answers to problems in printed linear texts, there is no guidance. To provide

[1] *Intrinsic Programming* Norman Crowder, US Industries (no date)
[2] Richard C Anderson, Educational Psychology in *Annual Review of Psychology*, Vol XVIII, 1967

even a modest amount of remedial text requires a book of daunting complexity.

The second major potential advantage of CBT over printed texts is in the area known as computer-managed learning (CML) or computer-managed instruction (CMI). Whereas teaching machines were designed principally to deliver specific lessons, a computer can serve a far wider range of purposes in course management. Figure 10.2 illustrates how the computer may be used to route students to resources appropriate to their needs. Of course, the computer-based lesson option shown here need not always use Control Data's PLATO system. Similar systems are briefly discussed in Chapter 17.

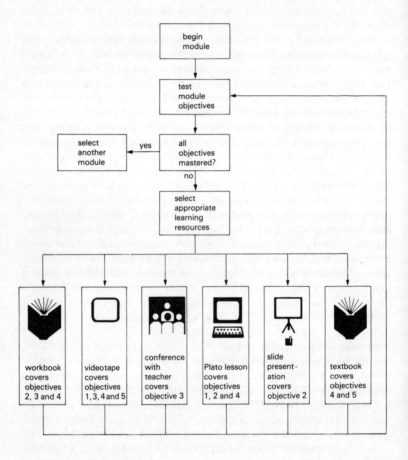

Figure 10.2 A CML system
Reproduced by kind permission of Control Data Corporation

At the start of a course the computer can assist in diagnosing the trainee's specific knowledge and skill deficiencies. His performance on an entry test can determine whether he needs further instruction in a particular subject and, if so, to what depth. The form this instruction might take could be audio-visual, printed, computer-based or live instruction.

A CML approach provides training design staff and management with performance data far more easily than a paper-based system. Pre- and post-test results, gain scores and so forth from validated programmes can establish the extent of trainees' success and their readiness for work in new procedures. At an earlier stage when programmes are still in draft form, the computer can monitor student responses to every question or problem, and can record in free-format any opinions or comments students care to make. Such data are invaluable for effective lesson development.[1]

A computer-based course development system enables the training designer to vary his teaching strategy and integrate different methods, without the awkwardness which often characterizes a mixed-media approach. Education and training specialists often talk about different approaches to teaching like case studies, simulation, drill and practice and so forth, as if they were mutually exclusive. Combinations of many of these methods may be applied in most courses, and frequently within particular sessions. This integration can be achieved with the use of the computer.

SIMULATION

Of all teaching methods simulation demonstrates most vividly the advantages of using the computer. The table in Figure 10.3 includes four types of simulation used in higher education and training. Some of these applications could be run, albeit in a rather clumsy way, using other presentation methods. For others, a non-computer simulation is not feasible. Let us consider one or two examples.

System facsimiles
The application which is called 'system facsimile' in the table will appeal to a wide range of businesses in which large numbers of customer or product records are filed. Typical of such businesses are television rental companies, airlines, public utilities, credit card companies, etc. The files of such businesses often contain tens of thousands of entries. An essential feature of the training of staff consulting these records is practice with a range of customer or product categories.

In the television rental company, for example, customers may pay the rental for their sets over a range of frequencies from weekly to six-monthly, and by a variety of methods from cash to bankers' order. Overdue payments may also be treated in a number of ways depending on such factors as the size

[1] Chapter 16 discusses this process in more detail

Type	Definition	Example
System facsimile	Reproduction of large-scale business system permitting *safe practice* on infinite examples	Air-line booking, TV rentals, credit card accounts
Process modelling	Demonstrates 'how it works'; enables study of effects of changing variables	Chemical plant, population growth, the effect of pollution on the environment
Apparatus operation	Using the computer to control selection, sequence and speed of practice items and give feedback	Radar, typing, flight simulation
Decision-making exercises	Presentation of problem situation requiring trainee to make a series of decisions to resolve problem	Fault-finding, action mazes, diplomacy, management games

Figure 10.3 CAT simulations in occupational training

and duration of the debt, the credit history of the customer and so on. The training will include intensive practice on a large number of cases drawn randomly from all types of customers. In the case of customers in arrears, practice may well be given on the appropriate action to take in recovering the debt. In a highly competitive service industry of this kind, sending the wrong letter at the wrong time can lose business. Practice with real cases is obviously a possibility but risky for the new recruit. It is much better to develop a file of dummy accounts large enough to provide extensive practice on a wide range of cases. This file can be stored in the computer. It will be capable of providing sufficient examples of account variation to give the trainee as much practice as necessary.

The phase of training immediately preceding practice using the dummy file will consist of demonstrations of the procedures to follow. These may be presented by the method most suitable to the trainees, taking account of available resources and the nature of the subject. Direct interaction with the terminal will not always be appropriate. But, for drill and practice in processing arrears, no other method could offer the quantity and variety of practice that can be achieved by storing the practice accounts in a computer file. In addition to the far greater number of accounts the computer can store, the trainer can include the capability to simplify or upgrade the complexity of the test examples, presented in relation to the ease with which the trainees deal with problems. An adaptive capability of this kind would be very difficult to administer in a conventional print-based mode.

Process modelling

There is another very powerful kind of simulation which we have called process modelling. As Figure 10.3 suggests, this type of simulation is fundamentally demonstrative in purpose. It seeks to answer the question 'How does it work?'

The example of the chemical plant cited in the figure was a simulation of a refrigeration plant producing ice and chilled brine for use in the manufacture of dyestuffs. The simulation was one element in a training package for operators which included audio-visual materials, manuals and printed performance aids. Following the audio-visual overview of the operating principle and components of a refrigeration system, the operator's understanding of the refrigeration concept is tested using graphical presentations of different stages of the process on a VDU.

Apparatus operation

Equipment simulators

Computer-based simulations of the operation of complex equipment have been well-known in the training of such professions as airline pilots and in military applications for some years. A complete reproduction of a DC 10 in flight will cost millions of dollars (possibly even more than the real thing) but is an essential feature of the training of the contemporary pilot. The resources required to develop a jet aircraft simulator are usually denied to the average company trainer. However, a less spectacular application than the flight simulator which will be within the technical and financial capability of many trainers has been demonstrated by the Royal Navy. This is described in Chapter 9, pages 121-122.

Drill and practice simulators

This kind of simulation enables operators to receive intensive practice of a manual skill and/or discrimination skill, and gradually increase their speed or accuracy of performance. Drill and practice is important in the related areas of keyboard training for data-input staff, typists transferring to word processors with new keyboard facilities, and others needing to use the terminal to access information programmes which are needed to perform other clerical procedures.

Language learning is another area where intensive practice with prompting is often desirable. Sequences giving drill in the use of particular grammatical formalities are easily developed and can be immensely effective. One interesting experiment in the field of adult literacy education is a project on basic word recognition. The problem, here, is to develop a tutorial sequence to enable low-motivated learners to build up the confidence to learn in what is, after all, a rather embarrassing situation. The learning programme ensemble consists of a computer program which runs on a Pet microcomputer linked to two cassette tape recorders. One of these carries a so-called 'empty structure tutorial'. This structure enables the tutor to present verbal material of his own choice on the VDU. The second cassette is used to synchronize the transmission of the spoken word or words, with their appearance on the screen. Using this system the student may receive as much intensive practice on word recognition as he can accommodate.

Decision-making simulations

Our final category of simulation demonstrates clearly how the trainer can exploit the strengths of the computer to achieve an effect that would be far more difficult to achieve through another medium. Situations frequently arise in both manufacturing and service industries in which managers and operators must choose one of a number of possible solutions to a problem. Sometimes the choice leads simply to another choice and so on.

In the training context, a series of nested, multiple-choice problems of this kind is known as an action maze. The problem which typically confronts the learner picking his way through the maze may be paraphrased as, 'Your choice leads to this change in the situation; what will you do now?' This kind of sequence occurs frequently in management training exercises simulating the running of a business or, in manufacturing industries, in the testing of the ability of a chemical plant operator to respond to emergency signals.

Management games

The computer-based management game is an interesting business application in the decision-making category. Typically, a game will involve teams of managers working as rivals. A common game scenario requires teams to establish and manage a production company. Teams must take decisions about the type and level of investment, production capacity, marketing strategy, and so on. At each stage, the consequences of their decisions are analysed by the computer and further decisions are required. Besides simply carrying out the necessary arithmetical and statistical functions, the computer will be used to simulate the passage of time and may randomly adjust external variables such as exchange rates, interest rates and pay rises. Games may include a requirement to use particular tools of financial management such as break-even charts and network analysis. Activities of such complexity will consume considerable resources. The expense may well be worth it since a well-designed game may remain valid over a period of years and be capable of use by a wide variety of staff.

INFORMATION RETRIEVAL

Training does not have clearly defined frontiers. Many other disciplines affecting human performance at work contribute to the acquisition and improvement of knowledge and skills. Ergonomics, the science of man-machine systems, is one such discipline. Information retrieval is another field of expertise which impinges on the work of the training designer. Information retrieval implies the use of the computer to store, sort and process masses of data, so that users may obtain virtually endless permutations of categories of the data stored. Thus economists may obtain information about products and sales in relation to such variables as numbers manufactured, social class of purchasers, annual volume of sales, profit, correlation with sales of other products, etc. A valuable application of information retrieval in education and training may be seen in the various computer-based abstracting and reference systems.

Both the individual and institutional trainers and educators have access to public information retrieval systems using television as a means of communication. The various categories of viewdata are described in more detail in Chapter 9. Many opportunities exist whereby a viewdata system could be integrated into an overall training system. For example, a course on financial administration for managers could include exercises requiring the participants to search and apply the stock market information of the day.

11. When is CBT worth considering?

INTRODUCTION

Computer-based training is not a panacea. It is quite inappropriate in some instances and quite out of the question as regards cost in others. We set the scene by looking at three situations where CBT may be appropriate. Two are hypothetical and the third is an outline of how the Barclaycard system developed. We then discuss the major factors involved in deciding whether to use CBT in a company.

THE AUDIENCE

Company training often involves employees being taken away from home for days or weeks to attend formal courses. There may be a dozen or so gathered from all over the country and accommodated in hotels or company hostels. Alternatively, the company may send out teams of instructors to conduct courses at local premises. This can be expensive in terms of hotel bills, travel, room and equipment hire, etc.

If the course only runs a few times a year, some employees may have to wait before they can attend it while others may go earlier than they would ideally like. If an employee misses the course that he should attend, through illness or pressure of work, a lot of subject matter may have been acquired in other ways and bad habits may have developed by the time another opportunity arises.

There are benefits to the company and to the employer in attending courses whether they are in-company or commercial. They include the opportunity for people from different backgrounds and from different locations to meet informally as well as in groups and this should therefore have a broadening effect on those attending – frequently on the instructors, too. Attending public courses may, in addition, provide fresh views and experiences that cast a new perspective on the job. Certain topics are also more suitable for group presentation, eg some managerial skills such as communicating. These and perhaps other benefits are real, but they are intangible and unpredictable in their extent, where the costs are substantial and quantifiable.

Let us consider two hypothetical situations where the use of CBT techniques would be appropriate, and one actual case study where the use of CBT techniques proved highly successful, and attempt to draw some conclusions from them.

Case 1 – the ABC Bank
The ABC Bank consists of hundreds of branches, each of which must carry out its banking functions according to standard procedures. Each branch is well provided with computer terminals but they are mostly of a specialized nature, and the data processing department which runs the system will not be especially anxious to have training clogging up its computers. Nevertheless, the training department decided that these standard procedures lent themselves to a CBT approach. Some of the main reasons were as follows:

1. the highly formalized procedures are boring to teach regularly and to learn in the classroom, but all trainees must attain minimum, measurable standards on all topics;
2. branches are often reluctant to release staff for several days, but a CBT terminal in the branch can be used for short periods at any time during the day;
3. no travel or other direct expenses are incurred;
4. the training department can still monitor and assess the progress of the students;
5. there is a large body of students over which to spread the cost of developing material;
6. branch banking staff are, or should be, familiar with the use of terminals;
7. local managers and specialists are available to supplement the CBT courses with hints, tips and expert comment, but are not called upon to give lessons;
8. procedures and rules change frequently – non-CBT systems and printed manuals cope with change awkwardly.

So, despite the fact that the proposals required one terminal in almost every branch to be dedicated to the training function, the training department persuaded senior management that a substantial investment in a CBT system was desirable and justified. The system that they installed, after a pilot project, consisted of a number of minicomputers, each of which could support up to 20 terminals at any one time. The minicomputers were installed in various parts of the country serving about 50 branches and each branch had one terminal. If someone dialled into the terminal network and found that the system was busy, he had to try again later. As more material was developed the 'busy situation' increased in frequency. When it became serious enough, more equipment was purchased.

As the system developed, training material was mounted on the system to train all branch personnel, from the manager down, in new procedures. After initial resistance by senior personnel and some hasty PR work by training management, the training terminals became accepted tools for all staff for relevant training.

The training department decided to have a central minicomputer linked to each of the other minicomputers in a computer network as shown in Figure 11.1. This allowed the trainers to develop and update courses, collect statistics and monitor use by transferring data between the remote minicomputers and the central system using telephone lines. It was considered that this permitted the training department to retain responsibility for the training despite dispersing the provision of the courses.

Thus, the ABC Bank made and justified its decision. The DEF Bank, with an almost identical problem, decided to install stand-alone microcomputers in 15 different branches, in a pilot project. The lack of central control was accepted as were the considerably higher administrative costs in distributing courses and collecting statistics. It was, however, considered that the higher capital costs and the need for skilled computer personnel made a mini- or mainframe computer solution too expensive.

Case 2 – The Worldwide Oil Exploration Company
This company had expensive drilling equipment and was very unwilling to have it sitting idle due to breakdowns and malfunctions. It needed engineers who could diagnose and repair faults rapidly. Most of the company's recruits were skilled in their relevant field but needed the specific expertise of drilling equipment maintenance and operation. After much thought and sophisticated costings the company decided to go for a combination of CBT, a computer simulation of the main control panel, high quality printed material, and videotape with a minimum of instructor involvement. The main reasons were as follows:

1. traditional instructor-led courses were unsuitable as the engineers were recruited spasmodically and courses would often run with only one student. However, instructors or supervisors were necessary for some of the practical work. It would also be difficult to train, and retrain, instructors in all the skills;
2. the mixed media approach reduced boredom; videotape, for example, was useful to demonstrate instrumentation, moving parts, etc and the knowledge of students was systematically assessed by tests in the CBT material which linked into the simulation;
3. the cost of employing and training these engineers is very high, so expensive training methods, if effective, can be justified.

Case 3 – Barclaycard
The previous examples have been hypothetical; this one is an actual case study. Barclaycard is one of the two main credit card companies in the United Kingdom, operated by the major banks. It is very highly computerized and there is virtually no aspect of the business (which includes issuing cards, collecting and posting remittances, replacing lost and stolen cards and

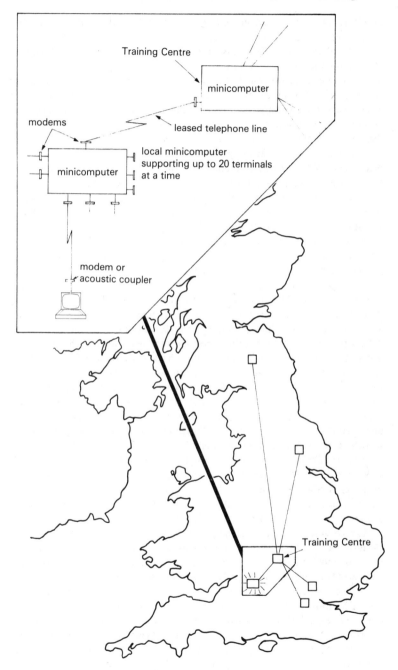

Figure 11.1 The computer network for the ABC Bank

monitoring customers' account status) that does not involve some action on the computer's part. Of course, virtually all of the 80 or so tasks require some form of human input. This may vary in complexity from straightforward procedures such as writing an account number on a pre-printed form, to quite complex processes such as deciding whether to increase a customer's credit limit. But in almost every case, including the two cited, the clerk will either access the computer to obtain or check information, or give the computer an instruction to amend the account data in some way. Thus, to find the account number to be entered on a document, the clerk may obtain the number from a particular program that lists the customers in alphabetical order. The decision about the credit limit may be made by inspecting another set of data that gives details of a customer's recent financial history. This information is accessed on VDU terminals, which are linked into the company's mainframe computer, by a large number of work-groups each consisting of eight or nine staff at seven different centres. Altogether, there are over 1500 people within the company who are trained to work in these work-groups. Thus, new staff joining work-groups require training both in the procedures appropriate to particular tasks, as well as in the selection and interpretation of the computer-based information programs that provide the information necessary to carry out those tasks.

Until 1977, lecture/demonstrations and exercises in the classroom were the main vehicles for this training. Courses for trainees from all the branch offices took place at the Northampton Head Office. In 1977, the company initiated a scheme to transfer most of the basic task training for the work-groups into computer-based form. Since all work-groups used computer terminals, in addition to the 500 or so data entry staff keying in information from customers' vouchers at terminals, it was decided to use the computer as the main vehicle for training. As IBM users, it was natural for Barclaycard to adopt IBM's authoring language, ITS (Interactive Training System). This was the precursor to IIS (see Chapter 17).

A team of authors was recruited and trained in authoring techniques and took up the formidable challenge of writing CBT lessons for some 80 or so procedures. Since the material to be learned was entirely textual, ITS proved quite suitable for the purpose. As lessons were completed, they were made available to trainees in the various regional offices.

The volume of training materials developed is high and the demands on the terminals used for production work are constant and heavy. So it has not been possible for CBT to be provided on the terminals in normal use. Hence, dedicated training terminals have been made available away from the normal work place. By now it is probably true to say that new entrants to Barclaycard learn most of the day-to-day tasks performed in work-groups through CBT courses. The experiences of Barclaycard have been widely quoted and it is certainly one of the most successful and largest users of CBT in the country. It is relevant to note that the skills taught are those connected with the use of terminals.

What help can these specific examples give in considering whether a CBT course is suitable, or whether a substantial investment in equipment is worthwhile to permit extensive use of CBT techniques?

Managers' attitudes

It is often found, as with the ABC Bank, that managers are not initially very enthusiastic about using CBT for their personal training. This is due mainly to a fear of the medium. Nowadays, school leavers are joining firms with no fear of sitting at and using microcomputers and terminals, but managers are often unfamiliar with a keyboard, let alone all the rest of the equipment, and are afraid of losing face by making fools of themselves. Thus, if it is decided that management should do some training using CBT, and there are commercially available courses from, for example, Control Data with PLATO, it may be worth the additional cost of taking them away from their subordinates so that they can be taught how to use the medium without feeling self-conscious. This fear of the medium is not, of course, peculiar to managers.

If you have a large computer with a timesharing network of terminals and some computer time to spare, the potential exists for developing CBT courses, subject to a few provisos. Data processing managers will frequently wish to regard the use of the computer for training as an ideal application when there is machine capacity to spare, but increasingly it will become rather a nuisance as the computer becomes heavily loaded or computer staff resources become stretched. Successful implementation and operation of the large machine CBT systems (IIS on IBM or ASET on Univac, for example) involves a substantial and continuing commitment on the part of the data processing department.

Assuming that it is feasible to set up such a system with suitable guarantees of continuity, at whom should the training be directed?

Clerical and data entry skills

The Barclaycard example shows how this 'piggybacking' approach has been very effective in training clerical staff and data entry clerks on identical terminals to those that they will use in their daily work, while a simulation with dummy data permits them to practise precisely the operations that they must carry out on the job, rapidly and accurately, on a routine basis. There are similar applications in telephone sales, order entry, airline bookings and many standard screen-based data entry functions. Companies with a large staff of clerks doing routine operations according to well-defined standards may be able to make very effective use of CBT, providing better, more stimulating training than traditional methods.

Data processing training

Another area where there is a lot of interest in training packages for these piggybacking systems is in the training of data processing personnel themselves, although this is not highlighted in the case studies. There are training modules for operators, programmers and analysts in considerable variety of topic and quality. A consideration of some of the factors that have caused this area to grow may be instructive. Data processing is a young, fast-changing industry that has traditionally had a rapid turnover of personnel. Terminals tend to be available for the staff to use at work and they are therefore used to them. There is a wide audience available that needs training and that is likely to be sympathetic to the medium. In addition, data processing training courses have been very expensive. Lastly, with the mobile employees in this field, companies may not be averse to minimizing the contacts they have with employees of competing organizations.

Non-computer related training

CBT offers potential advantages for general training in the following circumstances:

1. Fairly small numbers of people need training over an extended period. With CBT, the trainees can get the training they need when they need it, without causing lecturers to teach undesirably small classes.
2. Students cannot readily be released for a course. A terminal or micro-computer in the place of work can be available at all times. It may even be possible to take it home and study there. Indeed, this form of study will soon become widely used for general education and training.
3. Large numbers of people need training frequently. Trainers can become bored with presenting the same material repeatedly and the use of CBT may be appropriate in this case.
4. Students with widely differing starting skills need to attain the same level of finishing skill. The self-paced nature of CBT means that the more knowledgeable will complete the course rapidly without becoming bored, while those with little starting knowledge will progress at their own pace without becoming lost.
5. Certain topics need to be taught to all personnel, at all levels of seniority. If a topic such as plant safety procedures must be taught to all personnel who enter the plant, it might be appropriate to use CBT to avoid mutual embarrassment in the classroom (assuming that senior managers can be persuaded to use the terminal).
6. Travel and accommodation costs are high. The cost of CBT may be high, but it is becoming cost-effective in more and more applications, as the cost of computer equipment drops and better software is developed to help the authors of the training material. The costs of producing CBT material are discussed in a later part of this chapter, but they are continuously falling relative to travel and accommodation.
7. On-the-job training is inappropriate. Simulations of varying complexity can be written as part of a CBT course so that students can learn by seeing the effect of their decisions on the simulated model.

THE MATERIAL

A successful CBT course, as with any training material, will hold the student's interest. The very act of sitting at a terminal and seeing it respond to the student's actions is often very motivating for many new users despite, in many cases, an initial fear of the medium. This novelty effect has tended to make a large amount of poor and mediocre training material acceptable. As yet there is little evidence as to how long the cosmetic attractiveness of CBT lasts with individual students.

The most common fault in CBT is to use the terminal as an automatic 'page turner'. This involves displaying a screenful of training material with an instruction such as PRESS ENTER TO CONTINUE at the bottom of the screen. When the ENTER key is pressed another screen is displayed and so on. This is bad enough when you are reading from a well laid out screen with upper and lower case and up to 80 characters to a line, but with smaller screens and an output in capital letters, the effect is dreadful. The best screens are harder to read than a reasonably well printed page and a page is probably the best place for such information. Audio-visual methods may also be worth considering in certain circumstances.

It is necessary, on occasions, to present information using successive screens without interaction, but extensive and extended use is wrong. This may seem obvious when written down, but apparently it is not, as there are examples showing exactly this fault in CBT material released in 1982.

Computer-based training provides a tremendously flexible medium. Some aspects, eg videodisc and elaborate graphics, are prohibitively expensive for most users today, but the power that the interaction with the user provides, needs exploiting to the full.

The capability within CBT to analyse responses from the student and take action depending on those responses provides the author with a huge variety of potential paths through the teaching material, some of the routes being remedial, some reinforcing and some progressing the competent student rapidly through the course. The result of having these multiple paths through the course is that the material can take widely different times for completion. Not all the paths need be exclusively computer-based. The student may be sent away to study written or audio-visual material, to carry out an experiment, to do some maintenance on equipment or to see the tutor (see Figure 10.2). He would then probably restart at the point where he left off.

Testing at various stages in the course can be carried out by the computer with the results being produced for the instructor on demand. Questions can be selected from an item bank so that no two students get exactly the same questions. Numbers may be generated randomly within certain ranges so that the same complexity of problem is presented but with different numbers. For example Student 1 might get the question:

If a current of 1.25 amps is passing through a resistor of 5 ohms, what is the voltage drop across the resistor?

For Student 2, the same problem might be posed with the current being 2.03 amps and the resistor 7 ohms. The student is being tested on the formula for calculating the voltage and on similar multiplication skills, but the answer to the question cannot be passed from student to student.

CBT rarely stands alone as the teaching resource. It is most often used in conjunction with the printed page in student texts or course books and, not infrequently, to supplement classroom tuition. A CBT course will thus consist of a student text which will probably explain how and when to get the computer-based part of the course started, provide an introduction to the topics to be covered and contain teaching material for the different topics as necessary. The decisions about what to display on the terminal and what to print in the book are discussed in Chapter 2 in the section, 'Selecting the presentation method'.

THE COSTS AND BENEFITS

The costs
The production of high quality CBT courses is a challenging process requiring skills in training design as discussed in Part 1. It also demands a wide range of skills from analysing the training problem to the presentation of the course as a series of displays on a VDU, and the design of the related documentation. Once this has been done, the teaching material has to be written in an author language and entered into the computer (see Chapter 14), printed and other (audio, video, practical) material prepared. This is going to be the major cost in any course, but there are other costs that need to be considered.

Start-up costs
Start-up costs are apparent in two main areas:

1. *People.* Before CBT can be implemented satisfactorily, the trainers need to be taught the specialized skills of programmed learning and authorship, if they do not already know them, the specific knowledge of screen design and the authoring system to be used. The specialists with the subject skills will need some training in CBT as well.

   Some computer expertise will also need to be obtained; how much and for whom will depend on the computer solution selected. If a centralized facility is provided using terminals, data processing personnel will have to be trained to set up and run the system for the training department. If microcomputers are used, it may be satisfactory to employ certain trainers with a little extra knowledge and buy in specialist knowledge from outside, as necessary.
2. *Equipment.* If a central facility is already provided, it may be possible to add CBT at little or no cost in additional equipment. Conversely, it may be necessary to add memory, disk storage, terminals, etc to allow

CBT to run. It may also be possible to run the courses on micro-computers which were purchased for other purposes but are not in continuous use.

It is highly likely, however, that the introduction of CBT will lead to some additional equipment costs, the least of which may be terminals or microcomputers in the training department for course development.

On-going costs

1. *Course production.* Many statistics have been produced for the time it takes, in man-hours, to produce one hour of a CBT course. The figures generally vary between 100:1 and 200:1. There are so many variables that such ratios are only a guide. Variable factors include:
   (a) Is the course brand new, an existing one using other training methods, or an existing one that needs updating?
   (b) What is the duration of the course? Since a major attraction that we have claimed for CBT is that it is self-paced, it cannot be of a fixed duration.
   (c) What is included in the production figures? The whole process from preliminary discussions through design, writing, entering into the computer, review, validation and production of other material is likely to lead to a figure nearer to 200:1 or even higher.
   (d) Whose time is included? The team involved in developing CBT will include a data entry clerk or similar person, and liaison with computer personnel may be required.
   In addition to the people costs, there are the recurrent costs of the equipment used for course development, depreciation, maintenance, paper, etc and the costs of non-computer-based material. These may be substantial in themselves. (One bank recently paid £90,000 to reprint and distribute a five-volume printed programmed text.)
2. *Course presentation.* The costs for course presentation include the running costs of the equipment that is used, supplementary material that is handed out to students, and the time that the trainer and others have to spend running the course and helping in tutorial sessions, etc.
3. *Course updating.* Courses may need to be revised because of errors, changes in the subject matter or to improve the content. Courses that have been properly reviewed and validated by subject experts should be virtually error-free. Subject matter changes will depend on the topics covered. Improvements can always be made, but when and how many will depend on information collected from students completing the course.

The benefits
There are various specific benefits to be gained from CBT and several have been mentioned already. It may be very difficult to cost some, but the attempt should be made if a substantial expenditure on CBT is being con-

sidered. Not all the benefits will apply in all circumstances. Let us first consider how the students and their departments may benefit. These comparisons are with class-based, instructor-led training unless otherwise stated.

Student benefits

1. *More effective use of student time.* Students are generally expected to complete a course having achieved certain objectives. The self-paced nature of CBT and the use of pre- and post-tests, means that students with a higher level of initial knowledge can complete the course faster than those with less knowledge or those who are slow learners, but each should eventually complete the course satisfactorily if they are capable of so doing. This is motivating for the students as it gives the opportunity for the better ones to become productive sooner, yet the less able do not return to the job with gaps in their knowledge. It has also been shown in many cases that the majority of students complete a CBT course, having met the objectives, in significantly less time than with conventional courses. Less knowledgeable students are often inhibited from asking questions in class. There is no stigma attached to repeating and reviewing sections of a CBT course.
2. *The training is available when the trainee is ready for it.* Classroom-based training is seldom economic, and not usually very effective for very small groups (two or three people) but companies of all sizes have circumstances where one or two employees are ready for the next stage of their training, and have to wait until more are ready before the course can run. A CBT course can be taken by the students as and when they become ready, without any delay. Again trainees become productive more rapidly.
3. *The training material is presented consistently.* Lecturers can have an 'off-day' and days off through illness. They can also lack in-depth knowledge of the subject that they are teaching or may place unnecessary emphasis on those aspects of a topic with which they are more familiar. The subject expert, on the other hand, may be a poor lecturer and unsuitable to teach the course. The development of a CBT course brings the trainers and subject experts together as a team (see Chapter 13). It should be possible to guarantee that the topic is covered accurately to a sufficient depth to meet the course design objectives. Validation and testing can then improve the responsiveness of the course to students' answers. This responsiveness can go a long way to meeting the individual needs of each student. What CBT cannot do is digress in response to unpredictable questions or lines of thought, but these are often embellishments that the lecturer may be capable of adding, and do not necessarily contribute to the specific course objectives.
4. *Reduced travel time and expenses.* This varies considerably from one company to another. In cases where offices are dispersed over a wide

area, travel and accommodation costs may be a major factor in justifying CBT. It is also an easily quantifiable cost.

5. *Special short-term requirements can be met.* There may be occasions when changes in policy, operating procedure, legislation, etc require a substantial proportion of the company's employees to undergo a short amount of training fairly rapidly. Videotape is now being widely used to train employees, but it may be that a short CBT module is desirable, at least for those who need to achieve a measurable minimum level of knowledge about the changes.

The computer-based material can be as long as is needed to do the training. If a formal course is necessary, the content may fill only part of a day and the temptation is to stretch it to a full day to justify bringing people from far and wide.

A CBT module cannot be prepared and validated very quickly and company policy changes are often finalized at the last minute, so CBT will not always be appropriate. However, where there are adequate terminals or microcomputers available for the numbers who need the training and there is sufficient time for course development, it may be very cost-effective.

6. *The student is not away from his place of work.* This is a two-edged sword. Constant interruption is unsatisfactory for the student, but a manager may be more willing to let the student attend the course if he knows that the student is readily available to sort out serious problems. It may also be that the student can schedule a number of hours a week for a course. This is possible using CBT. It also means that the student is not away from home.

7. *Practical training can be made more effective.* A lot of practical training, whether workshop-based or on-the-job, has a very low student/teacher ratio – often one to one. The people doing the training may also be the production workers who are skilled in their jobs but have not necessarily any well-developed training skills. Into the bargain, on-the-job training may be fairly haphazard; the skills that the trainee learns can depend on the work going through the factory, office, etc at the particular time he is there. Because this training is expensive and often disruptive and haphazard, CBT can be very attractive in this situation, if appropriate. The use of simulations can be valuable. This applies in computer-related areas such as computer operator and data entry clerk training, and for training in process plant operation, equipment repair and maintenance, etc.

8. *CBT can be available at any time of the day or night.* CBT training material may run on mainframe, mini- or microcomputers depending on company policy. It is possible to make the training material available round the clock for shift workers, if that is a requirement, and it can be a particularly good time to provide training; night shifts, in some industries and jobs, do not have the same amount of work as

day shifts, and the computer equipment is likely to be less heavily used overnight, thus providing resources for the CBT courses.

9. *Training can be carried out from home.* Depending upon circumstances, it may be ideal for trainees to do part of their training from home where they can keep in contact with the office or works, but not be too easily interrupted. At the same time the monitoring capability of the CBT course ensures that the student has the incentive to work. Home-based training can work with either a portable micro-computer, a terminal that can be connected into the central computer providing the training, using the public telephone system or by viewdata using a domestic television.

Training department benefits

1. *Reduction in instructor involvement in a specific course.* A CBT course that is developed to replace a classroom-based course should reduce the amount of time the instructor would otherwise spend taking the course. The initial development costs will be higher, but once the course is running the time spent by the instructor may be very low. The CBT parts of the course eliminate instructor preparation time, which may be extensive if a new instructor is taking a course, as well as the time actually spent with the class. Some CBT courses may require a local supervisor or instructor to support or enhance the CBT material by monitoring exercises, giving feedback, discussing problems and so forth.

   Just as student travel costs may be reduced by CBT, so may that of the trainers if they are normally required to run courses in different parts of the country or world.

2. *Amendments can be speedily incorporated.* The parts of a CBT course actually on the computer can be updated and in use again very rapidly, particularly with a centrally provided mainframe facility. CBT, as has been stated, almost invariably has written or other material associated with it. The more volatile material should, therefore, be on the computer with the static in printed form (see Chapter 2).

3. *Easier and more accurate monitoring of student performance.* The ability of computer-based training to monitor and record statistics on the performance of individual students including, if necessary, the time spent on particular topics, can lead to considerable savings in the time of trainers in supervising, marking and recording the results of students' tests.

4. *Reduced space requirements in the training department.* The use of CBT may cut down on the space needed in the training department. If terminals or microcomputers are already available in the trainees' workplace, the savings will probably not be offset by the increased requirements at the other locations.

5. *Constant incentive to improve the courses.* The collection of data on

student responses and the paths students take through a course, together with their recorded comments on modules and the students' performance statistics, give the trainers a regular reminder to re-evaluate and improve the course. This gives the training manager a regular means of assessing the effectiveness of the course.

SUMMARY

CBT costs/benefits

Costs	Benefits

Start-up
  people
  equipment
On-going
course production including
  design
  authoring
  entry into computer
  correction
  review
  validation
  other media
course presentation including
  running costs of equipment
  instructor time
  time of computer personnel
course updating
	To students
	  more effective use of time
	  available when needed
	  consistent presentation
	  reduced travel time and cost
	  special short-term requirements
	    can be met
	  not away from place of work or
	    home
	  practical training made more
	    effective
	  may be available any time
	  home study may be possible
	
	To training department
	  reduced instructor time
	  easier student monitoring
	  accurate student monitoring
	  less classroom space needed
	  incentive to improve courses

12. From frames to screens

INTRODUCTION

This short chapter attempts to show how to bridge the gap between the design of learning sequences as described in Part 1 and the documentation needed to ensure effective presentation of this material on a VDU as computer-assisted training (CAT). It is our contention that CAT must be highly interactive if it is to be motivating and make effective use of the medium. Therein lies the problem of devising any formal method of documenting the frames of the author in a suitably flexible way for transfer to the screen. The method described here has been shown to work in practice, although it will, no doubt, need modification for individual company needs.

THE DOCUMENTATION

The detailed specification of the course presentation on the screen can be carried out with the use of four basic documents. These are:

1. the mainline chart;
2. the programme flowchart;
3. the response analysis form;
4. the screen layout form.

The mainline chart
The mainline chart develops naturally during the design process described in Chapter 1. It is effectively the straight-through path that will be taken by a student who is not requiring any remedial teaching. This is not quite true as will be seen when we discuss an example, but all the first-time teaching is included in the mainline chart (see Figure 12.1). We cannot be too didactic about this design process because there is neither a right nor a wrong way, but we suggest that the mainline chart is typed up approximately as it would appear on the screen. If you have an 80-character screen, have it typed at 80 characters maximum, but if you are using 40 characters and all capital letters, have it typed like that. You will soon get a feel for the way such text will appear when displayed and how cluttered the screen will appear as lines are added.

The same technique may be appropriate in a remedial loop of several

---

From M20

M30

Right, it will be useful to record both what sort of documents will be typed and the method used to produce them.

Words like 'TYPIST' include a wide range of activities and methods. In this case the job advertisement would have been much more effective if it had mentioned the method of typing to be used.

Incidentally how many kinds of typing can you think of? Type in as many as you can.

M40

Here's my list:

  Copy typing   Audio typing   Shorthand   Speedwriting   Word processing

You will see that you got all/some of them and perhaps you thought of some others.

This simple example shows how a job title can include many different meanings.

M50

It also helps those looking for jobs to decide their suitability for a vacancy if the advertisement tells them something about the products of their work.

So a question asking about the kind of document typed would be useful. Careful questioning about these details could produce this information on the card:

  'Copy typing of letters, proposals, reports and sales literature.'

Suppose an employer notifies a vacancy for a caretaker, what specific duties do you think might be mentioned in the advertisement?

M60

You will remember that the employer's complaint about the applicants for his typist job mentioned a number of drawbacks. Press the START button on your recorder to hear that part again.

Can you now list the capabilities or experience you think should have been recorded by Charlotte and added to the advertisement?

To M70

Figure 12.1 Part of a mainline chart

frames, so the concept can be extended. Also, if students are given a choice of paths at a point in a course, there may be several parallel mainline charts (see later examples). Any methodology, particularly one that is kept simple like this one, must be adjusted to suit your requirements.

Note that the mainline chart is a typed sheet with the 'from frame' at the top and the 'to frame' at the bottom. The author is otherwise free at this stage to lay out the mainframes as he likes. When he gets to use the screen layout form, he must think in great detail of the presentation. To do so now would be time-wasting and constricting. The experienced author may, of course, produce a mainline chart that can be transferred almost directly to a screen layout chart.

The programme flowchart

In Chapter 4 we discussed the requirements for branching in programmed learning. There is nothing new in this except that for the first time the computer has provided an efficient device to control branching in a painless and effective way for the student. Branching can prove very complex for the author if he gets too carried away by the power he has available to him. The programme flowchart provides an effective means of documenting your branching strategy and is also a warning to the wise if the flowchart begins to get rather complicated. We include in Figure 12.2 the programme flowchart corresponding to the part of the mainline chart shown in Figure 12.1.

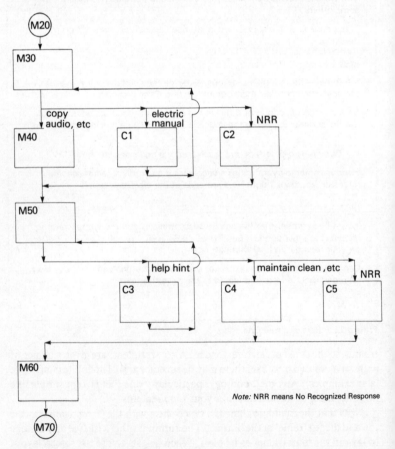

Note: NRR means No Recognized Response

Figure 12.2 Part of a programme flowchart

Note that the boxes in a vertical line correspond to the mainline chart. The C frames usually provide feedback to the student if an answer is matched with a predicted incorrect response or an unrecognized response. If you look, however, at frames M50 and M60 you will see that you can only get to M60 via C4 or C5. In this case, frame C4 is the frame which is passed through if the response is correctly matched. There may be several reasons for the author using this technique. In the example, this part of the course is concerned with training staff in an employment agency to take accurate and relevant information about vacancies, so that they can complete advertisements for their shop front displays or for newspapers. The main instruction is concerned with taking accurate details about a typist. At the end of frame M50 the author decides to add a question about the special duties that an employer might want a caretaker to carry out. It was obviously thought useful to add this as a reinforcement frame, either at the original time of writing or during a review. As it is supplementary to the main flow, it is quite acceptable to omit frame C4 from the mainframe chart. The programme flowchart will be drawn up together with a response analysis form which is discussed later. The response analysis form in Figure 12.7 corresponds to the programme flowchart in Figure 12.2.

Some examples of typical structures you may see in programme flowcharts are shown in Figures 12.3 and 12.4.

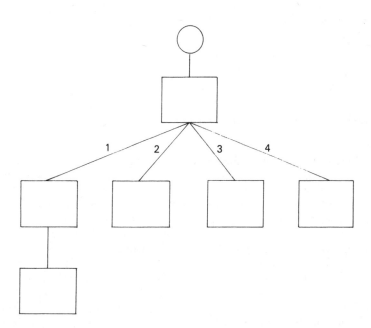

Figure 12.3 Branching in a programme flowchart

In Figure 12.3, a branch has been taken as a result of a decision made by the student, possibly from a range of choices, such as:

> select one of the following topics:
> 1. a telephone interview;
> 2. completing an application form;
> 3. a preliminary interview with a prospective employee;
> 4. finish the module.

Four mainline charts would start at this point; where they would end depends on the rest of the module.

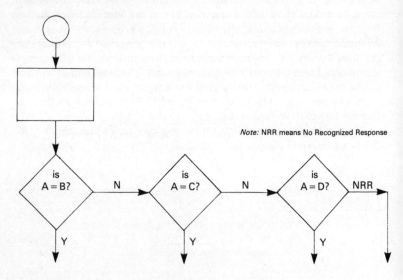

Note: NRR means No Recognized Response

Figure 12.4 The use of the lozenge in decision making

The situation shown in Figure 12.4 is frequently met. There are two common circumstances where the lozenge (◇) is used. The lozenge means 'make a decision about the path to take'. It could have been included after frames M30 and M50 in Figure 12.2 and in 12.3 where branching decisions are made, but the paths are so simple that the inclusion of an additional symbol clutters up the flowchart. If you are being rigorous, include it. The two common circumstances where it should be included are where you are doing several matches with different paths being taken as a result of each match, and where different paths are being taken as a result of the values in counters.

To exemplify these, consider an arithmetic test: What is 7 x 33? Predicted answers might be 231, 2@1 or 4ϕ where @ indicates that any character will be accepted at that point. Response matching is discussed later but note here that the order of checking is important, because in this case 2@1 will match

COMPUTERS & TRAINING

Dean Associates offer these services

CONSULTANCY
---

*Training System Design
(including Computer Based Training)*
●
Instructor and Author Training
●
*Computer Selection and Installation;
Systems Advice and Development*

PRODUCTS AND PROCESS DEVELOPMENT

Training Materials and Programmes
●
Research and Development

COURSES AND SEMINARS

Training Design Techniques
●
Computers and Training
●
Computer Programming
●
Microcomputers

All courses can be provided in-house

---

45 Canterbury Avenue, Sheffield S10 3RU, England.
Telephone: (0742) 303054

with 231 if you have not already looked for it. Thus, the sequence of the decisions is important and is specified by the sequence of the lozenges. The programme flowchart for this part could look like the one in Figure 12.5.

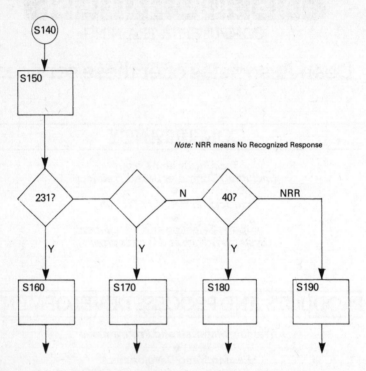

Note: NRR means No Recognized Response

Figure 12.5 Flowcharting the sequence of analysing responses

When you give a test you may wish to keep a total of the questions the student answered correctly. (You may also wish to note which specific questions were answered correctly.) The total might be held in a counter (C1). If the student got nine or ten correct you might send him to the next part of the course; if he got seven or eight you might tell him to reread part of the accompanying material; if he got four to six you might send him through some remedial teaching on the computer and, if he got less than four, you might send him to see the trainer.

Figure 12.6 shows how the flowchart in Figure 12.5 might develop if the question posed in frame S150 were the last in the test. Note how adjustments to counters and other administrative instructions are handled.

This simple concept for a flowchart is actually quite rigorous, as it specifies the sequence of checking matches (left to right) at any point. It also virtually ensures that you have considered that most important eventuality, the 'No Recognized Response', which, with some authoring systems, can

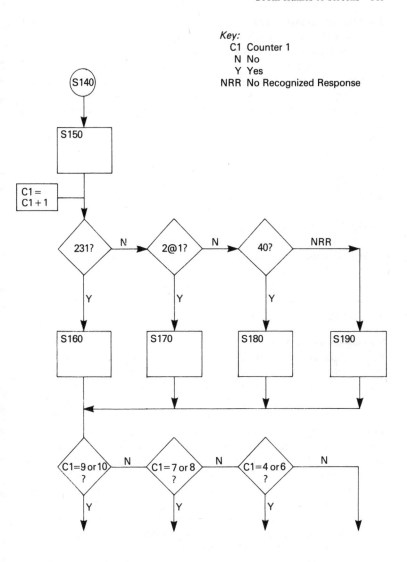

Figure 12.6 The use of counters in a flowchart

easily be overlooked. The flowchart is used in conjunction with the response analysis form which is discussed next. Obviously, the flowchart can become far more complex than those shown, but remember that its purpose is to act as an aid to the design team in producing a high quality course. Develop and modify it to suit your circumstances, but you must have something.

The response analysis form

This form is used to specify the responses that you wish to look for at any point, and the course taken if a match is found. Responses should be entered in groups with the feedback where appropriate, or the next frame number if it is a mainline frame. This is shown in Figure 12.7. Note that we have entered 'M30 response' in the 'then go to' column to indicate that the student is to have another try at answering the question in M30 without presenting the whole frame again. What you also need to do before the module is entered into the computer is to determine the strictness of the matching. This is discussed in detail later, but you might be happy to look for SPEED as the crucial part of the response SPEEDWRITING; likewise with WORD PRO-CESSING, you might be happy to look for WORD and assume that, if WORD were in the answer, they had meant WORD PROCESSING. It may be that you will not wish to specify the strictness of the matching when completing the forms initially, but come back to that on a second pass. What is almost certain is that validation will require modifications both to the words looked for in the responses to open-ended questions of the type shown in this vacancy taking example, and in the level of strictness in matching. It is suggested that you specify the matching as it would be coded for the specific author language you are using. Our example uses the rules of HAL which is a hypothetical author language developed in Chapter 14.

The screen layout form

This is the form upon which you mimic what is to appear on the screen in detail. You must indicate when the screen is cleared between one frame and the next. When different information is displayed depending on a student's response, you must be sure that at no time does the screen overfill. (If you permit scrolling, this is less of a problem.) It is not necessary for the screen layout form to indicate when counters are altered or statistics taken. This will be shown on the programme flowchart. The form is almost self explanatory (see Figure 12.8). You will note that the line numbers are not specified nor is the form limited to 25 lines, the maximum you will find on most terminals. The number of lines is limited only by the constraint of keeping the form manageable. You are thus frequently able to present the screen layout on one form – a part at a time – that the user will see, depending on his response. The form is approximately A3 size (11 x 7 inches).

The author will work with the relevant mainline chart, programme flowchart and response analysis form. The transfer of information to the screen layout form will usually be fairly mechanical, but the author will have to ensure that the standards that have been established are being followed (see Chapter 13). Figure 12.9 shows the completed screen layout form corresponding to the piece of instruction developed in Figures 12.1, 12.2 and 12.7.

There are several points worth making about the completed screen layout form. The different frames are clearly ruled off across the chart so that the reader can identify the breaks at a glance. The fact that the frame M30 starts in line 1 can be taken to indicate that the screen has been cleared to blanks

Frame no.	If response is...	go to...	and give this feedback...	then go to...
M30	COPY $ AUDIO $ SHORT $ SPEED $ WORD	M40		
	ELECTRIC $ MANUAL	C1	This is a type of typewriter. I asked for kinds of TYPING. Have another try.	M30 Response
	NRR	C2	Here's my list:- (Lhis as Frame M40) You don't seem to have any of those, but you may have thought of some others. What is important to remember is that a general Job Title like TYPIST means different things to different people	M50
M50	HELP $ HINT	C3	Caretakers often wear overalls to perform some of their duties. Now have a try at answering the question	M50 Response
	MAINTAIN $ CLEAN $ POST $ MAIL $ SECURITY $ LOCK $ HEAT $ BOILER $ POLISH $ LIFT	C4	These were the sorts of duties I was thinking of:- MAINTAIN FITTINGS CLEAN ENTRANCE HALL ACCEPT POST SECURITY CHECKING LOCKING & UNLOCKING OF PREMISES CHECK HEATING SYSTEM POLISH FLOOR CHECK LIFTS & REPORT FAULTS We are thinking along the same lines	M60
	NRR	C5	As C4 until last sentence Replace with:- I think that you would agree that it would make a difference if some of those were included or not.	M60

Figure 12.7 The response analysis form

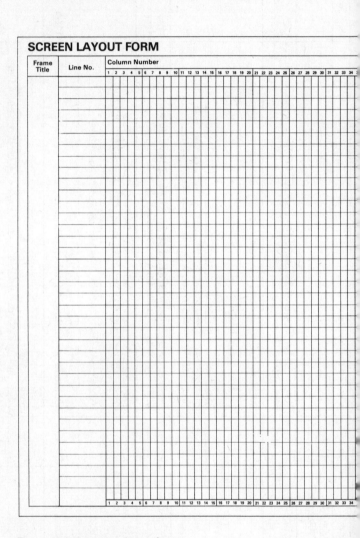

Figure 12.8 The screen layout form

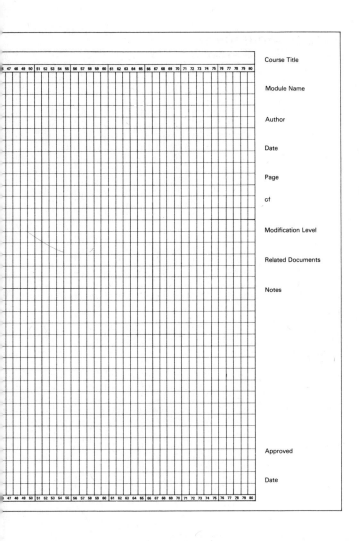

Course Title

Module Name

Author

Date

Page

of

Modification Level

Related Documents

Notes

Approved

Date

SCREEN LAYOUT FORM

Frame Title	Line No.	Column Number (1–35)
M30	1	Right, it will be useful to record
		and the method used to produce them
		Words like 'TYPIST' include a wider r
		case the job advertisement would h
		Mentioned the method of typing to b
		Incidentally, how many types of typ
		Type in as many as you can on one l
	13 or 18 (Note 1)	Here's my List:-
		COPY TYPING AUDIO TYPING SH
		You will see that you got (at)some of t ②
		This simple example shows how a job
	13	Electric and manual are types of ty
		Have another try.
		Accept M30 Response.
	13 or 18 (Note 1)	Here's my List
		COPY TYPING AUDIO TYPING SH
		You don't seem to have any of these
		What is important to remember is th
		different things to different peopl

Fiure 12.9 A completed screen layout form

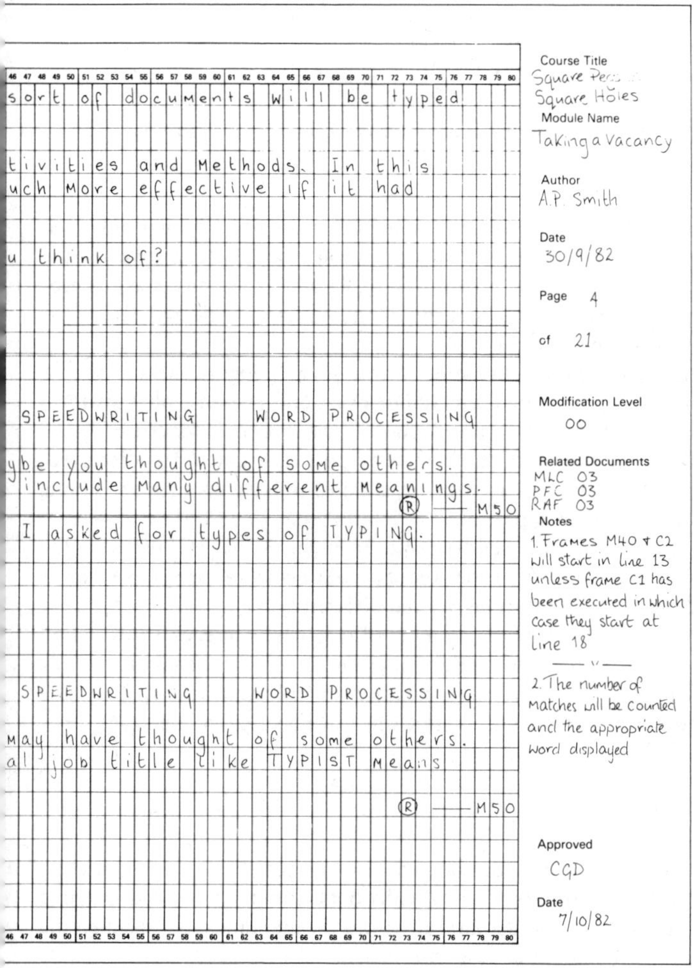

Course Title
Square Pegs...
Square Holes
Module Name
Taking a Vacancy
Author
A.P. Smith
Date
30/9/82
Page   4
of   21
Modification Level
00
Related Documents
MLC 03
PFC 03
RAF 03
Notes
1. Frames M40 & C2 will start in line 13 unless frame C1 has been executed in which case they start at line 18
——— v ———
2. The number of matches will be counted and the appropriate word displayed
Approved
CGD
Date
7/10/82

Grid content (columns 46–80):

```
sort  of  documents  will  be  typed

tivities and Methods.  In this
uch More  effective  if  it  had

u  think  of?

SPEEDWRITING    WORD PROCESSING

ybe  you  thought  of  some  others.
include  Many  different  Meanings.
                              (R) ——— M50

I  asked  for  types  of  TYPING.

SPEEDWRITING    WORD PROCESSING

May  have  thought  of  some  others.
al  job  title  like  TYPIST  Means
                              (R) ——— M50
```

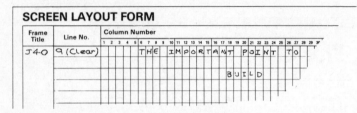

Figure 12.10 Indicating that the screen must be cleared before displaying the lines following

before frame M30 is displayed. With some screen displays you may only need to display two or three lines, in which case it will probably be better to use the lines near the middle of the screen, say 10, 11 and 12. In this case it is probably necessary to add a note indicating that the screen is cleared before displaying the text (see Figure 12.10).

The precise wording on the screen layout form in Figure 12.9 has altered slightly between producing the mainline chart and response analysis form and actually producing the screen layout. If the student enters ELECTRIC or MANUAL and none of the correct responses, frame C1 is displayed. After the text in frame C1 the student is asked to have another try. Frame M40 or C2 would then appear on line 18 rather than line 13. If there were no room, or the author felt it was desirable, he might clear the C1 text after the student's second try, so that the feedback text always appeared starting at line 13. Note (1) would then be worded differently.

Note (2) about counting the number of matches, is adequate instruction for the person writing in the author language. It is not necessary to include this in the programme flowchart as it is relevant only at this point. The value of the counter used is only of interest when displaying that message.

CONCLUSIONS

The combination of these four documents can provide all the information needed by the person producing individual computer-assisted training modules. They also build up naturally from the mainline chart through the programme flowchart and response analysis form, which will probably develop in tandem, up to the screen layout form. By the time that the screen layout form is produced, the ideas and the wording will have been extensively changed, so it is likely to be near its final form and will only require those alterations which may be suggested by validation and testing.

The precise way the documentation is used will depend on the authoring system, but a logical overall design process similar to this must be adopted to produce good computer-based training material.

13. Courseware development in CBT

INTRODUCTION

This chapter is in two parts. The first part discusses what an authoring system does, the composition of a design team and the major strategic decisions the design team need to take. The second part discusses the sort of detailed decisions that need to be made to ensure consistency between courses and authors. The presentation standards and guidelines need to be formulated at an early stage, so that when the writing of the course actually commences the authors can concentrate on presenting the material in the best way possible within these yardsticks.

PART 1: MANAGEMENT AND STAFFING

What does an authoring system do?

There are various programming languages widely used in computing. Some of these have been mentioned briefly in Chapter 7. They were designed and written for use in business or scientific computing. A typical business program may accept input data, check it for accuracy or acceptability and then perform fairly simple calculations using data from a file or files, before producing several fairly elaborate reports. COBOL was designed for just such a purpose. Similarly, scientific or engineering programs may be written in FORTRAN which can evaluate complicated formulae well and quite efficiently, but is not very good for producing reports.

When a trainer has prepared a lesson using CAT techniques and sits down to get it running on the computer, he does not require FORTRAN, BASIC or COBOL. He requires a language that will permit him to present questions to the student, analyse responses, give feedback and remedial help if necessary, etc.

Note that it is suggested that the trainer should be able to produce the teaching material on the computer (a suggestion that is discussed further in the next section). This implies that the language should be fairly easy to learn and use, and not require an in-depth knowledge of computing. This does not apply to most of the normal programming languages although BASIC can be learned quite quickly by many people, some of whom might not expect to have the aptitude. However, the types of features mentioned above are common to author languages and are peculiar to the needs of CAT; that is why special authoring systems have been developed. They do the specifics of CAT well, if they are good languages, and suffice for the majority of CAT requirements. There are circumstances where the use of an author language may not provide the complete or best solution. This may be the case with complex simulations or in the use of graphics. Professional computer experts may be needed to advise and to write some, or all, of the teaching material at these times, but the trainer must remain in charge to ensure that the best over-all training package is produced at the end of the day.

It is perfectly possible to write excellent tutorial lessons in programming languages like FORTRAN and BASIC and a lot of good material is available for schools and colleges in these languages, particularly in science teaching. Some of the best is distributed by CONDUIT.[1] These teaching programs are written in FORTRAN or BASIC because these languages are available on such a wide variety of computers, from large mainframe computers to micro-computers like the PET, Tandy and Apple. Nevertheless, CONDUIT still has problems in making programs transferable, and it is still necessary to distribute the programs in a number of ways for different computers. Stand-ardization and transferability in computing have proved very difficult. There are two main reasons for not writing CAT material in a traditional program-ming language if it can be avoided. The first is that the trainer is no longer in charge. The actual job of entering the lessons in the computer and ensuring that they work correctly, is now the programmer's. The second reason is that the cost is likely to be considerably higher in terms of development time and man-hours involved; the cost of CAT in man-hours is usually high enough anyway. The reasons should be very good before increasing the cost further.

The following table shows some figures that were obtained when a short piece of training was written in a variety of languages. They are not particu-larly significant on their own, but they agree generally with the figures that others have achieved. They show that the time taken to write the training material decreases with increasing sophistication of the authoring system.

System used	Time taken (minutes)
BASIC	380
PILOT (on Apple II)	280
STAF	240
IIS	180

Note: The systems PILOT, STAF and IIS are discussed in Chapter 17
BASIC has been described in Chapter 7

Figure 13.1 Writing the same piece of computer-assisted training material using different authoring languages

[1] CONDUIT, PO Box 388, Iowa City, Iowa 5244, USA. It publishes a journal called *Pipeline* twice yearly

Who is going to write it?
Various skills need to be brought together to produce good CAT material.
These include:

1. *Subject matter skills.* The accuracy of the course content is dependent
   on having a person who knows the particular area that is being taught.
2. *The ability to communicate.* Good instructors are experts in verbal
   communication, quick thinking and alert when answering students'
   questions, and they enjoy the challenge of the face-to-face contact that
   the classroom environment provides. These skills are useful adjuncts
   for a CAT course author, but are less significant than the ability to
   write clear, concise and interesting material. Yet we are not looking for
   someone who can just produce good documentation. The time that the
   student spends at the terminal must be highly motivating and lively.
   The course author must try to build into the course the best aspects of a
   one-to-one relationship. In the classroom, this relationship can only
   take place for a short time with any one student because of the
   numbers in the class.
3. *Clear knowledge and understanding of the target audience.* This skill is
   necessary for the material to be written in a style the student finds
   attractive, albeit probably subconsciously. The language used must fit
   the audience. If plant operators and supervisors are being taught about
   safety legislation, the legal jargon must be reduced to a minimum or
   else eliminated. A CAT course with the same overall objectives, but
   aimed at company lawyers, would use a very different vocabulary and
   probably several different examples. In other instances, the differences
   that should ideally be written in for various groups of students are
   more subtle than in the rather obvious example given. However, the
   cost of producing material tailored for each marginally different group
   would be prohibitive, so it is very important at the design stage to
   define the target audience for the course.
4. *Skill to use the instructional techniques that CAT offers.* There are
   various CAT techniques that are discussed in the second part of this
   chapter. To use these effectively, training and practice is naturally
   required. The author must, in addition, be persuaded of the merits of
   CAT for teaching. How easily the authors are persuaded may depend
   on the authoring system that is made available to them, and on the
   computer facilities that the company can provide, as discussed later.

SELECTING AUTHORS
It is natural to think first of the classroom instructor or lecturer, when considering whom to train as a course author. It is not necessarily the case that
good instructors make good authors of CAT courses, since the skills required
are different. Good instructors are good talkers who can handle the direct
contact with students and respond to questions. Good authors, however,
need to be good writers who can produce teaching material remotely from

the students, who can predict the questions that may arise in the students' minds and predict the misconceptions that students may have during a course. This ability to predict is difficult and for this reason, in particular, courses need to be thoroughly validated before being released for general use.

It may be, then, that an instructor can be selected to train as a course author, but there are others who may be more suitable. In some cases a performance-orientated person, such as a salesman, may be more successful as an author than a teacher who is often more interested in the topic than his trainees' learning. An expert in the subject matter to be taught may be better for a specific course, but it is important to get a person with the correct level of skill and knowledge for the target audience. For example, a highly competent researcher is unlikely to be suitable to write a CAT module for plant operators although his research may have permitted the plant to be built. The cost of training such a person in CAT, and their likely aptitude, must be considered against the fact that the individual will only be useful for a limited range of courses.

In some cases, a computer programmer may be the best person to write CAT courses particularly if they are computer-related, as so much of the early CAT material has been. Course authoring for CAT has much in common with simple programming and programmers can, therefore, be expected to be productive when coding, but unless they have subject or teaching skills to impart to the course as well, they are unlikely to find the task challenging for long. Figure 13.2 summarizes the position.

Possible authors	Pros	Cons (problems)
Instructors/ lecturers	Understand training Verbal communicators Immediate responses to questions/comments	Can they transfer their skills to written instruction? Are they good at predicting questions and answers?
Subject matter expert	Has a thorough knowledge of the material to be taught?	May not be a good communicator May be at the wrong level
Computer programmer	Likely to be a productive writer Able to exploit/ manipulate computer software	May not have enough to contribute to get long-term job satisfaction

Figure 13.2 Factors for and against possible authors

The design team
There are several roles that must be filled by the team that is to be responsible for the course. There must be:

1. A project manager/co-ordinator who will be in charge overall. This person will be responsible for seeing that deadlines are met, standards adhered to and that the different aspects of the overall project are drawn along together.
2. Course authors. The selection of authors has just been discussed. An author may also be a subject specialist or a trainer.
3. Subject specialists who will be involved in ensuring that what is being taught is technically correct.
4. Trainers.

There will also probably be:

5. Media specialists if the project involves film, tape/slide presentations, etc.
6. A computer professional to advise on what is practical and desirable. The role of this specialist will vary depending on the instructions given to the design team. If the team is told to use a specific author language to design the project, the computer adviser will tell the team what is and is not practical with that particular system. If the team has a fairly free hand to select an appropriate system that suits their needs, the role of this adviser will be different.
    It is quite likely that the data processing departments of even quite large companies will not employ a member of staff with the appropriate skills for this advisory role in what is a specialized area. In this case it may be sensible to consider using an outside consultant to assist, at least while a computer professional within the company is learning about the system. Of course, if a microcomputer system is selected, the data processing department may not be closely involved at all. Most specialist computer assistance will be needed for the CML rather than the CAT aspects of courseware development.

The organization and overall structure of the course
The design team must decide how the course is to be organized. This will involve setting objectives, producing estimates of course duration, selecting the media to be used and where each is appropriate, calculating numbers of students taking the course at any one time, determining the locations of students and course prerequisites. It is possible that some of these decisions may have been made by senior management before the design team is established. Some of this has already been covered in Part 1.
    Consider the situation where a company wishes to train its service engineers, who cover the country, in fault diagnosis and repair of a new piece of electronic equipment. This involves teaching the engineers some new diag-

nostic skills, telling them about the equipment for general knowledge to help them understand how it fits into the company's product range, and testing their ability to find a number of common faults and repair them.

The design team must decide, or find out from the service managers, how many engineers need to be trained over how long a period and the duration of the course. There may well be a film that has been produced for sales training that can be employed usefully to show how the product fits into the company's product range. The design team must decide whether to reinforce the message of the film, with a CBT module, to bring home points specific to the engineers. The best method of teaching the new diagnostic skills and of handling the fault finding and repair must be decided, and these decisions will have obvious implications for the equipment needed for the training. Deciding the structure of a course has been covered in Chapter 2.

Length of teaching units
The length of a teaching unit is influenced by a number of factors, including the topic being taught, how much the designers think, and later discover, that students can take at a time and the paths individual students take through the units. If there is the possibility of extensive remedial teaching, times in the unit may vary considerably between the fastest and slowest. It is good practice to include frequent reviews at convenient points in each unit. The length of teaching units has been discussed in the section 'Developing a modular structure' in Chapter 2.

The computer options
The design team may be required to recommend a suitable computer system to supply the CBT elements of the course, or it may be told that it has a certain system and to use that. For those in the latter position this section is superfluous.

We can consider the solutions under the general headings of systems on mainframe computers, minicomputers and microcomputers, although, as has been discussed, these differences are becoming increasingly blurred. A fourth option is to use a timesharing bureau.

Mainframe computer systems
Many companies have extensive terminal networks linked to one or more central computers. Or they may have a distributed system with terminals linked into a local computer. In these cases, the data processing hierarchy may be prepared to mount a suitable authoring system for the trainers, that will allow some or all of the terminals to be of potential use for training. It will, however, be only one application along with sales, finance, production control, payroll, etc, although the solution is often particularly appropriate when CBT is to be used for training users and potential users of these terminals. It applies to data entry, enquiry systems, and the training of computer personnel. There will, however, be occasions where it is sensible to install additional terminals on the network primarily to meet the training

need. This was the case at Barclaycard because the level of usage of existing terminals precluded adequate access for training. There is no reason why these additional terminals should not be set up in quiet training areas and used for training in topics totally removed from computers. This solution has advantages and disadvantages. The advantages are:

1. the authoring systems are powerful and provide good facilities for presentation and management of the learning;
2. the data processing department should help with difficulties with the hardware and software;
3. some of the course administration can be handled by the computer. It would, in fact, be interesting to know how many serious users of these systems actually use most of the facilities offered to monitor and control courses and students' progress. This is an aspect of computer-managed learning which is discussed in Chapter 16.

The disadvantages are:

1. trainers with little computing knowledge may feel intimidated by the system – its size, complexity and the remoteness of help;
2. it is usually expensive to get started;
3. training may not be treated with sufficient seriousness when the computer system is busy. This can lead to students becoming confused and frustrated whilst waiting for the terminal to respond;
4. it is essential to have professional computer expertise available at the end of a telephone.

Minicomputer systems
Minicomputers may operate CBT in a similar way to that described for mainframes, where the CBT system is often 'piggybacking' on the main system. This means that the CBT system is an additional facility that is probably added at a marginal cost on to the mainframe, the expense of which has already been justified for running other aspects of the business.

Where there are few companies that can afford a mainframe computer system solely for training, there are more that can consider 'dedicated' minicomputer systems, supporting half a dozen or more terminals, solely for training. These terminals may be supported in the same building as the minicomputer or they may link in from anywhere in the country using the telephone network. The advantages of such systems are:

1. the training department has control of the system. If it fills up with courses and the responsiveness of the system degrades, the training department is responsible and can do something about it;
2. there are sophisticated authoring systems available;
3. they should be capable of giving a very good response to users.

The disadvantages are:

1. they are sophisticated systems, so some computer expertise is necessary. How it is provided will depend on the circumstances;
2. the system involves substantial capital expenditure which may be difficult to justify if CBT is not proven within the company.

Microcomputer systems
One can purchase multi-user microcomputer systems which are similar to minicomputers, but which probably support fewer terminals. However, it is likely that microcomputers will be considered for CBT for use in one of two ways. The first and most important today is as stand-alone systems, ie single user; the second is in local area networks (LANs). The pros and cons of the two are similar because the LAN may be regarded as effectively providing a number of stand-alone microcomputers with the sharing of some more expensive resources. The advantages of the microcomputer are:

1. it is quite cheap to get started (a few thousand pounds);
2. the trainer is in control and usually has the microcomputer when he wants it;
3. it is flexible, and probably fairly cheap to attach non-standard devices, such as graphics tablets or special keyboards;
4. there is a wide variety of microcomputers to choose from (some might construe this as a disadvantage).

The disadvantages are:

1. the operating system is not very sophisticated. The trainer is responsible for copying diskettes, etc;
2. the authoring systems are not as sophisticated as for mainframes and minicomputers. There is often very little computer-managed learning;
3. the speed of response may be variable due to the relatively slow access to diskettes;
4. help may be very difficult to come by.

Timesharing bureaux
There are several CBT systems that can be used by hiring terminal time on commercial bureaux. The option may be attractive to companies investigating CBT and who wish to evaluate a sophisticated CBT system. Some of the bureau services offer a range of CBT courses on a variety of topics. This solution gets expensive if substantial use is made of the service but it may be economic as all the worries and costs of supporting the system are removed from the user.

PART 2: THE DESIGN PROCESS

Why is it important to have standards for presentation? There are two groups that benefit: first and foremost, the students are helped by having information and instructions displayed, and responses handled, consistently. A 'house style' will give students confidence as they take different courses. The second beneficiaries are the authors who have yardsticks to go by and so do not waste time thinking how to display, say, a multiple-choice question on the screen.

Of course, presentation standards of the type suggested in this section are not unalterable commands; they are merely guidelines to cover most circumstances. Where they are not applicable to the letter, they should be modified with a view to causing the minimum of confusion to the students.

A number of the criteria discussed in this section may be decided for you, if the authoring system that is to be used has already been selected. We shall assume here that the standards are being set down without undue restriction from the limitations of actual authoring systems. If a system is selected to fit as closely as possible the standards that have been established, some changes will no doubt need to be made to fit the author language.

Almost all CBT courses written today will use a visual display as the prime means of communicating with the student, so this will be assumed here. Chapter 6 discussed features of VDUs in some detail and it may be necessary to refer back for a description of some of the terms included here.

Screen features

Items that should be considered and given a level of importance include the following:

1. *Screen size.* Is a screen size of 80 characters by 24 lines necessary? This is very much a standard for interactive terminals on timesharing systems. Would a 40 character by 24 line display be adequate? This is common on many of the microcomputer systems and is being successfully used by Barclays Bank with a viewdata system.
2. *Upper/lower case.* Is it necessary to be able to mix capital and small letters on the screen? To be able to do this may be essential, in teaching languages or typing, for example, but it is almost always desirable if the lower case letters are well formed, as the readability of the material is then enhanced.
3. *Scrolling/split screen.* It is sometimes attractive to retain some information on the main part of the screen while asking questions about it. In this case it may be desirable to scroll part of the screen while retaining the rest. Some microcomputers have a facility for scrolling the bottom four lines of the screen while leaving the rest unaltered; other systems offer considerably more flexibility.

    It is also necessary to decide, in general, whether to have the course material scrolling off the top of the screen, or to clear it and present everything on a blank screen. It is probably less disconcerting to clear the screen when it gets full or you wish to change the topic. Scrolling is really a continuation of the old printing terminals. Although you are unlikely to wish to use it all the time, scrolling can be helpful in some circumstances, particularly if the split screen facility is not available.

4. *Highlighting of information*. This may be done by underlining, reverse video, flashing (rapidly gets wearing), colour, capital letters, etc. The most suitable way of highlighting will probably depend on the specific terminal selected.

5. *Forms presentation*. Many applications that involve data entry staff require forms to be displayed on the screen and completed by the trainee. These forms must look exactly like the forms they will be completing when trained. To permit this type of course to be presented satisfactorily, it may be necessary to have easy screen addressing and protected fields.

6. *Graphics*. Effectively used, graphics can be a significant enhancement to a course. Obvious areas are plotting graphs, histograms, fairly simple diagrams, etc. Graphics is not usually very easy to use without some specialist knowledge of a computer programming language. If it comprises a significant part of the material presented on the computer, it is likely to increase substantially the number of hours spent in course development.

Do not discount graphics; used judiciously it can have a startling impact, not least in selling the course and medium to management. However, always consider the alternatives, particularly good quality pictures and on-line drawings in a course book, which may be much more cost-effective and clearer to follow. The quality of graphics and the ease of producing pictures are both improving rapidly and the cost is falling, so that the use of graphics is going to increase.

7. *Colour*. There are basically two possibilities with colour. There is the capability of presenting characters, words and lines in different colours. Together with this system you will usually get the capability of character graphics in colour. This is common on viewdata systems. It is worth using if it is there and can often be used effectively, but it is rare that such rather crude colour capability will constitute a requirement for a system. Displaying characters in a variety of colours can be confusing to the student if it is done randomly. However, using colours to highlight different topics or groups can be very effective and speed the assimilation of the information.

The use of colour to highlight words in an otherwise monochrome display may be misleading to the viewer because those words may be over-emphasized. It may be more appropriate to display them in capitals or underlined or, possibly, in reverse video.

The other, and far more interesting, use of colour is to colour good quality graphics. This is becoming much more readily obtainable and, as with graphics on its own, the impact of colour can be dramatic.

However, all the comments that apply to graphics apply to colour so check out the system carefully. If you need good resolution graphics, for example, you may find that the system you are considering can only display very few colours at that resolution.

Asking questions and analysing the answers
Part 1 of the book covers the principles of good course design; if you have studied that section you will know the questions that you will wish to ask at various stages in a learning unit. Remember that you will probably wish the computer to analyse the students' responses to your questions and, whereas this gives you a lot more scope than if you were writing a programmed instruction text, the wording or structure of the questions needs to be formulated with much more care than is necessary for a classroom trainer who can use his common sense if an unexpected answer is given.

Response analysis
One of the major attractions of CAT as a technique is its ability to react intelligently to student answers to more or less open-ended questions. To do this, the author language must be able to take the student's reply and analyse it according to rules specified by the course writer. Exactly how the reply can be analysed varies with different author languages, but there are several factors that may be important. We shall discuss the more common.

1. *Exact match*. It is frequently necessary to match exactly the student's reply with the anticipated response. This is particularly so with arithmetic or language training. An exact match is often sought first, followed by other less precise matches. For example, the answer to a question on French vocabulary or comprehension might be 'un oiseau'. There might be three or more exact matches to be checked here, depending on the form of the question. Besides 'un oiseau', we might look for 'une oiseau' or 'l'oiseau' before looking for less precise matches like those discussed below.
2. *Extra words in the reply*. It is often good enough to look for a keyword or keywords in a response and, if you find them, to reply accordingly. If the answer to a question was 'Harry Truman', you might look first for the two words Harry Truman. If you allowed additional words, the following would be matched:
   Harry Truman, Harry S Truman, Harry S. Truman, I think it was Harry Truman.
   but, so would:
   Harry Fred Truman, James Walter Harry Truman, etc.
   so also would:
   I don't really know, but I am sure it was not Harry Truman.
   The last is an example of the so-called 'not' problem. It is foreseen as a potential problem, but in fact, with sensibly worded questions, students taking the course rarely try to outsmart the system so the

potential problem rarely becomes a real one. Some systems allow you to preclude certain words or character combinations from appearing in the response. This could possibly be used in cases where it was important to guard against unwanted negatives being included in the student's reply.

Having looked for Harry Truman, it might be sensible to look for the surname, if Harry Truman was not found. This would accept any set of words that contained Truman such as Truman Capote or Ben Truman. The returning comment to the student would then have to be appropriate. For example, you might say,

'You have the surname, but his full name was Harry S Truman. Incidentally, the 'S' was only an initial; he had no second name.'

3. *Words in any order.* In some questions you may wish to elicit more than one word where the order is not important. For example, 'Name the two English kings who fought the Battle of Hastings' could get the correct reply of 'Harold and William the Conqueror' or 'William the Conqueror and King Harold', etc. This facility is not as frequently used as one might think because you often wish to analyse the answer several times, looking for one keyword each time, to find how many anticipated responses are included in the reply. If you asked, 'Which countries were founder members of the EEC?', you would probably look for France, Germany, Italy, etc sequentially, checking the answer each time and recording which were found. The order is not important, but it probably is important to know which were entered correctly.

4. *Permitting extra characters in words.* It is usually of little importance whether the student can spell perfectly, so it may be adequate to analyse the response so that you can be sure the response sought has been given, if a match is found. With the Harry Truman answer, you might wish to look for a near match after looking for an exact match. If you looked for the consonants TRMN, you would pick up TRUEMAN or TRUMEN and could reply, 'Yes, but his name is spelt TRUMAN.'

Another way to use this same facility is to look for the stem or part of it, thus permitting various endings and the plural. If your question encourages a free form reply, this may be useful. Looking for the character string POLIC, you would accept POLICE, POLICING, POLICEMAN, POLICEMEN and POLICY. Depending on the author language and how you used it, you might find that POLITICIAN, POLITICAL, etc were accepted as well. So you have to take care if you do not want these sort of answers to be accepted.

It may be possible to permit differences at certain points in a word. For example, you might wish to accept COLOR or COLOUR as a reply. This might be indicated by COLO#R where the # indicates that additional or no characters may occur at that point. Similarly ELE#ANT would accept ELEPHANT or ELEFANT without differentiating.

5. *Upper and lower case.* In most situations, it is not important whether a reply to a question is entered in capital letters, small letters, or a mixture, but it is obviously important in some cases, for example language teaching. When it is not important, it is usually possible to change all the letters in the response to the same case before attempting any matches. Therefore, ALL, All and all would then be treated as the same response.

6. *Other facilities.* No two author languages provide exactly the same response analysis capabilities, but you cannot readily do sophisticated matching without most of the facilities discussed above. Additional facilities provided include:

(a) the ability to strip blanks from a response, so that you can effectively get a single word which may include commas, full-stops, etc. Thus, RED, WHITE AND BLUE would become RED,WHITEANDBLUE;

(b) recognizing the numeric parts of a reply. This may be important if numeric problems are generated in the course. If 'I think it is 25.1' were entered, 25.1 would be recognized as the numeric part;

(c) the ability to do virtually any analysis you wish by learning special skills beyond those that are normally necessary. This might mean learning a programming language for the particular analysis that you wish to do. It must be emphasized that it is exceptional for this to be necessary with most of the languages mentioned in Chapter 17, so do not expect to require facilities beyond those supplied as standard.

YES/NO (AND TRUE/FALSE) ANSWERS

Questions that ask for a YES or NO answer are not likely to be very frequent, or very often concerned with questions testing knowledge or understanding. There is, after all, a 50 per cent chance of getting the correct reply even if you have no idea of the right answer. Where YES/NO answers may be practical is when the student is given the option of doing a test or some more examples. If YES/NO is being used as a knowledge question, it may be necessary to allow for 'DON'T KNOW' and you may also allow the student to ask for a hint or help.

Slightly vague wording of questions can elicit a YES/NO response. For example, 'Do you think the omission of either of these items from the description makes very much difference? If so, which?' In this case the author is looking for one of the items to be entered or, perhaps, 'none of them', but a student may well answer 'YES' or 'NO' in response to the first question. So, a fairly simple little routine can be developed as shown opposite. Note that we suggest that such a dialogue is permissible, although it should not be used too frequently. Provided the responses are handled properly, such a dialogue prevents the course becoming predictable and stereotyped.

It is a matter for the design team, but it is probably adequate to look for a Y or an N as the first letter of the first word of the response. You may wish to

```
Question 5R

Do you think . . . ?

RESPONSE          FEEDBACK                        Branch

Item A            Yes, it is important to . . .   Next frame

Item B            Well, I should have said that
                  Item A was . . .                Next frame

YES               Which one?                      Accept
                                                  answer

NO or NONE        You think neither item makes    Next frame
or NEITHER        much difference. I am not so
                  sure . . .
```

restrict the student to a single word reply. That would mean that YES, YUP, YEAH, Y, etc would be treated as YES, and NO, NONE, NEITHER, NOPE, N, etc would be accepted as NO. Replies, such as YES, I THINK SO, YES OR NO, YES NO, I GUESS IT WILL would be treated as unexpected answers and would probably cause the terminal to display a message such as: 'Please answer YES or NO', and wait for the reply to be entered again.

The above strategy will normally be adequate unless a student is trying to beat the system. If you are administering a test and using the marks obtained, you may have to be more strict in your matching, so that the student has to enter only Y or N, say, as the response. Exactly the same considerations apply to the use of TRUE (T) or FALSE (F) as the response to a statement.

MULTIPLE-CHOICE QUESTIONS
It is beyond the scope of this book to discuss, in detail, the formulation of multiple-choice questions.[1] It should be noted, however, that the authoring systems will allow you to collect adequate statistics on student responses to evaluate the quality of your questions, although it may only be possible to pick out gross errors in wording with a validation of the type recommended in Chapter 15. We shall concentrate in this section on the type of response that should be insisted upon.

With all responses to multiple-choice questions it is easier if you insist on a small variety of responses. You must decide how restrictive it is reasonable to be. For a single correct answer, eg 'b', you may insist that the single character b is all that is acceptable, ie you look for an exact match on b. You may look for b as a word in a sentence. A word is often defined in authoring systems as a string of characters preceded and followed by at least one blank (or space). So 'I think it may be b' would treat the single letter 'b' as a word, but 'I think it may be b.' would treat the letter 'b' followed by a full stop (b.) as a word.

---

[1] *Objective Testing* City and Guilds, 3rd Edition, 1977 covers multiple choice and other questioning techniques

So, to be safe, you would probably need to look for 'b' or 'b,' or 'b.' just to be almost certain to recognize b as the answer. You would be dealing with a particularly erudite (and long-winded) group if you needed to look for 'b:' or 'b;', but you have to decide where you draw the line and how you approach the problem in the first place.

If you now permit the trainee to give more than one letter as the response, there are new combinations to look for. If the answer is a, b, d, these could reasonably be entered as 'abd', 'a,b,d', 'a,d and b.' etc. It is no good just looking for the letters in the reply since 'and' contains two of the ones you want. It now begins to get rather complicated. Just how to tackle this depends on the particular authoring system that you are using, but we do not consider that in this situation, with a formalized questioning technique, it is unreasonable to be somewhat restrictive in what you accept as valid responses. You may wish to recognize 'all', 'none' or 'don't know' in a longer response and then only to accept the letters, or the letters with full stops or commas. In this example, you would thus recognize 'abd', 'a b d', 'bad', 'b, a, d', 'a,b,d.' as correct. However, 'a,b and d' would get the response of 'Just enter the letter(s) of your choice'. If you are consistent and explain what is required, either on the screen or on accompanying material, the student will soon realize what to do.

Analysing the responses to multiple-choice questions is fairly complex, but it should only need to be done once with most authoring systems because you can write what is called a subroutine which you can access at any point within a course. This is discussed further in the next chapter.

MISSING WORDS
It is a fairly common technique in programmed instruction texts to write a sentence with a word missing and to continue with different material depending on the reply. For example, you might display,

```
There are 2.2lbs in a

Enter the missing word.  ■
```

The responses that you predict for such a question would depend on its context but presumably you would look for 'kilogram' or 'kg' as being correct. Sometimes it is difficult to predict responses, and validation and testing may be helpful, but you might look for 'gram' or 'gramme', 'quarter' or, possibly, 'hundredweight' or 'ton'. In the next section on open-ended questions we discuss the treatment of more bizarre responses.

The missing word technique of questioning makes the response analysis somewhat easier, in that you know how many words to allow for in the reply, but the similar open-ended question is often as good or better, and not necessarily harder to handle. This is a technique that helps you to add the right kind of variety to the training, if you wish to use it.

MATCHING BLOCK
This questioning technique presents the student with two lists and asks him to match each item in the first list with the correct item in the second (see Figure 13.3).

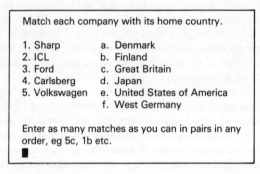

Figure 13.3 The matching block technique

This technique can be useful, but it may not be immediately obvious to the student how to enter his answers, so care must be taken with the instructions the first time the technique is used. With a fairly complicated format of this type, a standard method of presentation is particularly important. We shall be mentioning the use of touch-sensitive screens and light pens at the end of the chapter, but it is much easier for a student to respond to this sort of problem by touching or pointing to the pairs of his choice in succession.

OPEN-ENDED QUESTIONS
One of the main skills to be acquired by a CBT author is that of presenting properly worded questions and predicting the answers that students will give. You do not have to encourage wordy replies but you can produce a natural flowing question-and-answer technique. The question 'What does the C stand for in the initials EEC?' is asking for a single word, but allows students to enter their replies in free format if they wish. Remember, though, that your analysis of the response is, to a greater or lesser extent, dependent upon the goodwill of the student. You have to assume that the replies you will get to your questions are not designed to beat the system. And this is a reasonable assumption. If a student replies 'Community Club Committee Company Congress' in the hopes of getting the right word somewhere in the answer you may say that he is right or wrong depending how the answer is analysed, ie whether the correct word is sought before predicted wrong answers or vice versa. This may not matter if your reply to the student is helpful and provided the question is not part of a test. If you collect statistics and record the students' responses, you can very quickly pick up students using

these techniques. But it must be emphasized that this does not really matter except when administering tests. You must assume that the objective of each student is to complete the course successfully and this will be measured by the tests you devise. If students would rather play with than learn from the computer, they are the ones who will suffer. A far more serious problem arises when students enter replies that seem sensible enough, but which receive unhelpful replies from the computer. The most serious fault is probably for the computer to tell them they are right when they are wrong or vice versa. A gross error that is easy to make on some systems occurs in this example:

Question   At what age is life said to begin?
Answer   Forty-five.
Reply   Yes. Life begins at forty.

Because the author is allowing a free format reply, he is looking for the answer 'forty'. He ignores the fact that other numbers might, quite reasonably, be included. The same mistake can sometimes be made with numeric answers. If 40 were being looked for, a student might enter 400 by mistake. If additional characters were accepted he might get the same reply as above. Such errors can creep in all too easily and look so stupid when the student comes across them that there is a risk that he will lose confidence in the whole computer-based training programme.

Of course, mistakes do occur and it is important that the student does not end up thinking the wrong answer is right. The reinforcing feedback (life begins at forty) can be important in helping the student to realize that something odd has occurred.

Having now discarded the malevolent or mischievous students and retained the ignorant, let us return to the open-ended question format and response analysis. An important word of warning applies to much of CBT – keep it simple – while you are developing your own skills at authoring. It is better to have a simply structured course that works, than a complex one that aims to take care of every nuance, but fails. The two main areas where you may tend to get carried away are in response analysis and branching. Branching is considered in the next section.

As already mentioned, properly worded questions help you to design your response matching suitably. To ask the question 'What are the major tourist attractions in London' could elicit several pages of attractions and you can probably only cope with one line. 'Name one major tourist attraction in London' would probably keep the answer to one line but how do you predict the response? 'Name one major tourist attraction in Whitehall' would have two correct answers – Horse Guard's Parade and Downing Street. It would also have several anticipated answers such as the Cenotaph, Whitehall Theatre and, perhaps, the Houses of Parliament and Trafalgar Square. To be sure of matching the vast majority of answers that suggested Downing Street, you would have to look for Downing Street, Downing St, Number 10, No 10, Number Ten, Prime Minister's Home, Prime Minister's

House, Prime Minister's Residence, Official Residence of the Prime Minister plus others referring to the present Prime Minister.

We shall consider this analysis in some detail (see Figure 13.4), because the strategy is generally applicable. Remember that in most training, the case of the letters is not important.

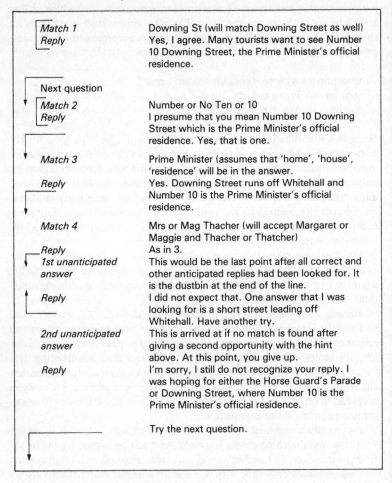

Match 1	Downing St (will match Downing Street as well)
Reply	Yes, I agree. Many tourists want to see Number 10 Downing Street, the Prime Minister's official residence.
Next question	
Match 2	Number or No Ten or 10
Reply	I presume that you mean Number 10 Downing Street which is the Prime Minister's official residence. Yes, that is one.
Match 3	Prime Minister (assumes that 'home', 'house', 'residence' will be in the answer.
Reply	Yes. Downing Street runs off Whitehall and Number 10 is the Prime Minister's official residence.
Match 4	Mrs or Mag Thacher (will accept Margaret or Maggie and Thacher or Thatcher)
Reply	As in 3.
1st unanticipated answer	This would be the last point after all correct and other anticipated replies had been looked for. It is the dustbin at the end of the line.
Reply	I did not expect that. One answer that I was looking for is a short street leading off Whitehall. Have another try.
2nd unanticipated answer	This is arrived at if no match is found after giving a second opportunity with the hint above. At this point, you give up.
Reply	I'm sorry, I still do not recognize your reply. I was hoping for either the Horse Guard's Parade or Downing Street, where Number 10 is the Prime Minister's official residence.
	Try the next question.

Figure 13.4 Analysing the responses to an open-ended question

Horse Guard's Parade would require a similar sequence of response analysis.

Presenting the training material on the screen
In this section, we take further the discussion on 'Selecting the presentation method' which was started in Chapter 2, and discuss the detailed decisions that should be made and adhered to in presenting your course. We will con-

sider the presentation of topics rather than pre- and post-testing. If you get the topic presentation right, you will have grasped the presentation techniques for the tests.

Using the computer for learning should be a stimulating experience for the student, so it is important to use the terminal to the full, provided that it is the appropriate medium. A well displayed screenful of information can always be displayed better on the printed page. If graphics are included on the screen, the same applies, only more so. Why, therefore, put static information on the screen? If you are leading the student through a module of a course, he does not want to be continuously switching from course book to screen and back. It is sensible to display a screenful of text or, perhaps, two without asking any questions. If you start displaying several in sequence without any student interaction, except 'Press ENTER[1] to continue', think again. One cannot, of course, be dogmatic, but be wary of too much narrative without useful interaction.

Many users will come to the terminal to study a CBT course apprehensive of the medium. They will find it potentially confusing. You will obviously know your target audience but it will always be good practice to do the same things in the same way during a course. This applies to standard instructions, screen layout for multiple-choice questions, YES/NO answers, student feedback, etc.

We have already commented on the instruction 'Press ENTER to continue'. This should normally be displayed in the same position on the screen, eg in the bottom right hand corner or in the same position relative to the last line of text. In this way, the student very soon gets used to the instruction.

It is not necessary to restrict the use of this instruction to a full screen of information. It is sometimes rather daunting for the student to have a whole screenful of information at a time, so it may be sensible to pause, with the screen partially filled, and add the second section when the student presses ENTER (see Figures 13.5a and b). Note that in Figure 13.5b, the 'Press ENTER to continue' instruction halfway down the screen has been deleted and re-displayed at the bottom of the screen. There are circumstances where you may wish to vary this instruction. For example, you may direct the student to another medium, thus:

Listen again to the conversation between the customer and the sales assistant and try to determine precisely where the misunderstanding occurred.
Press START on the tape recorder now.
When you are ready to continue, press ENTER.

---

[1] The ENTER key is pressed to indicate to the computer the completion of a line of typing. It may be labelled differently on some terminals. Make sure that you get the name right. In a terminal network there may be inconsistencies between terminals. Thus it performs a similar function to the carriage return key on a typewriter

```
   NESTED LOOPS

   As you will have realized from studying Page 7, the FOR-NEXT
   statements can be nested by enclosing one pair of FOR and NEXT
   statements by another. If you obey the rule about indenting the
   statements within the loop, it is easy to see that you have the
   nesting correct, eg

      100 FOR J = 1 TO 10
      110    FOR K = 2 TO 10
      120        READ A$(J,K)
      130    NEXT K
      140 NEXT J
       .
       .
                                                Press ENTER to continue.
```

Figure 13.5a A partially filled screen

With any standard questioning technique, whether it is multiple-choice, YES/NO, fill in the blanks, etc, it is important to be consistent in the wording and the layout. We shall consider the presentation of multiple-choice questions in some detail to show the factors that should be considered and then make more brief comments on other questioning techniques.

Consider the screen presentation in Figure 13.6. This may not be a particularly good question and, as already stated, the design of multiple-choice questions is beyond the scope of this book, but we can make some points on the layout.

1. If you are using letters as the identifiers for each statement, use lower case if you expect the student to key in a lower case letter. He may get confused if he thinks that perhaps he ought to use the SHIFT key for capitals. (Of course, a capital letter A, B or C would be a valid response.)
2. Always use the same layout for each possible answer. This may mean that you indent three spaces followed by the letter in lower case, a bracket and two spaces. If the possible answer goes on to a second line you must specify where that line starts, eg

```
   column    1 2 3 4 5 6 7 8 9 10
   first line          a )    T h e...
second line                   i s ...
```

NESTED LOOPS

As you will have realized from studying Page 7, the FOR-NEXT
statements can be nested by enclosing one pair of FOR and NEXT
statements by another. If you obey the rule about indenting the
statements within the loop, it is easy to see that you have the
nesting correct, eg

```
100 FOR J = 1 TO 10
110    FOR K = 2 TO 10
120       READ A$(J,K)
130    NEXT K
140 NEXT J
       .
       .
```

Statement 120 is the only statement in the second (inner) loop and it
is indented twice.

Statements 110 and 130 are only in the first loop, so they are only
indented once.

Each indentation is three character positions.

Press ENTER to continue.

Figure 13.5b The same screen (Figure 13.5a) with added text

Which of the following is correct?

There are approximately:
    a) 2.2 kilograms in a pound.
    b) 2.2 kilograms in a hundredweight (cwt).
    c) 2.2 pounds in a kilogram.

Enter the letter of your choice. ■

Figure 13.6 An example of screen presentation of a multiple-choice
question

You will probably wish to specify the normal line spacings between the heading, possible answers and instructions. These may be subject to change if you have a particularly full or sparse screen display and are, thus, guidelines rather than standards.
3. Give clear instructions about the method of answering. In some cases you may have more than one valid answer. If this is so, you must indicate it. For example, 'Enter the letter, or letters, of your choice.' Of course, if you use only that format when more than one letter is expected, your students may get wise to it.
4. Be consistent where you put the cursor. You may like to place your cursor on the next line, which is necessary for the answers to open-ended questions, or one space after the instruction as shown in Figure 13.6.
5. By pulling the part of the sentence 'There are approximately' out of each option, unnecessary repetition is avoided.

This should indicate the level of detail that is recommended for standard questioning techniques. For YES/NO or TRUE/FALSE questions the student should have a clear idea of what he is expected to enter although you may match other reasonable entries. For example:

Is Edinburgh called 'The Granite City'?
Enter YES or NO.

As already discussed, the YES/NO method of questioning should not be used extensively but it provides the opportunity to mention a technique that has a wider application. Some course authors like to abbreviate their instructions once they consider the student has had enough opportunity to understand them. In this case the line 'Enter yes or no' might be abbreviated to 'yes/no' immediately after the question, once the full message had been displayed a few times or possibly omitted altogether.
When presenting 'fill-in-the-blank' questions, it is generally easier for the course author to ask the student to enter the missing word on a subsequent line. This may be the best technique unless you are teaching form filling on the screen. We shall consider form filling below; for now, consider problems of this sort:

In the diagram on page 7, the flow of petrol to the engine is controlled by the_____.
Enter the missing word.

You must decide how the statements are to be laid out on the screen, whether the lines will be indented and, if so, by how much. You may decide to indicate the length of the word by the number of dashes in the space for the missing word. This is obviously a helpful clue. If more than one word is wanted, you must decide how to indicate this. One possible way is:

A common name for the accentor is the _____ _____.
Enter the two missing words.

Form filling
With many author languages there are problems with moving the cursor back up to the position of the missing words, and the benefits do not always justify the effort.

With form filling on the screen, where you are teaching specific skills and the lengths of fields are important, the effort must be put in. Form filling is one of the major areas of application for computer-based training, because, as discussed in Chapter 11, the cost equation is often right for this type of application. (When talking about form filling *on the screen* we mean that the person using the terminal has to enter data in specific areas of the screen according to titles and descriptions that are displayed (see Figure 13.7). It does not cover training people to complete printed forms.)

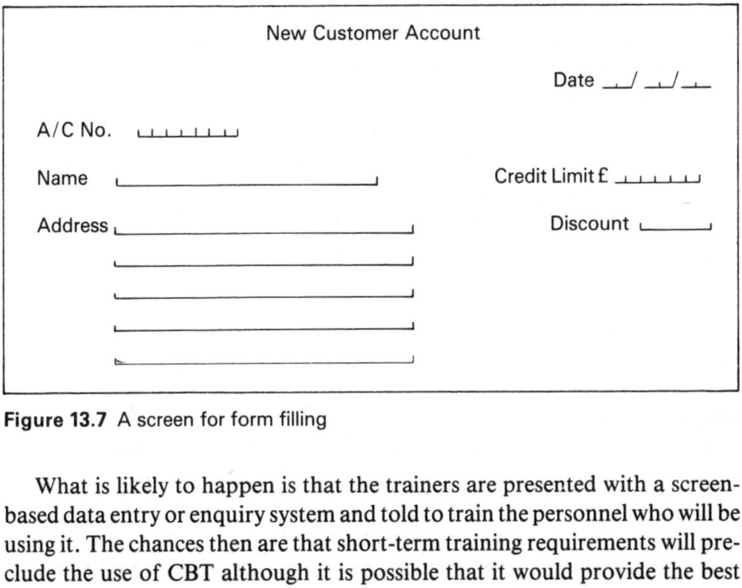

Figure 13.7 A screen for form filling

What is likely to happen is that the trainers are presented with a screen-based data entry or enquiry system and told to train the personnel who will be using it. The chances then are that short-term training requirements will preclude the use of CBT although it is possible that it would provide the best long-term solution. This is, of course, a generalization since many computer systems do not have an adequate authoring system of any sort, let alone one capable of handling form filling, and many firms do plan their training. What should happen is that the training department gets involved in the design stages so that the trainers can prepare themselves to do the job properly and acquire new training skills if necessary.

Form filling is an addition to all the other aspects of presentation, so all that has been written about response matching, etc is still relevant. In some ways life is easier because parts of the screen layout are already decided for you, but there are aspects of simulation that you may need to build into the system. It is hardly likely you will wish trainees to enter data into customer files on the live system, so you will probably wish to simulate what goes on with small dummy subsets of the data.

There are particular safeguards and features that can be built into the design of screens for form filling. These include:

1. specifying the length of a field so that either an error is indicated if the operator keys too many characters, or the cursor automatically skips to the next field;
2. numeric only fields so that only digits are accepted as valid;
3. check digit verification. This is a security feature that can be built into an account number, for example, so that the number keyed in by the operator is checked by carrying out some arithmetic on it, to see if it is a valid number. The chance of a random error getting through is very low;
4. protected fields. These are areas that are jumped over by the cursor. In Figure 13.7, only the areas indicated by the underlining would accept data. The cursor would either remain at the end of one field until the operator pressed the ENTER key, or it would automatically jump to the next field when the previous one was filled.

An authoring system that is good for form filling, a major area of CBT, will cater for these specific requirements. The author will be able to simulate the operation of entering a new customer into the system, including all the rules on credit limits and discount structure for new customers. Similar requirements are necessary for enquiry, order entry, hotel administration systems, computer operator training and a host of computer terminal-based applications. So, although form filling is a specialized area, it is still an important one.

Other screen features

So far we have discussed the design considerations for conventional screens, where the students reply using a typewriter keyboard. Since one of the major CBT systems that is available (PLATO) makes extensive use of touch-sensitive screens, these are obviously important. Other VDUs can have light pens attached. The use of aids of this type can make the interaction by the student much less inhibitive and error-prone. The design standards we have discussed are not markedly affected by the use of such devices; instructions will alter and there may be a tendency to use questioning techniques that lend themselves to pointing, eg matching block and multiple-choice. Too much of this type of questioning at the expense of freer form input might be disadvantageous, but the design team must base their decision on the target audience and the skills to be learned.

14. Using an author language

INTRODUCTION

This chapter describes a hypothetical author language (HAL) that provides the sort of facilities you should be able to expect in any author language for commercial use. These facilities are provided in a wide variety of ways. Some of the more recent systems are largely menu-driven – the trainer develops the training material by repeatedly selecting from choices presented on the screen – but the facilities are much the same. We then go on to describe additional facilities that may be necessary under some circumstances.

THE FRAMEWORK

The language that we are about to develop provides a system which will:

1. present text and questions on a screen;
2. accept responses entered using a keyboard;
3. analyse the responses;
4. store details of responses and the values of counters on a file;
5. branch to other parts of the learning programme;
6. provide feedback;
7. interface with subroutines written in computer programming languages.

We shall consider each in turn and then develop a short training sequence using HAL. Computer professionals may become irritated by the vague definitions and certain practical difficulties in implementing HAL, if anyone were to attempt to do so. Please bear with us, however, and try to accept the principles that we are illustrating.

FRAMES

The concept of learning frames was introduced in Part 1. In CBT the screen will be the principal feature of most frames but not necessarily the only one. In terms of our HAL, a frame will define a screen or part of a screen of information. Each of these frames will have a unique title in our author language, the frame label, which will be up to 20 numeric or upper case alphabetic characters, ie each character can be 0 to 9, or A to Z.

HAL commands or labels all start with a colon (see Figure 14.1). In these, all lower case letters are converted automatically to upper case. This removes the confusion of possibly having two different labels – :FRAME1 and :Frame 1.

:FRAME1 The frame title ends with the first space. This is a comment.

You may now enter text at any point on the screen up to the capacity of the screen.

You may use any valid characters, except a colon although, if you must have that we could probably provide it.

You may set up your screen layout exactly as you wish, although you will of course, have designed it carefully on screen layout forms first.

Figure 14.1 A HAL frame label and text

As the figure shows, after your frame label (:FRAME1) you may leave one or more blanks and then complete that line with a comment. Frame labels should normally start in column 1 for readability but it is not a requirement. Below that line, the screen is yours for you to enter any valid characters. The only restriction is that a colon in any place is recognized as indicating a HAL command or label, so is not acceptable.

If you have less than a screen of text to enter, as you almost invariably will, you may enter other HAL commands on the same screen. A screen is processed – checked for invalid HAL commands and stored – each time the ENTER key is pressed. The screen of information is assumed to finish at the lowest completed line.

To provide you with full control over your screen, it is necessary for you to be able to clear it as you wish. The command :C does that for you. Since the :C is a HAL command, it may appear on the same line as the frame label. Thus,

:FRAME100 :C
Now is the...

will cause the screen to clear when the course is run, and then the screen starting with 'Now is the...' will be displayed.

ACCEPT RESPONSES

When you have presented a frame to the student you will invariably want some sort of response, even if it is only pressing the ENTER key. There are anticipated responses (:A1,A2, etc) and unanticipated responses (:U1,U2, etc). HAL analyses the anticipated responses in the sequence A1,A2 ... An. Thus, as the author, you are in charge of the sequence of checking. This is important as you may wish to eliminate some wrong answers before matching the correct one, although you might tend to look for the correct answer first, possibly because you know what that is. For example, if the correct response to a question was 1940, you might want to accept 'nineteen forty' and permit extra words. In this case you could look for all or some of one, two, three, four, five, six, seven, eight or nine, before checking for nineteen forty.

The format of the anticipated response command is:

    :An rm:cm:si:branch label
        ↑
     space

Where: rm = response matches
        cm = counter manipulation
        si = statistics instructions
        branch label is the frame label to branch to if a match is found.

The only obligatory field is the branch label. If the response-matching field is omitted the branch is always taken, so any subsequent anticipated responses or unanticipated responses within the frame are ignored. HAL will warn you if you do this, but you may want to do it for testing purposes.

The unanticipated response command is processed differently. It is only ever reached if none of the anticipated responses are matched. At the first student attempt, the instructions following U1 are executed; if the branch label is omitted the student is returned to have a second attempt. If he fails to enter an anticipated answer the second time, the instructions in U2 are executed and so on, until the last U command in the frame is reached. The last U command must have a branch label otherwise it is optional. This is the point where you give up for that frame.

The format of the unanticipated response command is:

    :Un comment:cm:si:branch label
        ↑   ↑
     space   obligatory for last
                  U in frame

Where: comment = the feedback displayed to the student if this
                  point is reached.

    cm = counter manipulation
    si = statistics instructions
    branch label is the frame label to branch to if this U
        command is executed. (Usually omitted for
        unanticipated responses except for the last in
        a frame.)

All fields are optional. It is unusual to have no comments to the student but
they may be given in a frame reached by branching.

    The obligatory 'branch label' in the last :U command is a security feature
which prevents an omission by the author causing the training sequence to
continue, by default, in the next frame (see Figure 14.2). This is available on
some systems, but is notably lacking on others. We shall discuss response
matching in the next section.

:LABORTORY A frame to illustrate the use of An and Un.

Name one of the parties that has been in power in the United
Kingdom over recent years.

:A1 CONSERVATIVE$TORY$TORIES:
:YES, the Conservative Party is one. The other is, of course, the
Labour Party. :LIBSOCDEC

:A2 LABOUR$SOCIALIST
:YES, the Labour Party is one. The other is, of course, the
Conservative Party. :LIBSOCDEC

:A3 LIBERAL: Not really. They have been in power, but not
recently. Try again. :LABORTORY

:A4 COMMUNIST:
:I don't think you are really trying. Think which are the two major
parties in British politics and try again. :LABORTORY

:U1 I did not recognize your answer. One begins with 'L' and the
other with 'C'. Try again.

:U2 I am sorry, but I do not agree. I wanted either the Labour Party
or the Conservative Party :LIBSOCDEC

Figure 14.2 A HAL frame and accepted responses

Response matching
There are various levels of strictness in matching that you may wish to specify. The most strict is an exact match. For a single word response, if the answer is WESTMINSTER, an exact match will look only for the letters:

WESTMINSTER

with no blanks inserted within the string. If the correct answer were:

WESTMINSTER BRIDGE

the blank between R and B would be significant; if the student typed:

WESTMINSTERBRIDGE

it would not match.

Exact matching is less frequently used than the stratagem of looking for a word or words within the student's response, ie extra words are permitted. In HAL this is the default. If you look for a response with:

:A1 WESTMINSTER :FR300

the following will be accepted:

WESTMINSTER, WESTMINSTER BRIDGE, IT MAY BE
WESTMINSTER CATHEDRAL

etc. In this case, additional characters at the beginning, within, or at the end of the word would not matter, ie WESTMINSTERS would be accepted as would WESTMINSTERY. However, the order of the letters is important. If you want an exact match, you insert an X after the A in the command which thus becomes :AX1.

Alternative words or phrases
To keep the number of anticipated response commands to a reasonable level, you may look for alternatives by using the dollar sign $. This means that, if you put:

:AX3 WESTMINSTER$HOUSES OF
PARLIAMENT$WHITEHALL$PARLIAMENT SQUARE:F2

any one of the four groups would give a match if entered by the student, but because of the X in :AX3 the response WESTMINSTER BRIDGE would not.

Spelling
There are two circumstances when you may wish to match what you consider significant characters within the anticipated response. The first is when you are not particularly concerned about spelling as with COLOR and COLOUR. The second is when the word being matched may occur in a sentence in various ways – notably singular or plural. In either case, already defined rules may be adequate. If the answer is SPARKING, it may be

adequate to look for SPARK so that SPARK, SPARKED, SPARKS, etc would be accepted. If you thought SPARKLER was a possible response but a wrong one, you would either have to look for it before looking for SPARK, or be more specific with your match (:AX1 SPARKING$SPARKS$ SPARKED$SPARK) or reword your question so that SPARKLER was a totally unreasonable response.

In the case of COLOR and COLOUR, it is necessary to define editing rules. The insertion of an @ sign in the matching character string allows any single character at that point, and a # sign allows multiple or no characters at that point. Thus COL#R would accept COLOR or COLOUR, and FRATERNI@E would accept FRATERNISE or FRATERNIZE.

A technique frequently used, and one that is permitted by the default-matching rules described at the start, is to specify a minimum number of significant characters, often the consonants, eg RSVLT for ROOSEVELT. However, care must be taken with loose matching to avoid matching character strings that are not wanted. RLBLE or RELIABLE, unless an exact match, would accept UNRELIABLE as well as RELIABLE.

The use of counters

Counters can be used for a variety of purposes. They can:

1. keep track of the student's progress. This may mean keeping totals of correct and incorrect answers, but it may also mean keeping details of the student's answers to strategic questions, and deciding on the future direction depending on the answers;
2. be used as variables in arithmetic calculations;
3. control the progress of the student at various points.

In the counter manipulation section of :A and :U commands, counters can be used algebraically. A counter is a letter (upper case) followed optionally by a number, so A, R, C1, Z9 are all valid counters. Counters are automatically set to zero at the start of a module and can hold a very wide range of numbers. One normally only wishes to do fairly simple arithmetic on counters, eg $A = A + 1$, but complicated calculations are possible, eg $A = 5*(4.7 - 1.01/7)$.

To control the student's progress through the course, it is also necessary to make decisions of the type 'if the student has got three questions wrong go to a remedial loop'. The counter manipulation section can be as long as you need and there is an IF ... THEN statement similar to that provided in the BASIC computer programming language. Thus, the IF $C3 = 3$ THEN frame label will cause execution of the training module to branch to the frame label specified if $C3 = 3$, otherwise the counter manipulation section will continue. Note that, if the branch is taken, the statistics instructions in the anticipated answer command will not be executed. Other comparisons apart from equals may be made. These are: greater than (>), less than (<) and not equal to (< >).

Counters may be altered or tested at various points in a frame. They have been shown coming after a response match as this is a common place to use them. Another point where they may be used is immediately after a frame label.

Statistics instructions
The statistics instructions can be used to record on a disk file the answer entered by the student, the values of any counters, the frame label and any remarks by the course author. If the letters STR are included in the statistics section, the student's response is recorded. If any counter is included, its value at that point is recorded. If the letters FR are included, the frame label most recently passed through is recorded. Any comments in the statistics section between quotation marks are also recorded.

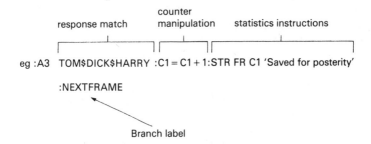

Statistics instructions are shown in the response-matching part of the frame, but statistics instructions may also be included at other points.

PROVIDE FEEDBACK

We have now defined most of the syntax, or command structure, of the basic author language. Feedback to the student is provided by branching to a new frame. If a systematic design structure is developed, as discussed in Chapter 12, it is easy in HAL to control the path that a student takes through a course.

Feedback can be provided in three ways, two of which have already been introduced. You may branch to a frame that displays the feedback to the student. With an unanticipated response you may include comments after the :Un. This is useful because you will then automatically branch back to the last frame label. You have the option with the unanticipated answer command to branch as well. However, if you branch and ask a supplementary question, and then return to your original frame, :U1 will be executed again when the next unanticipated answer is met. The condition is *reset* when you leave that frame (see Figure 14.3a and b).

If you are using part of your CBT course for testing, you may wish to return varied comments to the student when the answers are correct, such as

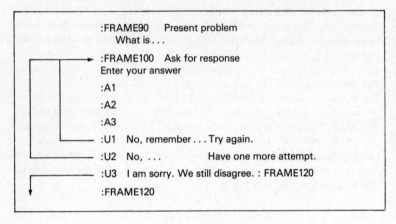

Figure 14.3a Providing feedback with unanticipated responses:
remaining within the frame

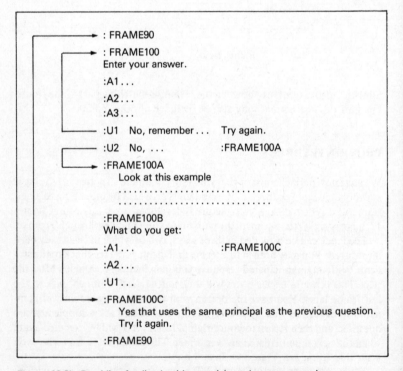

Figure 14.3b Providing feedback with unanticipated responses: going
outside the frame and branching back

'Correct', 'Good', 'Well done', 'Right', etc. To do this, and any other things that may occur more than once in a course, such as presenting a diagram, it is convenient to be able to branch to a subroutine. A subroutine is a piece of your HAL course that is reached by branching from one or more frames. The subroutine then executes, and eventually returns to the point immediately after the command that branched to it (see Figure 14.4).

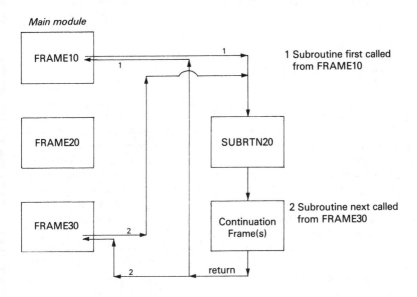

Figure 14.4 Repeated use of subroutines

This command can occur at any point where a frame label is valid. The command format is :S frame label 1 frame label 2. If the :S command is inserted within a screen display, frame label 2 is not necessary. If, however :S is used at the point where the frame label is given as a label to branch to, frame label 2 must be entered (see Figure 14.5).

```
:FRAME50
    You will remember that this diagram was developed previously
:S SUB20
    What does valve 1 control?
:A1 WATER:S SUB60 FRAME60
```

Figure 14.5 The use of the :S command

There is no reason why a subroutine should not consist of several frames but it must come to an end sometime. To indicate that you wish to return to the main part of the course, you enter the return command. It has the format :R. There may be several return commands within your subroutine. Each will return to the same point. You should not exit from subroutines in any other way except with :R unless you are exiting from the module altogether. Subroutines can save tedious repetitive coding, and keep down the total amount of code that you have to write.

INTERFACING WITH SUBROUTINES WRITTEN IN COMPUTER PROGRAMMING LANGUAGES

This may sound rather a specialized requirement for a language that is to be used by trainers, but let us consider what this facility can provide. HAL, as described so far, will work well for most screen-based training material. It does not provide facilities for graphics or recognizing other peripherals such as printers, plotters, graphics tablets, voice, audio cassettes, slide projectors, videotape, videodisc, etc; we shall add facilities for supporting graphics and a printer at the end of the chapter. The other facilities, however, tend to be specific to the computer, the type of peripheral and its make, so it is not possible to provide general functions to support all the peripherals that are available and new ones that are likely to come.

To overcome this problem, it is necessary to provide the ability to interface with subroutines, written by programmers in programming languages, that will support non-standard devices and facilities. The HAL command to do this is :CALL. The format is :CALL subroutine name (parameters). This permits you to pass data to the subroutine, as variables in the parameter string, and to receive data back in the same way. Being subroutines, they return to the point immediately after the :CALL command when they have finished.

:CALL type subroutines should cause no difficulty to course authors because they will appear in the author manual as additional commands. An example of a :CALL subroutine might be :CALL TIME (T1) where the time in seconds would be put into the variable T1. Another might be :CALL TOD (T1,T2,T3) where the time of day would be returned with the hours in T1, the minutes in T2 and the seconds in T3.

DEVELOPING A SHORT PIECE OF TRAINING MATERIAL

We shall now use HAL to write the small session that was developed in Chapter 12 as part of a course for staff in an employment agency. You will need to refer to Figures 12.1, 12.2, 12.7 and 12.9 on pages 159-171. What you read here would be entered directly into the computer using the keyboard and screen. We are *not* telling you to develop your course at the terminal. The course has been thoroughly developed on the forms described in Chapter 12, before coming anywhere near the screen. The amount of detail you include and the way you use the screen layout form will vary depending on who will be entering the course at the terminal. If one of the course authors is doing the entering, less detail will be necessary than if a clerk or secretary, with some relevant training, is doing the job. We have here, and in Chapter 12, assumed that the course authors are doing the entering.

Assuming you are using a screen of 80 columns by 24 lines, you would key in the information exactly as it is shown in Figure 14.6, if that matched your design standards, down to, say, the end of frame M30A, which is the line :U1 :M40. You would then press the ENTER key to get the HAL system to check what you have entered and store it. The sorts of immediate checks that it could carry out are discussed in the next section. If HAL reported any detected errors, you would correct them at this stage, and then go on to the next part of the coding by clearing the screen or scrolling a part of the text off the top of the screen, leaving blank lines at the bottom. Frames and lines would be entered in the order in which you keyed them in on the screen, but the HAL system would provide facilities for you to open up gaps to enter new parts where you needed them. You could also delete sections or move them.

On first studying Figure 14.6 you may feel that it is a bit cumbersome, and decide that it will not be very easy to enter your CAT course. However, there is not much more to learn once you have grasped the sort of things you can do in an author language. Of course HAL has not got all the facilities, but there again, you do not want to have to learn a large amount before you can get started. Some enhancements are discussed later in the chapter.

ERROR CHECKING AND COMPUTER VALIDATION

Our HAL is now defined in a basic form and we have developed a short instruction sequence. That is fine if you do not make any errors either in writing the material or in entering it. If errors get through to your finished course or module, they may, depending on their severity and the students taking the course, have a catastrophic effect either on the attitude of the students to CBT or, if the errors lead to incorrect tuition, on their future work. The latter is highly unlikely in a properly designed and validated course and cannot be checked by the computer, but lesser faults can cause irritation to students. The most common fault of this kind is poor response matching. Again, the computer cannot pick this up, but validating and collecting student responses as statistics should help to refine weaknesses.

The computer can carry out its own validation of the training material both as you enter it and when you have written the module. This prevents errors creeping in due to mistakes in writing the HAL commands. While you are entering the material, it can check for syntax errors and that certain rules are obeyed. Examples of the type of error that would be picked up at the entry stage are:

The part of the programme preceding frame M30 will be here.

1 :M30　:C　:T = 0　Clear screen and set counter T to zero.

Right, it will be useful to record both what sort of documents will be typed and the method used to produce them.

Words like 'TYPIST' include a wide range of activities and methods. In this case the job advertisement would have been much more effective if it had mentioned the method of typing to be used.

Incidentally, how many kinds of typing can you think of? Type in as many as you can. :M30A　**2**
:M30A

3 :A1 COPY:T = T + 1:AUDIO:T = T + 1:SHORT:T = T + 1:SPEED:T = T + 1:WORD:
T = T + 1:M40
:A2 ELECTRIC$MANUAL:
This is a type of TYPEWRITER. I asked for kinds of TYPING. Have another try.
:M30A
:U1　:M40
:M40

Here's my list:

Copy typing　Audio typing　Shorthand　Speedwriting　Word processing

　　:M40A　**4**

5 :M40A　:IF T　5 THEN M40B

You will see that you got all :M40C
:M40B　:IF T = 0 THEN C2

You will see that you got some :M40C
6 :M40C
of them and maybe you thought of some others.　:S ENTER　M50
:C2
You don't seem to have any of these, but you may have thought of some others. What is important to remember is that a general job title like TYPIST means different things to different people.　:S ENTER　M50
:M50

It also helps those looking for jobs to decide their suitability for a vacancy if the advertisement tells them something about the products of their work.

So a question asking about the kind of document typed would be useful. Careful questioning about these details could produce this information on the card:

'Copy typing of letters, proposals, reports and sales literature'.

Suppose an employer notifies a vacancy for a caretaker, what specific duties do you think might be mentioned in the advertisement? :M50A
:M50A

:A1　HELP$HINT　:Caretakers often wear overalls to perform some of their duties. Now have another try at answering the question. :M50A
:A2　MAINTAIN$CLEAN$POST$MAIL$SECURITY$LOCK$HEAT$BOILER$
POLISH$LIFT

Figure 14.6 An example of HAL code

Notes

1. The frame M30 starts with the screen clear command (:C) that clears the screen and puts the cursor in the top left hand position on the screen. Remember, only HAL commands and comments are acceptable on a line after a frame label. We also set the counter T to zero. This is not essential if T has not already been used as all variables are set to zero at the start, but it is good practice in case you are careless in your use of variables.

2. The branch to the next frame (:M30A) is necessary to allow a branch back to this point from the anticipated response at :A2 in frame M30A.

3. Anticipated response match A1 looks for the various keywords one at a time, so that a count (in variable T) can be kept of the number found. Each attempted match automatically goes on to the next match within A1 until the matches are exhausted. If any of the words match the branch to frame M40 takes place, otherwise the next response match (in this case A2) is attempted.

4. The branch to M40A at the end of frame M40 is indented to avoid confusion between the branch instruction and the actual frame label which must start in column 1. HAL will not get confused but you might.

5. Frames M40A, M40B and M40C are used to save you entering the same text twice over. By testing the value of T we can tell the student that he got all or some of the anticipated kinds of typing.

6. Frames C2 and M40C use the subroutine ENTER. This subroutine, which is coded at the end, displays the message 'Press ENTER to continue' and waits until ENTER is pressed. It then clears the screen and returns to the calling point. Both frames C2 and M40C then branch to frame M50.

7 :T1 = 1:C4
   :U1:T1 = 0:C4
   :C4

These were the sorts of duties I was thinking of:

Maintain fittings   Clean entrance hall   Accept post   Security checking
Locking and unlocking of premises   Check heating system   Polish floor
Check lifts and report faults
      :C4A

8 :C4A   :IF T1 = 0 THEN C5

We are thinking along the same lines. :S ENTER M60
   :C5
I think you will agree that it will make a difference if some of these are included
or not. :S ENTER   M60
   :M60

You will remember . . . etc.

The rest of the course would be included after this point. It would probably
terminate with subroutines of a general nature such as the ENTER subroutine.

9 :ENTER   Subroutine to wait for ENTER and then clear screen.

                                                Press ENTER to continue.

   :U1::C:R

Figure 14.6 An example of HAL code (continued)

Error	*Example*
Frame label more than ten characters	:FRAME98765432
Duplicated frame label	You enter :F20 when that frame already exists
Unknown command	:B or :Z entered where a command is expected
Duplicated anticipated response number	:A2 repeated within frame

Some of these would be warnings and some would cause the entry process to
stop until you had corrected the error.

When you have written your module or part and wish to test it, it is very
convenient to be able to run it straight away as though you were the student.
Before HAL will permit you to do that it validates your HAL code. At this
stage it can look for errors that it could not pick up earlier. Examples are:

7. In frame M50A we use a new variable T1, which is a totally different variable from T, as an indicator to show whether any of the key words in anticipated response A2 have been found.

8. T1 is tested to determine whether to add the comment in frame C4A or C5 to the list displayed in frame C4.

9. The ENTER subroutine only displays the message 'Press ENTER to continue' on the right of the screen, and waits for ENTER to be pressed. The unanticipated response command :U1 is the only one, which means that no matching is done; the Return command :R is obeyed regardless of what has been typed before ENTER is pressed. (Remember that the ENTER key is a special key on the keyboard that has to be pressed to indicate to the computer that you have typed as much as you want to on a line.) The :C command clears the screen after ENTER has been pressed and puts the cursor in the top left hand corner. The two colons are necessary because 'comments to the student' are expected here. In this case the clear screen instruction (:C) is effectively the comment.

Error	*Example or explanation*
Branching to non-existent frame	Branch to FRAME10 when it does not exist
No return in subroutine	:R omitted in subroutine
Return without subroutine	:R found outside a subroutine
Screen may overfill	There are possible circumstances where more lines may need to be displayed than the screen can display. Scrolling would occur.

On some microcomputers with diskette drives, this process may take several minutes if you have a substantial module, ie 15 minutes or more of training. But it is necessary to ensure that the module cannot stop with some unpredictable and incomprehensible error while the student is running it. Whether you are forced to validate every time you make a minor change in development is not crucial. What is very important is to be able to do this computer validation before students get at your course. If a system does not validate in this way, it is adding an unnecessary and time-consuming chore to the testing process. Even at the end, it is impossible in a substantial module to be sure that a potentially disastrous error is not still lurking somewhere, for example, a branch to a non-existent frame label. Computer validation removes this uncertainty.

SOME OTHER FEATURES

We shall now discuss one or two other features that might be added to HAL to give it more flexibility. One addition that we might want is the facility for handling form filling. Form filling has been discussed earlier and requires very specific features such as protected fields and highlighting, but one aspect is screen addressing and we shall add that. We shall also add support for simple graphics and a printer.

Screen addressing

Screen addressing means that you issue a command to move the cursor to a particular point on the screen and start displaying from that point. Considering a screen of 24 lines by 80 columns, you have 1920 addressable points for the cursor. The top left position is usually point (0,0), so the column can go up to 79 and the line up to 23 (see Figure 14.7a).

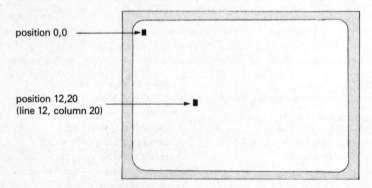

position 0,0

position 12,20
(line 12, column 20)

Figure 14.7a An 80-column screen with the points 0,0 and 12,20 indicated .

We can thus define our screen addressing command as:

:@line,column

We might have a frame: :FRAME90
:@10,60 Wrong. Re-enter.
:@10,30
:FRAME80A

This would display a message against a particular response and place the cursor to allow the student to enter another attempt (see Figure 14.7b).

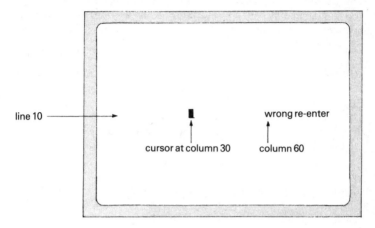

Figure 14.7b How the HAL commands in FRAME90 are displayed

Cursor addressing adds a new level of flexibility for you in your use of the screen, as well as a new level of complexity in designing your course.

Printing
It may be useful at various points in a course to print something for the student to take away with him – perhaps an insert for his course book or a summary of his performance. There are two forms of printing that you may wish to use. The first gives the student the option of receiving a printed copy of the material displayed on the screen. You might give that option with certain important screens. The second allows you to print information directly on the printer without displaying it.

The command :PS will print the contents of the screen at the point where the command is executed. The format is :PS.

The command :P will print output within that frame, instead of displaying it, from the point at which :P is executed until a :PE command is reached. The :P command is automatically switched off at the end of the text part of a frame, eg by a :A command. The formats are :P and :PE.

Screen graphics
We have discussed screen graphics, its advantages and disadvantages. Sophisticated graphics can become complicated both to use and to define, so we shall define a simple graphics submode. Two new HAL commands define the beginning and end of graphics submode. They are:

      :GB   for Graphics Begin
and :GE   for Graphics End.

Between these two commands, a special plotting language is recognized.

When discussing plotting, it is sensible to start, by default, with the origin at the *bottom* left hand corner of the screen at x = 0, y = 0. We then have a sheet of graph paper with an x maximum of the width of the screen and a y maximum of the height of the screen, both in millimetres. We can define the following commands:

PLOT (x,y)	draw a straight line from the current point to x,y
MOVE (x,y)	move from the current point to x,y
WRITE (x,y,ang,height,text)	write the 'text' starting at x,y of height 'height' and at angle 'ang'
CIRCLE (x,y,rad)	draw a circle of radius 'rad' and centre x,y

Other commands could draw arcs, rectangles, polygons, pie charts, histograms, etc.

A sequence using graphics might look like this:

```
:GRAPH1    A frame to plot a simple graph
           A graph of temperature vs time
:GB
MOVE(10,30) PLOT(210,30) MOVE(10,30) PLOT(10,210)
MOVE(10,30) PLOT(30,60) PLOT(50,90) PLOT(70,110)
PLOT(90,130) PLOT(110,140) PLOT(130,148) PLOT(150,155)
PLOT(170,162) PLOT(190,170) PLOT(210,176)
WRITE(9,100,90,5,Temperature – °C)
WRITE(90,22,0,5,Time – minutes)
:GE
:@21,0
What is happening to the rate of increase in temperature with
increasing time?
:A1 FALL$DROP ....
```

The above would produce on a suitable screen, the display shown in Figure 14.8.

Such graphics are still fairly limited. For example, the axes in the graph (Figure 14.8), although labelled, have no scales on them. With a little more sophistication the graphics could remain quite easy to use while providing comprehensive facilities including colour.

REVIEW

We have developed our hypothetical author language to a reasonable level of sophistication. It still has some omissions, mainly those concerned with dis-

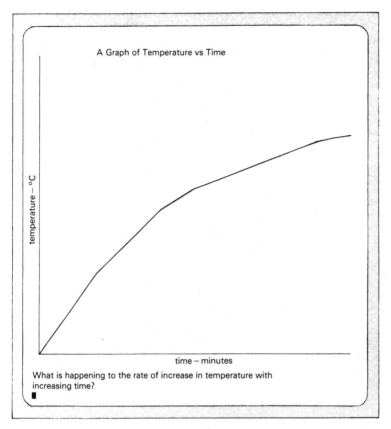

Figure 14.8 A graph drawn using HAL plotting commands

playing counters and accepting and evaluating numeric responses. This capability and the ability to generate random numbers are particularly important for drill and practice in arithmetic skills, but they are also generally useful for mathematics, accounting and science.

We have emphasized the importance of the computer validating the code for coding correctness. We have not described in any detail how you would edit your modules as you developed them. This is an important area, as poor editing facilities can make an otherwise excellent system very difficult for the trainer to use, but such a discussion would rapidly get technical.

Do not think that the way this language has been developed means that all authoring systems look like this to use, although several have more than a passing resemblance. Most will provide all the basic facilities described, or very similar ones, although some use different techniques to achieve much the same end.

SUMMARY OF HAL COMMANDS

Command	Description
:An	Match the student's response with those anticipated after this command.
:AXn	Match the student's response exactly.
:C	Clear the screen to blanks and put the cursor in the top left hand corner (position 0,0).
:CALL	Call a subroutine in another computer programming language.
:R	Return to the point immediately after the last :S command.
:S	Branch to a HAL subroutine. Return when a :R command is executed.
:Un	If none of the anticipated responses match with the student's response, obey the unanticipated response commands in the sequence :U1 for the first unanticipated response in the frame, :U2 for the second, etc.

Some advanced commands

:@	Move the cursor to the point specified by the parameters
:GB	Go into graphics mode
:GE	End graphics mode
:P	Print the following text until :PE is executed
:PE	Stop printing text; switch display to screen
:PS	Print the screen contents, as displayed, on the printer

15. Testing and evaluation

INTRODUCTION

This section discusses the methods of evaluation of the CBT courses as they are written. The necessity of collecting statistics on the paths that students take is discussed and the use of interviews and questionnaires is considered. The difficulties of comparing the CBT course with the previous method of training are often very extensive and highly subjective, but some evaluation of this type should be part of the plan from the beginning. This relates back to the training objectives that were discussed at the very beginning in Chapter 1.

COURSE REVIEW AND REVISION

When the course author has completed a section of the course, which may vary from ten minutes or so to an hour, it is ready for *peer evaluation*, the reviewing and assessing of a course. If the course is the first that a team has developed, it is essential to review the beginning before too much has been written, to see that agreed objectives are being met and that the course structure is progressing as planned. With most substantial CBT courses there will be a course book, but there could also be videotapes, videodiscs, tape-slide presentations, lectures, etc. These must be available in a suitable form to permit a sensible evaluation to take place.

What is peer evaluation going to look for?

1. *Content.* The course must teach the subject matter that has been specified in the initial objectives.
2. *Accuracy.* The internal assessment verifies that the subject matter taught is accurate and sufficient.
3. *Presentation.* The quality of the presentation on the screen must be consistently high. If a screen with 80 characters by 24 lines is being used, the usage of this large area must be effective and uncluttered. This has been discussed with examples in Chapter 13.
4. *Adherence to presentation standards and guidelines.* The purpose of presentation standards is to make the medium as unobtrusive and sympathetic to the user as possible. The author should not be permitted to use different screen layouts according to whim. Peer evaluation

should pick up occasions where the standards have not been adhered to. This will cover such items as:

○ YES/NO responses – are Y or N accepted in capital or small letters?
○ Multiple-choice questions; are the choices preceded by a letter and a right hand bracket, eg a)?
○ Instructions for continuing to next screen – is the same instruction given each time (press ENTER to continue)?
○ Headings;
○ Highlighting;
○ Use of capital letters.

At the same time as these standards are being checked, the screen presentations of standard formats must be studied to see that they match the guidelines. For example, the layout of the following should adhere to guidelines:

○ YES/NO responses – is the instruction clearly given in a standard format in the same place on the screen each time?
○ Multiple-choice questions – is the letter for each choice against the left hand margin, and are three spaces left before the first word? Are continuation lines indented by eight characters? Are two blank lines left between choices?

Unfortunately, or perhaps fortunately, standards do not cover all eventualities and it takes judgment at the peer evaluation stage to assess whether the course has the right 'feel'. This depends, of course, on the supplementary material as well, but in considering the computer-based element the 'feel' is influenced by such factors as:

○ Instructions to the students progressing with them. For example, at the start, it may be standard to ask the student if he is familiar with the terminal. For new students it may be necessary to tell them to press RETURN or ENTER after entering their replies, but only for the first few times. When to stop is a matter of judgment and experience and may depend on how they do initially.
○ Remedial loops. How patient are you when the student appears to be rather stupid? What style of comment in these circumstances is most helpful?
○ Humour. A dangerous commodity but in the right hands it can make a course if the other elements are right. Remember that a joke is never so good that it can be repeated in the course, so beware if remedial loops can be gone through twice.

5. *Use of the author language.* Just as there should be a set of standards and guidelines for course presentation, there must be standards for using the author language if the writing and, importantly, the amendment of the course is to be efficient. These standards have been discussed earlier and cover such items as labelling, branching, response analysis and use of counters. The use of these standards must be checked, but there are other techniques that may help the writer if he is aware of them, many of which cannot be written down to cover all

eventualities. An experienced author may be able to help a novice by giving hints after reading the actual code. A fresh approach can also occasionally surprise the more experienced author with an elegant or effective solution to a particular problem. A study of the code the author has written may lead to amendments that are not detected by the student but which save on computer time, storage requirements in memory or on disk, and most importantly on author time in later modules.

This is not all that studying the code can achieve. In testing the course as a user, it can be very difficult (or impossible) as well as time-consuming, to attempt to enter all the predictable responses to each question. Studying the code produced by the author allows the evaluator to see just how responses are being analysed, how branching is being handled and how statistics are being kept. It is probably better to run through the course as a user before looking at the coding. This means that the first view taken is that of the student.

6. *Statistics.* Statistics are kept for two main reasons – to measure student performance and to aid validation of the course. Chapter 16 discusses the sort of statistics that may be collected. Here we shall consider what use to make of them during validation and testing. Figure 15.1 illustrates both these points.

```
TEST  RESULTS                    FOR STUDENT 006 OF BRANCH 2254

   DATE            PAGE              QUESTION            ANSWER          RESULT
              0000000006638   -   REVERSALS DEBIT    -   Y        -   RIGHT
                        B     -   REVERSALS ENTRY    -   N        -   RIGHT
                        B     -   REVERSALS CREDIT   -   N        -   RIGHT
                        B     -   REVERSALS          -   Y        -   RIGHT
                        B     -   REVERSALS DATE     -   110581   -   RIGHT
                        B     -   3LA               -   *        -   UNKNOWN
                        B     -   SEQUENCE NUMBER    -   DI404972319 -  RIGHT
                        B     -   ACCOUNT NUMBER     -   30378984  -  RIGHT
                        B     -   AMOUNT            -   2113     -   WRONG
                        C     -   DEBIT             -   Y        -   RIGHT
                        C     -   ENTRY             -   N        -   RIGHT
                        C     -   CREDIT            -   N        -   RIGHT
                        C     -   REVERSALS         -   Y        -   RIGHT
                        C     -   REVERSALS         -   110581   -   RIGHT
                        C     -   3LA               -   STO      -   RIGHT
                        C     -   SEQUENCE NO       -   DI410000020 - RIGHT
                        C     -   ACCOUNT NUMBER    -   60419576 -  RIGHT
                        C     -   AMOUNT            -   1190     -   WRONG
                        D     -   DEBIT             -   Y        -   WRONG
                        D     -   ENTRY             -   N        -   RIGHT
                        D     -   DATE              -   110581   -   RIGHT
                        D     -   CREDIT            -   N        -   WRONG
                        D     -   REVERSAL          -   Y        -   RIGHT
                        D     -   3LA               -   STO      -   RIGHT
                        D     -   SEQUENCE NO       -   DI410000040 - WRONG
                        D     -   ACCOUNT NUMBER    -   50488887  -  WRONG
                        D     -   AMOUNT            -   6850     -   WRONG

   NO. OF ANSWERS CORRECT    19         TOTAL NO. OF QUESTIONS ANSWERED    27
              PART CORRECT    +          NO. OF ANSWERS NOT CHECKED
                             ---         NO. OF ANSWERS CHECKED            27
                             19          NO. OF ANSWERS UNKNOWN             1
   NO. OF ANSWERS WRONG      7          PERCENTAGE OF ANSWERS CORRECT  = 70%
```

Figure 15.1 An example of statistics collected on a live system

The time taken for the course, or parts of it, is important since the course objectives will have given target durations. The time that students spend on different parts of the course may be found to be unrelated to the relative importance of the topics covered in these parts.

The detailed statistics of the exact path that each student has taken through the course, and the answer to each question, are enormously important during the testing phase. These statistics are obviously going to be voluminous and it is unlikely that they will be collected once the course is in regular use. By following the exact paths that the students follow, the whole structure of the course can be checked.

Peer evaluation will lead to a course review that decides the changes that should be made and may, if the evaluation has covered an early section of a course, lead to revised objectives or a new approach to subsequent parts of the course. Any revisions as a result of peer evaluation must be completed before the next stage of course validation.

COURSE VALIDATION

Validation should only be carried out on courses or sections where the CBT part is complete. Supporting material must be virtually, if not entirely, complete. With printed material this is not difficult; photocopies can be used. With videotape, videodisc or slides, changes may not be so easy. What follows may sound like an ideal; it will not always be possible. However, the nearer that the validation can approach the format suggested here, the more certain you will be that a thoroughly tested product is going into use.

The students selected should match exactly those who will be taking the course in the future. If it is a course for apprentice motor mechanics, for example, the validation group should be taken from apprentices with a similar degree of experience. A small group of half a dozen or so should be started on the course exactly as though they were taking it normally. The course author can hope to get the following data when the students have completed the course:

○ pre- and post-test results;
○ the time each student has spent both using the computer and in the overall course;
○ the responses of all the students;
○ the students' evaluation of the course;
○ any difficulties the students may have had.

Most of this information will be collected automatically. The time spent on the course as a whole will be recorded by the person in charge of the testing, but the time spent using the computer can probably be recorded as a statistic.

Test results and all responses will be automatically recorded as statistics and it may be sensible to ask the student to evaluate the course at the terminal, perhaps as a series of multiple-choice questions. In addition it may be thought necessary to interview the students as well. The subjective information the author wants is:

○ suitability of the English used
○ subject matter
○ questions
○ presentation
○ enjoyment
○ time taken
○ supporting material

There are two quite different circumstances under which course validation can take place. The new CBT course may be replacing an existing one using different teaching methods, or it may be a new course. In the first case it should be easy to compare the pre- and post-test results of the students taking the existing course, with the results of those taking the CBT course. It is important that the original objectives state the yardstick for success as clearly as possible. For example, it may seek to do as well as the existing course, to do a specified amount better as measured by the post-test, or to do as well in less time. A course can only be validated against clear objectives.

It is relatively rare for there to be an existing course that matches exactly the CBT course, because most training requirements change fairly rapidly, and a rewrite of a course is a good time to revise it. Whether or not the CBT course is replacing an existing one, an intelligent evaluation will need to consider most of the following points and possibly others:

1. Are the pre- and post-test results consistent?
2. Were students who could not cope identified early and directed to the instructor?
3. Do the more knowledgeable students progress too rapidly through the course and get good results? Is it too easy for them?
4. Do the remedial loops help those students who use them, ie has the lack of knowledge that caused them to go into the loop been rectified by the additional material?
5. Is response matching adequate? Are the anticipated responses being handled correctly and have the authors overlooked responses that they should have anticipated?
6. Do the results suggest that the explanation of part of the course is poorly presented, or too easy?
7. Did the students have difficulty in administering the course themselves or were the instructions unclear? For example, if videotape was needed could they use it easily and obtain the correct piece of material?
8. Are there any remedial sequences which no one visits?

An example of what can happen in a course that has not been thoroughly validated and tested is given below. This is part of an actual run by a student taking a chemistry lesson on gas chromatography. The student should have had some written material to refer to during the lesson. This student was already having some difficulty when the following happened (note that this lesson uses a printing terminal and only capital letters):

> LOOK AT FIGURES 2 AND 4, WHICH ARE
> CHROMATOGRAMS OF BENZENE/CYCLOHEXANE MIXTURES
> OBTAINED AT 90 DEG C USING TWO COLUMNS OF
> DIFFERENT POLARITY. WHICH ONE OF THE
> CHROMATOGRAMS (FIG 2 OR FIG 4) WAS OBTAINED USING
> SE30, A METHYL SILOXANE STATIONARY PHASE?

student I HAVE NOT GOT ANY FIGURES HERE

> YES – SINCE SE30 IS NON-POLAR AND WILL NOT SEPARATE
> THE MIXTURE.

> NOW LETS RETURN TO THE QUESTION WITH WHICH YOU
> FOUND DIFFICULTIES EARLIER ON IN THE EXERCISE.

> .
> .

> And so on for a page and a half with the student getting more
> and more confused, until

> .
> .

> NOW – WHICH CHROMATOGRAM WOULD YOU PREFER TO
> USE (FIG 1 OR 2) FOR ROUTINE QUANTITATIVE ANALYSIS?

student LOOK IVE TOLD YOU I HAVE NO FIGURES

> PLEASE ANSWER THE QUESTION BY TYPING 1, 2 OR
> NEITHER

student OK ILL GUESS 1

> YES – WHY?

student ITS SEPARATED MORE

> NO! ...

> .

> .

As a learning experience the lesson was a disaster for this student. It should be said that this was exceptional and the course was generally successful. But it points to several areas that can be overlooked during course development. Things obviously go catastrophically wrong at point 1. First, the student does not have the required printed material. Why not? Were the instructions unclear or non-existent at the start of the course? Second, the student response is interpreted as the correct answer. Something is wrong with the response matching. The trouble is that in looking for the word FOUR as part of the correct response, the letters FUR are looked for, in that order, in any word in the response. That combination occurs in FIGURES, so the response is accepted as correct, much to the confusion of the student.

The student's response at 2 is indicative of the sort of attitude that users often build up towards the computer. The computer was expected to know that the student did not have the figures.

One further point is that the student appears to be ignorant of how to get out of the course; it is patently obvious, from studying the whole session, that he was completely lost and should have stopped. Again, were the instructions adequate or should the course have recognized how the student was faring and advised him to get help?

To suggest that a validation run on half a dozen students will provide all the answers for the evaluation may seem a little unrealistic but we have not finished yet. In our ideal world you will make changes to the course as a result of the first validation run and then put another group of students through the same process. With a refinement process such as this, it is possible to end up with a course that you are confident meets the objectives set at the beginning, or such revised objectives as experience may have shown to be desirable.

Out in the real world where trainers work, time, cost and production problems will mean that you have to decide the final format of the videotape months before the course is ready, or else it is not there when you want to do course validation, or the training manager demands that a new module is inserted only a few weeks before the course goes live. However, if the course teams are clear about the validation process, much can be achieved by doing as much as possible of what is suggested here.

FOLLOW-UP

Classroom-based courses, which have a large amount of teacher contact, should alter in response to the perceived needs of the students, because of the class feedback the teacher receives. If there is an omission, the teacher can go away and learn the relevant material.

With a CBT course it is not so easy to maintain a continuous watch. Once the validation is over, there is a temptation and a likelihood that the project will be regarded as complete; in some circumstances it may be. With other courses, revision may be forced by changes to the subject being taught. Maintenance for a piece of electronic equipment for example, may change because new components replace the original ones. A large number of subjects may change gradually or subtly over a period, or the emphasis may alter. A classroom course, largely due to the sensitivity of those running it, can and should react to these changes. The lack of this gradual development in a CBT course is not likely to be highlighted in comments, because the students will not know what they are missing, nor is it likely to be shown in the tests which were, after all, designed to meet the original objectives.

A problem with all courses, whatever the medium, is that too rarely is any systematic evaluation made as to how well the course is preparing the students for the next stage, ie the actual needs. This is true whether the course teaches car maintenance, COBOL programming, or sales techniques. Your CBT course may be well received by the students, enjoyable and produce good post-test results, but it is always capable of improvement. A questionnaire or interview with them, their manager or instructor will confirm that the course meets its overall objectives but it may indicate that certain topics were not covered in enough depth or were omitted, while others were over-emphasized. A regular review meeting, say every six months, should consider the status of each course, its usage, relevance, need for improvement, etc so that it does not carry on for years becoming increasingly out of date.

This follow-up process should lead to detailed refinement of the product, so that faults or omissions found at this stage will not generally lead to recrimination, but will be treated as positive steps towards a better product.

16. Computer management of instruction

INTRODUCTION

Computer-managed learning (CML) and computer-assisted training (CAT) are the two parts that combine to make up computer-based training. Throughout Part 2, we have referred to the subject generically as CBT, because in most circumstances, the two are intertwined. All authoring systems provide some aspects of CML such as statistics or student testing. What we will discuss here are the aspects of CML that are found with the more sophisticated CBT systems, where the authoring system is a major component of the system rather than the complete system itself.

In Part 3 we have, so far, discussed how to write modules of training material. The assumption has been that such modules will take an hour to an hour and a half to complete, depending on the mix of computer-based and other training methods. If an apprentice is taught a technique and sent away to do it practically, the module may take a morning.

The overall design and planning of a course of indefinite duration was described in Part 1, so now we need to bring the two together. We must consider the administration and management of a CBT course. Most of what is described here can be done perfectly well by a trainer or competent secretary, provided they are systematic and organized and there is always someone available who can help. This is precisely the sort of job – boring, time-consuming and error-prone – that the computer can do very well. Unfortunately, it is a complex process for the computer to do well, and the sort of facilities described here are only provided with CBT systems running on minicomputers and mainframes and not necessarily with all of them. It is by no means essential to do any of the course management on the computer, but it must be done somewhere if the training is to be methodical and complete.

Computer-managed instruction (CMI) or computer-managed learning (CML) does not, of itself, require the trainers to use the computer to present the training material; this was done with a project called CAMOL (Computer Assisted Management of Learning).[1] The computer can keep details of the courses and modules that each student has completed, whether it was lecture, audio-visual, practical, etc. It can record any marks and issue instructions to the student about the next modules to take and the sequence. It can also report to the supervisor on student progress.

[1] *CAMOL – A Technical Overview* Educational Products Group, ICL, 1978

There are several functions of CML that can be considered separately and, at the lowest level, virtually all CBT systems provide some, notably statistics, and the ability to direct the student to new material, depending on cumulative performance or a (series of) test(s). We shall consider the following:

○ Registering courses and students
○ Testing and record-keeping
○ Directing the student through the course
○ Restart facilities
○ Course maintenance
○ Reporting
○ Running a CML system

REGISTERING COURSES AND STUDENTS

Courses will probably consist of a number of modules, some of which are computer-based even if they incorporate other media, and some are in other media altogether or consist of a practical experiment. It should be possible to establish a course structure defining the path that students will go through, depending on various criteria at each critical point, and this will have been done at an early stage of the design process. Figure 16.1 shows formal pre-tests and post-tests, but the process need not be as formalized as that. You can accumulate data on student performance during the module, but this is rather more difficult to plan and validate.

The course structure is then established and will consist of a student progress chart, of the type shown in Figure 16.2, which will be recorded in the computer. This indicates how that particular student will be assessed at each stage in a course. All students on a given course will normally have the same progress chart. It is then necessary to register the students for the course, so that records can be established of their progress and, possibly, for security purposes. If the company has a widely used terminal network, it may be quite inappropriate for anyone who can get into the system to be able to use the training programmes. Also, as trainers, you will wish to ensure that those who do sign on to your courses are properly equipped with the essential supporting material.

TESTING AND RECORD-KEEPING

We have discussed testing and monitoring the student's progress within a module. If you are using CML, the important information should be stored as part of the student record and accumulated as he progresses through the course. It is not essential or necessarily desirable for all, or even most, of the testing and assessment to be carried out by the computer. It is quite possible

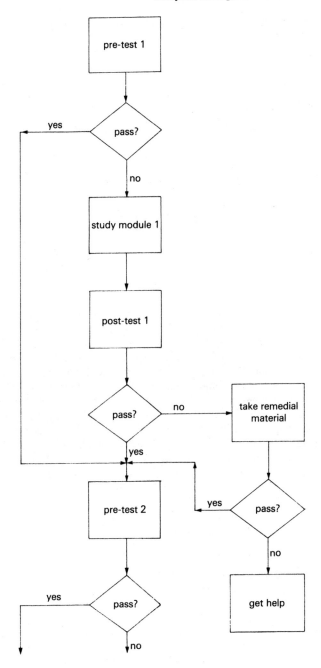

Figure 16.1 The sequence of pre- and post-testing

Student number	1543	Student name	F J Bridge
	Module	Success criteria	Next module
No	Description		
1	Introduction	—	2
2	Basic principles	70% in post-test	Pass 3
			Fail 2A
2A	Film on I/C engine	—	2
3	Compression and expansion	80% in post-test	4
		60% in post-test	3A
		Less than 60% in post-test	Instructor

Figure 16.2 An example of a student progress chart

to administer tests or assess a piece of practical work and then enter the marks for these into the computer. The marking can be done using marked documents of the type illustrated in Figure 6.14.

Whenever one discusses keeping any type of personal records on the computer, the problem of privacy can become an issue. In this case, if properly handled, there should normally be no problems. Handling the records properly involves making it quite clear what data are being collected and why, and being willing to let the student see his own records if he wishes. The fact that handwritten comments on the individual in his personnel file may be far more derogatory and inaccurate than those on the computer, as well as being virtually inaccessible, is not strictly relevant. The 'Big Brother' image and the power of computers to record and access vast amounts of data, mean that you must be prepared to be seen to be above board in your use of personal information.

So, what data will be kept? It will depend on what you require but may include any or all of the following:

○ Course name
○ Student name and number
○ Date started and date completed for each module
○ Marks in tests
○ All responses ⎤ these can take up a lot of disk storage
○ All frames passed through ⎦ but are useful for validation
○ Time spent on each module
○ On remote terminal systems you may record the locations of the terminals used.

DIRECTING THE STUDENT THROUGH THE COURSE

The course structure must be established in the computer so that the information is available to direct the student. It may be quite adequate for the author language to direct the student to, or suggest, the next topic, depending on its own information accumulated in counters. If more sophisticated CML is being used, it will be possible to prevent the student, if it is important to do so, from taking modules that are out of sequence, or from going to the next learning assignment before he has passed a given test. Of course, the instructor should be able to override such restrictions for classes or individuals if necessary.

It is with large numbers of students and strict training procedures, for example in the British and American forces, that these prescriptive aspects of CML pay off. Substantial savings in staff time can be made in recording students' progress and in directing them on to the next topic. It can also save the students both time and frustration, when they have completed a test or module, by giving immediate feedback of how they have performed and what to do next. CML can also save the student time by being specific about the parts of the previous module that he has not learnt adequately. The student is therefore directed to remedial material only for his weak areas. A less sophisticated approach would make the student study remedial material that covered all topics with a resultant waste of the student's time and demotivation. The alternative to CML may be to seek out the instructor, who may be busy, and get the next topic or module from him. A well-run CML system releases the instructor to spend more time helping the students with their difficulties, and informs him, by means of reports, of those students who are struggling and where they are having difficulty. Two examples of the instructions that might be given to students at the end of a module are shown below (see Figures 16.3a and b).

The 4-stroke engine

You have now completed:
    Module 4   The Inlet and Exhaust Valves

You got 70% in your computer assessment and 60% for your practical.

You understand most of the topic but need more instruction on how to adjust tappets.

Before proceeding to Module 5, you should watch the videotape 'Adjusting tappets' and then take Module 4B.

You should then see your instructor.

           To print this screen press P.

Figure 16.3a Example of instructions to students at end of module

---

The BASIC language

You have now completed:
  Module 3   The FOR ... NEXT Loop.

You got 98% in your computer assessment. Well done.

You should now code the problems on Page 5 of your course book and enter them as instructed in Module 1. If you have difficulties, consult your instructor.

When ready to continue, study:
  Module 4   DO WHILE and DO UNTIL.

Figure 16.3b Example of instructions to students at end of module

RESTART FACILITIES

Restart facilities permit the student to terminate the course at any point, not necessarily at the end of a module, and to restart at that point when he next signs on to the course. It may not, in fact, be sensible to restart at precisely the point where the student finished, in which case he will restart at the nearest sensible previous point.

It is possible that the computer system may break down for some reason while students are signed on and studying courses. In this case the restart capability will allow the student to continue from the nearest previous point that it can. When a system with sophisticated CML is running, it periodically records all the crucial details of each student's progress including all counters, time since signing on and the point in the module that the student has reached. This is called a checkpoint. If the student's terminal ceases to function for any reason in the middle of a course, he will automatically restart at the last checkpoint when he next manages to get into the course.

This is obviously an advanced facility and is not available with the smaller systems. If restart is not available, there are one or two alternatives that can help. You will realize that a student who gets to the latter stages of an hour's module will be displeased at finding that the system has suddenly stopped. He will be even more disenchanted if he then finds he has to start again from the beginning when the system becomes available again. One obvious method is to write short submodules (of eight to twelve minutes' duration) that normally run straight into one another but each self-contained enough for a student to be able to start at the beginning of any of the modules. Problems may arise in breaking long modules down if counters are normally accumulated throughout the long module. However, if the initial design incorporates the submodule concept, the adequate handling of counters can be planned. It will be necessary to have an appendix to the course book indicating the submodule structure and explaining how to start at any of them.

Some training material can be studied in a variety of sequences and it may be possible to allow the student to select his own path through the subject, by making a choice from a menu or series of menus. The last of a series of menus may present modules of eight to twelve minutes' duration. If it is necessary for the student to complete all the modules before finishing the course, it will be necessary to keep records including that information.

COURSE MAINTENANCE

We have claimed previously that it is often easier to maintain and amend CBT courses than conventional courses. We have also repeatedly stressed that very few CBT courses use the computer alone. The changeability of the information is therefore one factor to consider when deciding the best medium for specific teaching material. If you have had a thousand course books printed and bound, you will think long and hard before modifying the odd page in order to put over a few points more clearly. If, however, this same information is in computer-based form, it may be a matter of an hour or less to implement the changes and make them available to all students. This is not to suggest that unvalidated parts of courses should be put up in this way; it is rather that inadequacies thrown up by ongoing validation of student responses and comments should be corrected. Obvious examples occur when the response matching for a particular question is not quite good enough, and an alteration or addition solves the problem.

Other aspects of course maintenance involve adding, replacing, and deleting modules. The implications of altering the module structure in a course may be far-reaching, as it will alter the information recorded in the computer for the student progress chart (see Figure 16.2). The CML system should not allow you to add or delete modules unless you also restructure the student progress chart.

It is also quite possible to use a module or a group of modules in more than one course. If you start altering these, you have to be careful or you may cause confusion even to the most sophisticated CML system.

REPORTING

The instructors need reports on the students' progress while authors need information about the courses. The training manager may need additional reports on the utilization of the system, on the times students take for courses and where they are located.

Student reports

The information that instructors and management can obtain about each student on a course will depend on the system, but they generally wish to know how far the students have progressed, the results of the tests, the time spent at the terminal and, most important, which modules they have mastered, ie if an acceptable level has been achieved. A report might look like the one in Figure 16.4.

Student Report   7/5/82

Course: The 4-stroke engine

Student name   F Smithson   Student number 1153   Date started 6/4/82
                                                        Date last used 7/5/82
                                                        Time on system   1:36

Module	Pre-test	Post-test	Pass/Fail	Time (min)
1	32%	80%	P	32
2	56%	90%	P	51
3	42%	68%	F	13
4				
5				

Figure 16.4 A student report indicating the student's progress

It is also possible to obtain a student summary report, so that an instructor can have an overall view of how the students under him are progressing on a particular course (see Figure 16.5).

Group Summary   7/5/82

Course: The 4-stroke engine   Instructor: G French
                                                  No registered: 37

Module	Students beginning	Average marks Pre-test	Post-test	No pass	No fail	Average time (min)
1	35	47	85	33	2	37
2	32	51	82	29	3	41
3	27	38	80	22	2	25
4	3	61	–	–	–	–
5	0	–	–	–	–	–

Figure 16.5 A group summary for a particular course and instructor

Course reports

A huge amount of information about student responses, the values of counters and the paths that students take through the course can be recorded on disk files. It is usually only practical to accumulate this information soon after release of the course, as the last stage of validation. If you try to keep recording for all courses, you will soon find that your friendly data processing department becomes distinctly unfriendly. It may be important to make good use of this information for the first 20 or 50 students who take a course and then cease to collect it. The sort of summary that you can obtain is shown in Figure 16.6, but it could be far more exhaustive if the values of counters were frequently recorded and reported.

Course Analysis

Course:　The 4-stroke engine　　　　　　　　　　　No registered: 74

Date:　　　　1/5/82 to 2/6/82
Module:　　　1
Frame label:　M1L10

Response (number responding)	*Branch to frame*
help (1)	M1L10H
VALVES (1)	M1L10C
They are cylinders (1)	M1L20
Silinders (1)	M1L10A
Sparking plugs (2)	M1L10　Unanticipated
Cylinders (2)	M1L20
valves (3)	M1L10C
hint (3)	M1L10H
don't know (5)	M1L10G
cylinders (22)	M1L20

Frame label: M1L10G

yes　(2)	M1L10
YES (1)	M1L10
y　　(1)	M1L10
n　　(1)	M1L10H

Figure 16.6 A course analysis giving every response at each frame

Another report that you can produce will print student comments. Depending on the CML system and how you use it, it may be possible for students to make comments at any stage in the course, at specific points, or only at the end. This facility does not use up a large amount of disk space, so it is sensible to keep it going permanently and print comments every month or so when the course is in general use (see Figure 16.7). Other reports that will be of use to the course authors and to the training manager will give summaries of the level of use of the courses. An example is given in Figure 16.8.

Management reports

Training management will wish to know how much the various courses are being used, how long students take to complete the courses and the utilization of terminals. We shall give examples of the information that might be included in a course usage report (see Figure 16.9) and in a terminal usage report (see Figure 16.10).

Course Comments

Course: The 4-stroke engine

Date: 1/5/82 to 2/6/82
Module: 1
Frame label: M1L500

Student no	Comment
1011	I enjoyed the programme, but got a bit muddled with the diagram on Page 7.
1017	Good.
1019	I am sure I was right about the big ends but I was told I was wrong.
1055	I got a bit bored in the middle because I had to wait ages for the computer to answer me. Otherwise OK.
	etc

Figure 16.7 Comments on the course from the students

Cumulative Course Summary   10/6/82

Course: The 4-stroke engine

Module	No started	No completed	No pass	Average time (min)
1	94	94	93	39
2	93	75	75	45
3	72	63	60	27
4	63	47	47	50
5	46	43	43	31

Figure 16.8 A cumulative course summary showing the use of a specific course

Course Usage Report 10/6/82

1/4/82 to 10/6/82

Course	No registered	No started	No completed	Average time (hr:min)	Total time	Sessions
4F The 4-stroke engine	120	94	43	3:12	175:18	517
792 Milling machine theory	29	29	27	4:17	123:02	286
.	.	.	.	.	.	.
.	.	.	.	.	.	.
.	.	.	.	.	.	.
Totals	542	483	450	3:48	2100:07	3276

Figure 16.9 A course usage report showing how all courses are being used

Terminal Usage Report 10/6/82

1/4/82 to 10/6/82

		Connect time (hours)		
Terminal	Student	Author/supervisor	Total	Location
V27	128	3	131	Bayswater
A1	0	116	116	Trainers
V1	111	0	111	Group Room 1
V4	107	0	107	Group Room 1
V5	107	0	107	Group Room 1
V2	102	0	102	Group Room 1
A3	0	100	100	Trainers
.	.	.	.	.
.	.	.	.	.
Totals	1026	275	1301	

Figure 16.10 A terminal usage report showing which terminals are being used

RUNNING A CML SYSTEM

Certain aspects of the administration of a system with sophisticated CML features require specialist skills which at least one member of the training department should acquire, with the data processing department providing back-up. The CML administrator will be responsible for setting up the course modules and the linkages from the student progress chart. He will assign numbers to students at the request of instructors. He will produce standard reports and advise training personnel of other reports that could be produced, although the data processing department may write the programs that print the reports, once the layout has been agreed. He will also be responsible for monitoring the performance of the system and the use of computer resources.

The CML administrator may receive various specialized reports showing, for example, response times for students, ie the time the student has to wait after completing his entry before the computer responds. A wait of more than a second or two is not usually acceptable unless something is happening, or the student is warned. Other reports might inform the administrator of the amount of disk space he has allocated to him and how full it is, and the amount of central processor time the courses are taking up. This would indicate the training load on the system. He would also get an error report if anything went wrong, whether the system recovered automatically or not.

Whether the CML administrator spends his whole time running the training system depends on the level of usage; if a high level of sophistication in the computer management of the learning is being paid for, it is not going to be cheap. You should therefore plan to use it widely if you get it. Having said that, several companies do have such systems yet only use some of the simpler facilities the systems provide.

17. Some authoring systems

INTRODUCTION

This chapter discusses a selection of authoring systems that are available commercially. The facilities provided by the different systems vary widely, as do the costs and the sizes of computers they run on. There are not many systems that run on a wide variety of computers, so if you already have your computer, your choice may be limited to one or two authoring systems. The CML aspects of computer-based training only tend to be provided, in more than a rudimentary form, on the systems for larger minicomputers and mainframes.

The market place for authoring systems is developing very rapidly – at least the systems suppliers think and hope it is. There are new systems coming on to the market regularly and those already there are developing, so you may have to investigate other systems as well as studying relevant ones from this list in detail.

AN ALPHABETICAL LIST OF AUTHORING SYSTEMS

System: **COMBAT**
Supplier: Mills & Allen Communications Ltd,
               1-4 Langley Court,
               London WC2E 9JY
               Tel: 01-240 1307
Runs on: DEC LSI 11/23 for the authoring system and on DEC LSI 11's and
               Apple II's for the presentation system; other machine
               implementations are planned.
Description: COMBAT is a recently introduced authoring system. It consists of
               three components:
               ○ The preparation (or authoring) system that allows authors to
                 develop the training material
               ○ The delivery (or presentation) system that presents the training
                 material to the students
               ○ The management system that provides the administration and
                 monitoring facilities
                   Because COMBAT provides fairly comprehensive facilities, the
               preparation and management functions have been separated from
               those of delivery. This means that students may study training

material written in COMBAT on a microcomputer, while a minicomputer is needed for the larger and more complex authoring and administrative processes.

The preparation system is designed to be used by trainers who are not computer experts, and to achieve this the system restricts the author to a series of templates which he can use to produce the course.

To provide flexibility, there is a development of the programming language PASCAL, called Author PASCAL, that can be used by trained programmers for more sophisticated use. (The PASCAL system is USCD PASCAL).

Mills & Allen Communications offers a complete package of the system, documentation and education.

System:	**EDUTEXT AND MICROTEXT**
Contact:	Division of Information Technology and Computing,
	National Physical Laboratory,
	Teddington,
	Middlesex TW11 0LW
	Tel: 01-977 3222
Runs on:	A wide variety of computers from small microcomputers upwards. The smallest systems, eg cassette tape-based BBC microcomputers and PETS with diskette drives, run MICROTEXT which is a subset of EDUTEXT.
Description:	EDUTEXT is an authoring system which is easy to use; this makes it attractive to the trainer. It does, however, have good matching capabilities and a number of sophisticated facilities that make it suitable for producing advanced courses.

EDUTEXT has been developed to permit new commands to be added to the language. This means that commands to control special devices can be added easily. This is important today as the pace of development is rapid, and devices such as digitizers, plotters, slide projectors, video cassette players, videodiscs, etc are likely to become widely used in education and training.

EDUTEXT is a new system so there is not a lot of user experience, but if the National Physical Laboratory achieves its aim of making EDUTEXT portable across a large range of mainframe, mini- and microcomputers and it is a reliable system, it should prove popular. The CML aspects are limited at present.

MICROTEXT is a subset of EDUTEXT and permits authors to write and present courses on small microcomputers. MICROTEXT probably runs on a smaller and cheaper microcomputer (BBC model B microcomputer) than any other author language worth the name. It does not have some of the important facilities of a comprehensive author language, such as a full arithmetic capability or the capability of filing statistics.

System:	**IIS (Interactive Instructional System)**
Supplier:	IBM (UK) Ltd
	Contact your IBM salesman or local IBM office.

Runs on: IBM medium and large computers (4300 and 370 upwards) and compatible IBM look-alikes.

Description: IIS comes as two program products from IBM for each of which the customer pays a monthly rental; they are IIAS (Interactive Instructional Authoring System) and IIPS (Interactive Instructional Presentation System). The authoring system is used to develop courses and the presentation system for running the courses. The reason for the split is that IBM, amongst others, also sells CBT courses, and it may be quite adequate for a lot of customers only to have IIPS in this case.

IIS uses one of two main methods for course entry, both of which assume basic course structures. The first method, course structuring facility (CSF), uses a worksheet approach for the author. There are several different worksheets on which the author enters the text, questions, matching requirements for responses, etc. These are then entered into IIAS and generate the modules of the course. The other method, simulation exercise facility (SEF), is particularly suitable for simulations of other computer applications such as data entry, operating, enquiry, etc. It is a powerful alternative to CSF in most circumstances. There is a more basic author language called Coursewriter that gives the author considerable flexibility, but is also more difficult to learn and to write.

There are extensive CML facilities, and a wide range of reports can be produced on student performance, responses, course details, usage and machine utilization. Students may also send comments to their instructors via the terminal.

IBM provides a selection of courses written in IIS that companies may purchase for training purposes. They are currently all computer-related, covering such topics as running computer operating systems and teaching about various IBM products. These can be run under IIPS with no authoring skills within your company.

System: **MENTOR II**
Supplier: PMSL Computer Services,
Hays Lane,
Mixenden,
Halifax,
West Yorkshire HX2 8UL
Tel: 0422 247521

Runs on: Terak microcomputers and others; also on SEL 32 minicomputers.
Description: MENTOR II is a recently announced CBT system. It is a sophisticated system with a powerful screen editor designed to make it easy to use. It has graphics capabilities and supports videotape and videodisc as standard.

MENTOR II is written in UCSD Pascal and has been designed to make it relatively easy to support non-standard devices. The fact that it is written in Pascal means that it should be quite possible to mount MENTOR II on a variety of micro-, mini- and mainframe computers.

MENTOR II has good CML facilities that can be tailored to meet the customer's requirements.

PMSL did market a CBT system, called MENTOR, which ran on Univac mainframes. They no longer market this, but existing customers are supported.

System:	**PASS**
Supplier:	Deltak Ltd,
	Banda House,
	Cambridge Grove,
	Hammersmith,
	London W6 0LE
	Tel: 01-741 4711
Runs on:	Apple II microcomputer with dual diskette drives. 64k bytes of memory are necessary for the development system and 48k bytes for the presentation system.
Description:	PASS (Professional Authoring Software System) was produced by Bell and Howell and is marketed by Deltak. It is a flexible course authoring system with some CML functions for student adminis-tration. The colour graphics facilities of the Apple II are supported, as are several character sets and type fonts. Videotape and videodisc interfaces are available and other devices can be attached.

PASS is one of the more powerful authoring systems currently available on microcomputers but it is limited to the Apple II microcomputer. PASS provides extensive documentation including self-study training material.

System:	**PHOENIX**
Supplier:	Westinghouse Management Systems SA,
	1 High Street,
	Edgware,
	Middlesex MA8 7DF
	Tel: 01-951 1615
Runs on:	IBM medium and large computers (4300 and 370 upwards) and compatible IBM look-alikes.
Description:	PHOENIX is a product of Goal Systems International Inc and is marketed in Europe by Westinghouse. It is claimed to be upward compatible from IBM's IIS. This means that courses written in IIS should be easily converted to run under PHOENIX.

PHOENIX provides EASE (Easy Authoring System for Education) which adopts a structured approach to course develop-ment. It is an interactive development system, so that authors sit at VDUs to enter their courses. EASE prompts the authors and so takes them through the course entry process. Detectable errors are displayed immediately so that they can be corrected at once.

PHOENIX permits the author to include algebraic and trigono-metric formulae in the course, and permits test or drill and practice questions to be selected from an item bank, so that a student taking a test for a second time will get different questions from the original test. Students can pass comments to the instructor at any time.

Overall, the CML aspects of PHOENIX are extensive and it is probably one of the best CML systems available. Westinghouse also claims that performance of PHOENIX is very good in terms of its utilization of computer facilities such as central processor time.

System:	**PILOT**
Suppliers:	Various
Runs on:	A variety of microcomputers including Apple II, PET, SHARP, Tandy, and on some minicomputers.
Description:	There is no standard for PILOT, so the quality of different implementations varies. As an authoring system it has most of the facilities you would expect, and usually allows the author to use the BASIC language for non-standard or more sophisticated purposes. At the simple level, it should be perfectly comprehensible to the trainer with no computing skill; the problems will come with the need for more advanced facilities or because of the characteristics of the particular system on which it is being used.

PILOT was developed primarily for education and most of the implementations are not properly maintained or extensively documented, so potential users should check carefully what to expect if they are planning serious use of PILOT. Some systems, notably Apple PILOT, are well documented. Apple PILOT supports the graphics capability of the Apple II, sound, and has an animation package.

Generally, PILOT should be satisfactory for small scale use and to permit you to 'test the water'. It has very little of the CML facilities of larger systems, although some implementations will permit the collection of statistics on student responses, marks, etc.

System:	**PLATO**
Supplier:	Control Data, Control Data House, 179-199 Shaftesbury Avenue, London WC2H 8AR Tel: 01-240 3400
Runs on:	Control Data bureaux and large Control Data computers. There are also Control Data microcomputers that run the Micro PLATO presentation system.
Description:	Control Data has spent many millions of pounds developing and marketing PLATO and it is probably the most sophisticated CBT system commercially available today. PLATO makes extensive use of a touch-sensitive screen so that students can carry on some of their dialogue with the computer without using the keyboard. The quality of the graphics that can be displayed is also high, permitting displays, for example, of aircraft instrumentation for pilot training; animation is also possible.

The author language, TUTOR, is designed to be used by the trainer and does not require programmers despite the extensive capabilities of PLATO. It does, as one would expect, require fairly extended exposure for a trainer to use some of the more sophisticated facilities.

PLATO also provides a very extensive CML system with course and student administration.

PLATO is provided at a number of Control Data learning centres where students can go to study courses normally provided by Control Data. For a fee, the student works in a carrel sitting at a PLATO terminal to study a specific course. PLATO can also be provided by installing terminals within your company which are then linked into a Control Data bureau over the telephone network. Very large organizations may consider installing their own PLATO system.

Micro PLATO microcomputers can be purchased to run PLATO courses that are distributed on diskettes. They are, thus, presentation systems, Micro PLATO microcomputers can also link into bureaux as terminals.

There is a recently announced stand-alone author and delivery system that currently offers a subset of the full PLATO capability.

System:	**SIMPLER**
Supplier:	Modular Computer Services,
	Blackburn House,
	London Road,
	Coventry,
	Warwickshire CV3 4AL
	Tel: 0203 504150
Runs on:	Modcomp minicomputers.
Description:	The SIMPLER system bears a marked similarity to PLATO using the same touch-sensitive screens or ordinary visual display units. It also uses TUTOR – the same author language as PLATO. It does, however, run on Modcomp minicomputers so it is not nearly such a large system to install. Using the touch-sensitive screens, SIMPLER provides high quality graphics and animation. It is not essential to use touch-sensitive screens where other, cheaper terminals are appropriate.

The SIMPLER system can run on a dedicated minicomputer supporting varying numbers of students up to 30 or more. It is also possible to use the minicomputer to support other applications outside the training area, at the same time as CBT is running, if a sufficiently powerful configuration is installed.

The computer-managed learning aspects of SIMPLER, while quite extensive, do not attempt to match those of PLATO.

System:	**STAFII**
Contact:	Professor PB Ayscough,
	Department of Physical Chemistry,
	University of Leeds,
	Leeds LS2 9JT
	Tel: 0532 31751

Runs on: Most computers from the largest mainframe to a microcomputer
            with diskettes that runs CP/M. It needs a FORTRAN compiler.

Description: STAF was originally written for the teaching of chemistry and was
            designed to be transferable between different makes and models of
            computer. Teaching material developed in one institution could
            then be sent to any other with STAF, regardless of which computer
            the institution used.

            STAFII is an improved version of STAF that is suitable for use
            in training. It has a clearly defined structure that is flexible but
            author's coding is rigorously validated by STAFII to ensure that
            detectable errors are highlighted and eliminated during develop-
            ment; this is something that is not done by some of the systems for
            small computers, eg PILOT.

            STAFII is primarily an author language with no pretence at
            sophisticated CML. However, statistics on student performance,
            responses, comments, etc can be recorded and printed. Graphics
            and form filling require subroutines to be written in FORTRAN.

            The transferability is an important aspect of STAF and makes
            it unique. It may be attractive to companies who want to evaluate
            the potential of CBT but not to commit too much money, as
            material written for a small computer would transfer to a larger
            one at a later date.

            Unfortunately, support is not on a commercial basis at the time
            of going to press, but that may change.

System: **TICCIT**

Supplier: Plessey Co Ltd,
            Grange Road,
            Christchurch,
            Dorset BH23 4JE
            Tel: 0202 486344

Runs on: A computer supplied with the system from Hazeltine Corporation
            using Data General Nova/Eclipse minicomputers.

Description: TICCIT (Timeshared, Interactive, Computer-Controlled,
            Information, Television) has developed steadily since its inception
            as a research project in 1968. It is supplied as a complete system
            capable of supporting from 20 to over 200 teaching terminals
            simultaneously. TICCIT provides three main functions. There is
            an authoring procedure (APT) that Hazeltine claim is more than an
            author language and helps the user with the whole instructional
            design process. There is also an authoring language (TAL). The
            third component is the instructional management system. This
            provides the CML functions that one would expect from a sophis-
            ticated purpose-built system of this type.

            TICCIT uses a colour television screen as the output device, a
            special keyboard, with added functions, and a light pen for input.
            The system is flexible enough to support other devices for special
            training needs. Graphics and colour are supported as standard.

            The system is developing steadily and systems for smaller
            numbers of terminals are likely to be available soon. A recently
            announced microcomputer acts as a presentation system when used

on its own. It can also link into a full TICCIT system for development purposes.

System:	**WISE**
Supplier:	WICAT Systems Ltd,
	Edgbaston House,
	3 Duchess Place,
	Edgbaston,
	Birmingham B16 8NH
	Tel: 021-454 7782
Runs on:	WICAT's own minicomputers.
Description:	WISE (WICAT Interactive System for Education) has recently

entered the British market and is a sophisticated authoring system designed to be easily used both by the CBT expert and the novice.

It is a menu-driven system with several attractive features including good graphics, colour, videodisc support and an interface to link to programs written in computer programming languages. The WICAT minicomputers can support several users simultaneously and are also being sold as general business computers.

There is a management system, called SMART, that provides the CML functions when run with WISE. WICAT is beginning to market this system strongly in the United Kingdom and it is likely to be of interest to organizations with a substantial training requirement.

Summary
and conclusions

The decision to use CBT within a company is one with far-reaching effects that are way beyond the confines of the training department. It has been an objective of this book to provide those involved in making such a decision with the questions to ask in the information-gathering stage. It has also been an objective to help those who are, or are likely to be, involved with CBT, to understand enough about the overall field to be able to do their jobs more efficiently and identify areas of weakness not covered here that they may wish to pursue.

The aspect too often ignored by newcomers eager to use the existing technology at their disposal, is that of good methodical training design. The place to develop good CBT courses is at the desk, not sitting thinking at a terminal, provided that the course authors are aware of the potential and limitations of the authoring system and computer system to be used. Good CBT courses usually adopt a mixed media approach – avoid media myopia! Although we have only included a short chapter on testing and validation, the topic recurs at many stages. It is an essential adjunct to the design and writing processes.

Computer-based training is expensive, even on the smallest systems. Whether it is economic and cost-effective will depend on the circumstances, but costs are moving in the right direction for more and more applications to be worth considering. New developments are also opening up opportunities. It will, for example, soon be possible and economic to provide a small system, similar to the 'Speak and Spell' systems for children, that will instruct operators in start-up procedures for machinery, fault finding, etc. With voice recognition, the trainee will have both hands free to do as instructed.

What of the future? The principles of good training design will remain unchanged. The methods of delivering the training will alter with videodisc, voice input and output, home study, etc and there will also, sadly, be a plethora of authoring systems provided by different suppliers all offering much the same thing, but in slightly different ways. This is a field with a large growth potential and many manufacturers and others will be wanting a share of the market. The authoring techniques described in this book will gradually be extended and develop as the so-called intelligent tutoring systems become more accessible for general training. They are currently confined largely to university and forces research.

We, the authors, are very enthusiastic about CBT and have a vested interest in its success, but we have attempted to be reasonably objective and trust that you, the reader, will have appreciated that CBT is not appropriate in all training situations. Equally, it may be justified only for test marking and reporting if you have large student numbers. So, our conclusions are:

○ conduct a thorough feasibility study;
○ use CBT where it is appropriate;
○ select the appropriate system within the limitations of your organization;
○ get the training design right;
○ use the facilities of the CBT system as fully as you economically can;
○ test, evaluate and review;

and good luck.

CBT CHECKLIST

Since the price range for CBT systems discussed in this book is so great, you may have to be selective in the questions that you answer.

General
Why are we considering CBT?
    Are they good/sufficient reasons?
Is it appropriate?
    On what scale?
Can a pilot project be carried out?
What facilities do we need?
    Is a good authoring system on its own adequate?
    Do we need sophisticated CML?
Have we technical support in the company?
    Is external help identified?
What training do the trainers need?
Is the cost of CBT justified?
    Have we been realistic in our costings?

Course specific
Is this course to be integrated into an overall training scheme using CML?
Is the time scale realistic?
Have we defined the target audience?
Who comprises the design team?
Are we making the most effective use of CBT and other media?
Are we using systematic instructional design techniques as covered in
    Part 1?
What sequencing and presentation standards have we for screen design?
How is 'entering' of the course into the computer to be organized?
    Will the authors do it or will a clerk or typist?

How do we plan the validation and testing?
What statistics do we wish to collect?
Have we considered the impact of this on the disk storage requirements?
Is the administration of the course properly planned?

Some DO's and DON'T's

1. **Do** ascertain the level of commitment of senior management before starting.
2. **Do** check the support available from the suppliers of the authoring system that you propose to use.
3. **Do not** cut corners on author training.
4. **Do** make sure that you know the full capabilities of the system you propose to use.
5. **Do** define the responsibilities of the members of the design team.
6. **Do** develop and adhere to your own design standards.
7. **Do** incorporate CML, if using it, into your plans from the beginning; it is not an addition.
8. **Do** research and analyse course content thoroughly.
9. **Do not** set too ambitious a timetable – it will take longer than you think.
10. **Do not** skimp the programme design before writing frames.
11. **Do** consult the subject expert.
12. **Do** exploit a mixed media approach where appropriate.
13. **Do not** develop your course sitting at the terminal.
14. **Do not** get carried away by the medium – branching, graphics, etc.
15. **Do not** allow departmental divisions to impede progress.
16. **Do** keep sponsors briefed on progress during course development.
17. **Do not** publish your course without testing it adequately.
18. **Do** brief local management on how to use the completed course.
19. **Do not** assume that the course is complete immediately it is published; it will change with time.
20. **Do** maintain complete documentation.

Glossary

Acoustic coupler A device that permits a terminal to be linked to a computer using an ordinary telephone line; the telephone receiver fits into it.

Adjunct materials Materials which support the core of the teaching programme, usually printed or audio-visual.

Algol A programming language primarily used for scientific work.

Alphanumeric A combination of alphabetic and numeric characters.

ALU *See* Arithmetic and logic unit.

Analogue signal A continuously varying signal. (*See* also Digital signal.)

Applications package or program A program, or group of programs, written to perform a specific function such as accounts, word processing, and computer-based training.

Arithmetic and logic unit (ALU) The part of the central processing unit of the computer that carries out arithmetic and logic commands.

ASCII The American Standard Code for Information Interchange is a widely used code for representing characters as a 7 bit code.

Audio-visual Presenting information by means of sound and pictures.

Author The person who produces the CAT course.

Author language A high-level language specifically designed for authors of CAT courses; there are various author languages.

Authoring system The system within which the author language runs; it provides such facilities as editing, checking, file handling, etc.

Backing storage The means of storing information permanently on magnetic tape or disk; it is permanent and cheaper than computer memory, but access to the information is slower.

Bar code A method of coding information as a series of bars; widely used in shops and libraries.

BASIC Beginners' All-purpose Symbolic Instruction Code is a high-level programming language that is fairly easy to learn; it is widely used on microcomputers and minicomputers.

Batch processing A method of running jobs through the computer whereby one job is completed before the next is started.

Binary A system where a switch is on or off; represented as 1(= on) or 0(= off).

Bit A binary digit; it can either be 0 or 1.

Branching A strategy of lesson development in computer-based self-teaching programmes whereby students may be routed to different remedial sequences within a module appropriate to their answers to questions and problems.

Bureau A centre that provides facilities for customers to use time on the computer and pay for what they use.

Byte 8 adjacent bits that are treated as a group.

CAI *See* Computer-aided (assisted) instruction.

CAL Computer-aided (assisted) learning. (*See* Computer-aided instruction.)

CAPS lock A key on many keyboards that locks the letters in so that they display as capitals, but has no effect on the way other keys operate.

Card punch A machine that punches holes in a punched card according to a code; one type is attached to a computer; another is operated via a keyboard.

Card-reader A machine that reads holes in a punched card and transmits the data to the computer.

Cassette A container for magnetic tape.

CAT *See* Computer-assisted training.

CBL Computer-based learning. (*See* Computer-aided instruction.)

CBT *See* Computer-based training.

Central processing unit (CPU) The central part of the computer; it contains the control unit, arithmetic and logic unit and memory.

Character graphics Graphics produced by combining special characters on the screen.

Check digit verification An additional digit added to a number to allow the computer to verify, by means of a calculation, that the number is highly likely to be correct; used for customer numbers, account numbers, etc.

Chip An integrated circuit, one type of which is a microprocessor chip.

CMI Computer-managed instruction (*See* Computer-managed learning.)

CML *See* Computer-managed learning.

COBOL Common Business Oriented Language; a programming language very widely used for business programming.

COM Computer Output Microfilm (or Microfiche); a method of storing pages of computer output in a very compact fashion on microfilm or microfiche, which is a postcard-sized negative holding over 100 pages of computer output.

COMBAT An authoring system for CBT.

Computer-aided (assisted) instruction (CAI) Teaching using the computer as a means of tutorial instruction.

Computer-aided (assisted) learning (CAL) *See* Computer-aided instruction.

Computer-assisted training (CAT) Training using the computer as a means of tutorial instruction.

Computer-based training (CBT) A generic term covering CAT and CML.

Computer-managed learning (CML) The use of a computer to direct students through their training and produce statistical reports on student performance or system utilization.

Computer network A group of computers linked together so that data can be transferred between them.

Computer program A series of instructions to the computer that cause pro-grammed events to take place.

Computer validation In CBT, this means the checking of a course entered by an author to ensure, as far as possible, that the rules of the author language have been obeyed.

Control unit Co-ordinates the operation of the CPU and executes instructions.

Course author The person who writes a CAT course.

Courseware The material comprising the content of training courses.

CP/M A widely used disk operating system for microcomputers.

CPU *See* Central processing unit.

Criterion frame A point within a program which tests student understanding of the preceding program segment.

Criterion test *See* Post-test.

Cursor An indicator to show where the next character will be displayed on the screen.

Data base A related collection of data stored in a computer readable form.

Data collection The acquisition of data directly into the computer from monitors, sensors and measuring devices; it sometimes includes data keyed in by plant personnel.

Data entry The keying of information into the computer, usually by skilled clerks.

Data preparation The production of data for entry into the computer; it may include data entry, punching cards, etc.

Data processing (DP) The use of the computer to carry out business functions.

Digital pad A simple means of entering data into the computer avoiding the use of a keyboard.

Digital signal A signal varying in discrete steps. (*See* Analogue signal.)

Digitizer A means of turning a series of points on a diagram or map into digital co-ordinates.

Direct access The capability of going directly to a piece of information without having to scan over other pieces of data to find it.

Disk A direct access storage device that consists of a circular disk with magnetizable surfaces that rotates at high speed.

Diskette A flexible direct access storage device with less capacity and also less reliability than a disk, but cheaper; frequently called a 'floppy disk'.

Diskette drive The mechanism that holds diskettes to access the information stored on them.

Disk pack A series of disks built up to make a removable pack capable of storing many megabytes of data.

Distributed processing The processing of data at different locations in a network.

Dot matrix A rectangular matrix of dots each of which can be highlighted. Different combinations make different characters.

DP *See* Data processing.

Drill and practice In CBT, it means using the computer to provide intensive practice with feedback to develop mastery of basic routine skills such as keyboard operations and arithmetic.

EDUTEXT An authoring system for CBT.

ENTER key A special purpose key on a terminal keyboard which, when pressed, indicates to the computer that the user has completed entering data.

Entry test A diagnostic test given to assess a trainee's readiness to start a module.

Evaluation The assessment of the effectiveness of training materials during use; it can include the comparison of the chosen presentation method with other methods, a survey of trainee reactions and a review of operating costs against estimates.

Expert systems An aspect of artificial intelligence where the computer program 'learns' as it goes along.

Fax The transmission of pictures over the telephone network.

Feedback Output, usually displayed on a screen, to tell students how successful they have been in solving problems.

Field A computing term that refers to a part of a record or an area of the screen that is designated to hold a specified piece of information.

Floppy disk *See* Diskette.

Form filling Entering data into forms displayed on the terminal screen.

FORTRAN A high-level programming language widely used for scientific work.

Frame The basic unit of instruction in initial learning; used for the incremental presentation of subjects and procedures; three frame types have been identified: the teach frame, the practice frame and the test or criterion frame.

Games paddle Devices attached to microcomputers for games playing.

Graph plotter A device to draw pictures, etc on paper under control of the computer.

Graphics Displaying pictures, diagrams or graphs on a screen or other device using the computer.

Graphics tablet A means of digitizing information for computer processing.

HAL *See* Hypothetical author language.

Hard disk *See* Disk. Also refers specifically to a disk permanently enclosed with the read/write mechanism; a unit becoming increasingly common in microcomputers.

High-level language A computer programming language with aspects similar to the English language which makes it easier to write and understand.

Hypothetical author language (HAL) An author language devised specifically for this book to show some of the features of such languages.

IIS Interactive Instructional System; an authoring system for CBT.

Input Data that is fed into the computer.

Instruction A command to the computer to carry out an operation.

Intelligent terminal A terminal that can do some processing itself.

ITS Intelligent Tutoring System. A type of expert system for CAI. ITS also refers to a precursor of IIS.

Job aid A device providing guidance on the performance of a specific task or skill designed for use on the job; usually printed but may be an artefact; used in those situations where it is not feasible or not worthwhile to commit the procedure to memory; also known as a performance aid.

LAN *See* Local area network.

Laser A high energy light beam that can be controlled very accurately.

Leased line A telephone line that is made permanently available to the user; it is not necessary to dial a number to get a connection.

Light pen A pen-like device held by the user that points a beam of light at a VDU so that the user can select choices from and interact with information on the screen.

Live system A course or module that has been handed over for general use.

Local area network (LAN) A network within a building, linking computers, word processors, etc.

Magnetic ink character reader (MICR) A machine for reading magnetic ink codes from cheques, etc into a computer.

Magnetic stripe A strip of magnetic material stuck to a card or object holding information that can be read by a suitable reading device.

Magnetic tape A commonly used form of storage where a large amount of information can be stored cheaply on a long (2400 feet or more) length of coated plastic film.

Magnetic tape cassette The type of cassette used in tape recorders; used as a cheap form of data storage on microcomputers.

Mainframe computer A large computer with extensive disk storage and many facilities installed to carry out the DP functions of an organization.

Marked document reader A device that reads specially designed forms or cards with marks entered on them; used for testing in CML.

Matching A term in CAT; it means comparing elements in a student's response with possible answers that the course author has predicted.

Matching block An objective questioning technique used in CAT.

Matrix A rectangular array of points or dots treated as a unit.

Megabyte One million bytes.

Memory The part of the CPU that holds the data being processed; it may be several megabytes.

MENTOR An authoring system for CBT.

Menu A list of choices presented to the user on a VDU. The user makes a choice or choices from the menu.

Menu-driven program A computer program that progresses by presenting successive menus to the user as prompts for each step.

MICR *See* Magnetic ink character reader.

Microcomputer A small computer using a microprocessor chip, usually costing hundreds or a few thousand pounds.

Microfiche (microfilm) *See* COM.

Microprocessor A CPU where the control unit and ALU are included in a single chip.

Microsecond One millionth (10^{-6}) of a second.

MICROTEXT A subset of EDUTEXT specifically for microcomputers.

Minicomputer It comes between a mainframe and a microcomputer in power and price.

Modem A device to alter a digital signal into an analogue signal and *vice versa* for transmission of data over a telephone line.

Module One of an articulated series of sessions within a course; a module includes all the relevant study material and exercises to enable learners to master a defined area of the subject of study.

Monitoring The automatic collection and analysis of data using a computer.

Multiple-choice question A form of questioning where the student selects one or more choices from a selection of more or less plausible answers to a question.

Multiprogramming A method of using a single computer more efficiently. More than one program is resident in memory and each is executed in turn.

Network A linked group of machines which may be computers or terminals; there is always one computer in a network.

Objective A description of the purpose of a course or module, in terms of the capabilities that learners will acquire.

OCR *See* Optical character recognition.

Office of the future A generic term for the use of modern technology, especially machines that incorporate microcomputers, in the office.

On-line enquiry The enquirer asks a question using a terminal linked to a computer and the answer, from a data base, is transmitted back within a few seconds.

Open-ended question A questioning technique used in CBT whereby the student is allowed to enter a reply in his own words.

Operating system The computer software that co-ordinates the operation of the computer and peripherals.

Optical character recognition (OCR) Printed information can be read optically by a suitable reader directly into the computer; some readers require stylized character fonts, others can read handwritten data.

Output Data that is produced from the computer; it may be in a human or machine readable form.

Overview Introductory or organizing sequence at the start of a module including description of objectives and a synopsis of the content.

Package An integrated collection of study materials for a particular topic; not to be confused with applications package.

Paging Displaying text on a VDU a page at a time. The old text is completely cleared before the new text is displayed. *See* also Scrolling.

Paper tape A medium for computer input/output where data are stored by punching holes, according to a code, into a long strip of paper tape.

PASCAL A programming language of growing popularity.

PASS An authoring system for CBT.

Performance aid *See* Job aid.

Peripheral A device attached to the CPU and controlled by it.

PHOENIX An authoring system for CBT.

PI *See* Programmed instruction.

PILOT An authoring system for CBT.

PLATO An authoring system for CBT.

Plotter *See* Graph plotter.

Post-test The test or examination administered at the end of a course or module to assess the extent of learning; also known as criterion test.

Practice frame A frame which tests understanding of a point and prompts the response with some hint or support.

PRESTEL A public viewdata system run by British Telecom for business and the home.

Prerequisite An item of skill or knowledge expected to be within a student's capability at the start of a course.

Pre-test A test administered immediately before trainees start a module; includes similar questions to those in the post-test enabling measurement of learning achievement or gain score.

Printed graphics The use of a suitable dot matrix printer to print graphs, diagrams, etc; the quality is not as good as the plotted output from a graph plotter.

Printer A machine that produces output from the computer as printed information.

Printing terminal A terminal that has a printer as well as a keyboard; generally there is no visual display.

Program A series of computer instructions that, when executed, cause the desired actions to take place.

Programming language A clearly defined language that comprises a series of commands. These commands are combined to produce programs.

Programmed instruction (PI) Two interpretations are current:
1. the presentation method by which subject matter is explained and tested cumulatively in single-sentence steps by a teaching machine or printed text; this is the most common interpretation;
2. a system of instructional design in which the training outcome is determined by the design process.

Protected field An area on a VDU that has been specified as unavailable to the users; the cursor skips over to the next unprotected field.

Punched card A card that is used with card punches and card readers.

RAM *See* Random access memory.

Random access memory (RAM) Computer memory that can be altered by programs.

Read only memory (ROM) Computer memory with information permanently stored in it that can be read but not altered.

Register A storage area in the CPU for holding temporary information; use of registers speeds processing.

Remedial material A sequence of a learning programme to which students are branched when their responses to problems indicate a more than trivial misunderstanding of a teaching point.

Response The reply a student gives to a question or problem (turning a page or pressing the ENTER or RETURN key do not count as responses).

Response analysis A CAT term for the process of analysing a student's reply to a question, particularly an open-ended question.

RETURN key Synonymous with the ENTER key; the two names are used interchangeably.

ROM *See* Read only memory.

Rule set A sequence of one-concept statements comprising the entire content of a module; a valuable first step in authorship.

Screen The surface of a display device where information is presented.

Screen graphics The display of graphical information on a screen.

Scrolling Moving text, usually, upwards and off the top of a screen; it may be used to look at text that cannot all be displayed at once; it is sometimes possible to scroll backwards to look at text that has scrolled off the top of the screen. *See* also Paging.

SHIFT key A key found on typewriters and terminals to give access to capital letters and special characters.

SIMPLER An authoring system for CBT.

Simulation A computer model of a real life situation that alters depending on the actions of the student.

Simulator A device which closely resembles work apparatus in appearance and function; permits demonstration and practice of the operating procedures.

Software house A firm with analysis and programming expertise that will write and implement computer solutions for customers.

Speech synthesis The production of speech using microprocessors.

STAFII An authoring system for CBT.

Student monitoring The recording of a student's progress for subsequent use by the instructor or for directing the student to further training material.

Subject matter expert An authority on the theory and practice of subjects and procedures to be learned; used by authors to verify content, accuracy and suitability.

Subroutine A part of a program that can be executed repeatedly from different points in the program.

Task analysis The process of dividing and subdividing jobs into tasks, and tasks into steps.

Teach frame A frame introducing and explaining a new concept or procedure; includes a trainee response.

Terminal A device to input data to and receive data from the computer; it is linked to the computer by a communication line and frequently consists of a keyboard and screen or printer.

Terminal network A network that links terminals to one or more computers.

TICCIT An authoring system for CBT.

Timesharing A method of allowing a terminal network to share access to the computer.

Topic synopsis A short summary of a training topic written before the process of detailed analysis begins.

Touch-sensitive screen A screen that transmits to the computer the co-ordinates of a point when it is touched by a finger.

Track A path along which data are recorded; disk storage devices store data on a series of concentric circular tracks.

Validation The process of trying out and revising a module or course with a sample of typical students, before distributing the finished product.

VDU *See* Visual display unit.

Video cassette A cassette of magnetic tape upon which films and sound may be recorded.

Videodisc A system for playing back films and sound from specially produced disks; videodiscs are direct access devices.

Viewdata A system of selectively displaying information stored on a computer, on a television screen; the selection is made by the user keying numbers on a simple keypad; it uses the telephone network to transmit the data.

Visual display unit (VDU) A terminal with a screen and a keyboard.

Voice input The input of spoken words directly into the computer.

Word processing The handling of text by the computer; includes entering, editing, storing and formatting of the text for printing; a word processor is used which includes CPU, VDU, backing storage and printer at least.

Work station A terminal that provides fairly extensive facilities for the user such as a screen, keyboard and printer.

Index